ECO-DISASTERS IN JAPANESE CINEMA

T0385860

Eco-Disasters in Japanese Cinema

Rachel DiNitto, Editor

Published by the Association for Asian Studies
Asia Shorts, Number 21
www.asianstudies.org

The Association for Asian Studies (AAS)

Formed in 1941, the Association for Asian Studies (AAS)—the largest society of its kind, with over 6,000 members worldwide—is a scholarly, non-political, non-profit professional association open to all persons interested in Asia. For further information, please visit www.asianstudies.org.

Photo by Armin Fuchs — pianist, composer, Aikido master, and professor at The Hochschule für Musik Würzburg, Germany.

Library of Congress Cataloging-in-Publication Data available from the Library of Congress

SHORTS

Series Editor: David Kenley
Dakota State University

ASIA SHORTS offers concise, engagingly written titles by highly qualified authors on topics of significance in Asian Studies. Topics are intended to be substantive, generate discussion and debate within the field, and attract interest beyond it.

The Asia Shorts series complements and leverages the success of the pedagogically-oriented AAS book series, Key Issues in Asian Studies, and is designed to engage broad audiences with up-to-date scholarship on important topics in Asian Studies. Rigorously peer-reviewed, Asia Shorts books provide cutting-edge scholarship and provocative analyses. They are jargon free, accessible, and speak to contemporary issues or larger themes. In so doing, Asia Shorts volumes make an impact on students, fellow scholars, and informed readers beyond academia.

For further information, visit the AAS website: www.asianstudies.org.

CONTENTS

Introduction — Rachel DiNitto / 1

Toxicscapes

1. Temporality and Landscapes of Reclamation: Johnny Depp Goes to Minamata — Christine L. Marran / 13

2. Hedorah vs. Hyperobject; or Why Smog Monsters Are Real and We Must Object to Object-Oriented Ontologies — Jonathan Abel / 29

3. The Toxic Vitality of Kiyoshi Kurosawa's *Charisma* — Rachel DiNitto / 45

4. Plastic Garbage in Kore-eda Hirokazu's *Air Doll* — Davinder L. Bhowmik / 59

Contaminated Futures and Childhoods

5. Environmental Anxiety and the Toxic Earth of *Space Battleship Yamato* — Kaoru Tamura / 73

6. Miyazaki Hayao's Eco-Disasters in Japanese Cinema: Rereading *Nausicaä* — Roman Rosenbaum / 89

7. You Can (Not) Restore: Ecocritique and Intergenerational Ecological Conflict in *Evangelion* — Christopher Smith / 105

8. *Jellyfish Eyes* (2013) and the Struggle for Reenchantment — Laura Lee / 119

Nuclear Anxiety and Violence

9. The Reimagination of *Godzilla*: The Concealment of Nuclear Violence — Shan Ren / 137

10. The Walking Nuclear Disaster: Nuclear Terrorism and the Meaning of the Atom in *The Man Who Stole the Sun* — Eugenio De Angelis / 151

11. Representing the Unrepresentable: *Hibakusha* Cinema, Historiography, and Memory in *Rhapsody in August* — Adam Bingham / 165

12. *Hibakusha* Film as Genre, and the Slow Violence Depicted in Morisaki Azuma's *Nuclear Gypsies* — Jeffrey DuBois / 179

13. Nuclear Visuality and Popular Resistance in Kamanaka Hitomi's Eco-Disaster Documentaries — Andrea Gevurtz Arai / 191

Ruined and Apocalyptic Landscapes

14. Diverging Imaginations of Planetary Change: The Media Franchise of *Japan Sinks* — Hideaki Fujiki / 207

15. Technology, Urban Sprawl, and the Apocalyptic Imagination in Hiroyuki Seshita's *BLAME!* (2017) — Amrita S. Iyer / 221

16. Stranded among Eternal Ruins: Three Films about "Fukushima" — Aidana Bolatbekkyzy / 237

17. Disaster and the Landscape of the Heart in *Asako I & II* (2018) — Dong Hoon Kim / 249

List of Films Discussed in This Volume / 263

About the Editor and Contributors / 265

Acknowledgments

There are many people to thank for making this volume a reality. I need to start by thanking my colleague Dong Hoon Kim for encouraging me to teach a class on Japanese Environmental Cinema. I also want to thank all the students in the many versions of that class for their sustained interest in and enthusiasm for the topic. The class was and continues to be a pleasure to teach. University of Oregon supported my research and teaching in the environmental humanities with a Sustainability Fellow position and a Sustainability Award for Excellence in Teaching. Thanks to Sarah Stoeckl for running the Fellows program and to Mark Carey for all his support for the award.

This book started with a collection of excellent seminar papers by four graduate students in my Environmental Cinema class (Aidana Bolatbekkyzy, Kit McDunn, Shan Ren, and Kaoru Tamura) that they then presented as part of panel I organized for the online Western Conference of the Association for Asian Studies in fall 2021. Thanks to Marc Yamada who kindly, and unknown to me, relayed his enthusiasm for the panel to the Asia Shorts Book Series Editor David Kenley. Without David's interest and encouragement, this volume would not have come to light. I thank David for supporting the book in its infancy and seeing its potential.

I want to thank all the contributors for their insightful and compelling chapters and timely turnarounds as I pushed them to meet deadlines. The chance to work with scholars from around the globe has been inspiring and humbling. I especially enjoyed the opportunity to exchange ideas with both people I knew and those not normally in my orbit. Special thanks go to Christine Marran, Hideaki Fujiki, and Stephen Rust for being generous with their time and comments as they helped me work through and improve on the introduction to the volume.

Jon Wilson and Jan Bardsley at the Association for Asian Studies helped tremendously with everything from big concepts to small details. Jon was always willing to answer any and all questions. I appreciate his patience and humor as he guided me from the review process to seeing the book in print. I have long benefited from Jan's mentoring and was delighted to hear she recently became Chair of the

AAS Editorial Board. I thank Jan for her support, enthusiasm for the project, and help in marketing the book. My thanks to everyone on the Asia Shorts/AAS team. I also greatly appreciate the comments by the anonymous reviewers. The volume is much improved thanks to their extensive feedback.

A special thanks goes to Armin Fuchs for generously allowing me to use his stunning photo of Mt. Fuji for the cover. Last, a true debt of gratitude to all the filmmakers for their inspiring films.

Introduction

Rachel DiNitto

Japanese cinema is known for its spectacular scenes of disaster—from Godzilla's destructive rampage through Tokyo, to the multiple cataclysms of an animated, futuristic neo-Tokyo, to the destruction of the entire archipelago. These fictional cinematic disasters often reference historical disasters, including the Great Kanto Earthquake in 1923, the Asia-Pacific War (1931–1945), the Great Hanshin Earthquake in 1995, and numerous other tsunamis, landslides, and floods. Most recently, visceral images filled Japanese screens when the northeastern coastline was ravaged by a record-breaking earthquake and tsunami that triggered meltdowns at the Fukushima Daiichi nuclear power plant in 2011 (the triple disaster is known as 3/11), causing the worst nuclear disaster since Chernobyl.

This volume explores disaster in Japanese cinema as a powerful means for addressing environmental crisis. In addition to the catastrophic spectacles listed above, Japanese directors have used images of disaster and destruction to produce pertinent and timely visual commentaries on a multitude of environmental threats, from the slow violence of industrial pollution to the instantaneous decimation of atomic bombs. These films exceed the bounds of any single genre or approach. They range from the documentary to the monster film, from the cult film to the studio blockbuster, and from activist cinema to entertainment. *Eco-Disasters in Japanese Cinema* reads these films for their commentary on environmental crises while being attentive to both the historical inflection points of Japan's environmental disasters and the following intersecting themes that address local and planetary environmental destruction: toxicscapes, contaminated futures and childhoods, nuclear anxiety and violence, and ruined and apocalyptic landscapes.

Eco-Disasters in Japanese Cinema is the first volume dedicated to a multi-genre exploration of environmental themes in Japanese cinema.[1] It is not a comprehensive overview of Japanese disaster or environmental cinema, nor does it address the environmental impact or sustainability of the film industry in Japan. The chapters cover films from 1954 to 2020, highlight important moments in disaster ecocinema, introduce films not well known outside of Japan, and analyze films that may not have previously been read through an environmental lens.[2] *Eco-Disasters in Japanese Cinema* illustrates the profound diversity, debates, and plurality of voices when it comes to films that feature systemic assaults on the environment. The volume showcases a range of directors, eras, audiences, and genres; the authors of the chapters bring perspectives from multiple places in America, Asia, Australia, and Europe.

The earliest eco-disaster examined in this volume is Minamata disease, and it is also the subject of the most recent film examined herein. In 1932, the Chisso Corporation, a chemical company, began dumping its methylmercury-laden wastewater into Minamata Bay, destroying the marine life and fishing community dependent on the Shiranui Sea. While methylmercury was discovered as the source of the destruction in 1959, Chisso, the government, and medical institutions concealed this information until 1968, and lawsuits are ongoing sixty years later. Minamata disease is one of the "four big pollution diseases" in Japan, along with Itai-Itai disease from cadmium discharged into the local water source and agricultural soil by Mitsui Mining (1912), Niigata Minamata disease caused by methylmercury poisoning of the Agano River basin by industrial plants (1956), and Yokkaichi asthma air pollution from sulfur dioxide emissions from petrochemical industrial complexes (1961). The capitalist excesses of Japan's rapid modernization, lauded as a postwar economic miracle, yielded a spate of environmental catastrophes polluting Japan's air, land, waterways, seas, and residents.[3] These catastrophes are illuminated and critiqued across the multiple modes of cinema discussed in this volume.

This volume also recognizes nuclear harm as a form of environmental damage. Japan's tragic history with the nuclear includes not only the atomic bombings of Hiroshima and Nagasaki in 1945 but also American nuclear testing in the Pacific Ocean, specifically Japan's third nuclear exposure, symbolized by the *Lucky Dragon No. 5* incident in 1954. This Japanese tuna trawler was caught in the fallout from the American Castle Bravo thermonuclear weapons test at Bikini Atoll that irradiated an area almost three times as large as predicted and released radioactive isotopes into the air, sea, and land. This atomic history has been recorded in documentary and fiction films that depict nuclear victims, known as *hibakusha*, and it spawned the *Godzilla* series of radioactive monster films.

Starting in the 1950s, the US government ran a successful propaganda campaign to embed nuclear power in Japan, overcoming the memory of the atomic bombs and widespread public opposition to the nuclear.[4] Since the 1970s, Japan has experienced numerous accidents at their nuclear power plants that have led to radioactive releases and fatalities—and including cover-ups at the Mihama, Monju, and Tōkaimura plants—culminating in the Fukushima Daiichi explosions and meltdowns. Given the severity of the accident and its impact on Japanese cultural production and the public imagination, it is not surprising that the Fukushima disaster looms large in this volume. Several chapters in *Eco-Disasters in Japanese Cinema* analyze films made in Fukushima's wake: *Himizu* (2011), *Land of Hope* (2012), *Jellyfish Eyes* (2013), *The Whispering Star* (2015), *Little Voices from Fukushima* (2015), *Shin Godzilla* (2016), *Asako I & II* (2018), and the animated *Japan Sinks* (2020). But we also reread the nuclear harm and anxiety in films from the 1970s, 1980s, and 1990s that deal with both the fear of an unrealized nuclear apocalypse and the reality of actual harm to low-level nuclear workers and the communities that housed these toxic facilities. The films in this volume are bookended by nuclear crises, and the story is not over yet: as I write this introduction, the Japanese government has started the controversial ocean dumping of tritium-laced wastewater from the Fukushima Daiichi plant, despite protests both local and global.

Minamata and Fukushima were watershed moments in Japan's environmental history. *Eco-Disasters in Japanese Cinema* addresses disasters that occur at varying temporal and geological scales, and it tends also to the environmental harm ecocinema scholars Murray and Heumann term "everyday eco-disasters."[5] This is a recognition that these disasters are regular occurrences that impact our everyday lives and our ability to meet our basic human needs. The films in this volume cover a range of environmental crises as well, including widespread industrial pollution as a result of urban sprawl powered by Japan's economic recovery after the war. In the postwar years, Japan experienced air pollution severe enough that schoolchildren collapsed when playing outdoors, and ocean waters clogged with waste, red tides, and sludge so extreme that Tokyo and Osaka proclaimed their bays to be dead bodies of water. In more recent years, Japanese consumer culture has exacerbated the plague of plastic pollution, and the archipelago is particularly vulnerable to the rising coastal waters of climate change. Given the accreted nature of these environmental crises, many of the chapters employ the framework of slow violence to illuminate this ongoing harm. Coined by postcolonial ecocritic Rob Nixon, "slow violence" describes the incremental, unspectacular, often invisible harm that disproportionally affects the disempowered.[6] In Japan, this means people like fishermen, farmers, subcontracted cleanup workers at nuclear plants, and citizens who are financially yoked to these toxic facilities and systems for their livelihood. Documentary filmmakers like Tsuchimoto Noriaki and Kamanaka Hitomi are akin to Nixon's activist writers, using their medium to critique this unequal suffering and express their environmentalist perspectives through lenses that document the poor and disenfranchised.

Eco-Disasters in Japanese Cinema engages disasters actual and imagined. A series like Japan Sinks depicts the destruction of the Japanese archipelago from natural disasters—earthquakes, volcanic eruptions, tsunamis, and flooding—images that would have resonated strongly with anyone living in Japan. While the distinction between natural (tensai) and man-made (jinsai) disasters is still commonly used within Japan, Eco-Disasters in Japanese Cinema argues that there are no purely "natural" disasters. For example, while the origin of the 2011 Fukushima Daiichi disaster in Japan was natural (the earthquake and tsunami), the disaster was long in the making when we consider the unresolved safety issues at many of the plants and the placement of nuclear power plants on fault lines along the coastal zones. The narratives created about the trauma, loss, and destruction were socially and culturally constructed. Many of the chapters in this volume discuss these disasters as man-made or anthropogenic, widening the scope of how we define the disaster film genre by bringing an ecological lens to representations of destruction beyond the "natural." While some films view the threats to or from nature as external, reinforcing a divide between humans and nature, others recognize the deeply intertwined human-nature relationship as an essential step in redefining and addressing these disasters. Eco-Disasters in Japanese Cinema responds to calls from Japanese environmental literary scholar Masami Yuki and historian Brett Walker to read Japanese cultural production not via reified images of Japan's purportedly harmonious relationship with nature or via a contemporary popular culture alienated from the natural world but as a response to a modern history of engineering the environment, a process often called Japan's "war on nature."[7]

Japanese Ecocinema

Eco-Disasters in Japanese Cinema aligns with recent efforts to integrate Japanese film studies into global contexts, including environmental studies.[8] While environmental studies has been slow to come to Japan, ecocinema studies is itself a fairly recent development in the West. The field was nascent in the 2000s and primarily Eurocentric. Volumes such as Chinese Ecocinema: In the Age of Environmental Challenge, the first in global film studies to have "ecocinema" in the title; Ecology and Chinese-Language Cinema: Re-Imagining a Field; and Ecocriticism in Japan were instrumental in widening the scope of ecocinema and environmental studies into East Asia.[9] Eco-Disasters in Japanese Cinema is an important addition to this growing body of scholarship.

The films in this volume are primarily produced in Japan and are in the Japanese language. The national framework illuminates Japan's environmental history, countering perceptions of Japan as a culture in harmony with nature. We argue that the "relationship to one's material surroundings matters," as is evident in films made during the pollution crises of the postwar era and again in the wake of the Fukushima Daiichi nuclear accident.[10] However, we are not suggesting these films represent a homogeneous, culturally specific, national response to eco-disasters. We recognize the national focus limits our ability to fully capture environmental crises, especially planetary events like nuclear accidents or the rising tides of climate change. As Christine Marran argues, culturally specific, nature-based Japanese biotropes—such as the pathos of cherry blossoms—are often anchored in classical poetics and assume a homogeneous, ethnic, national response to disaster, making them ill-equipped to address the challenges of the Anthropocene.[11] While the crises at stake take place on the archipelago, they also reference broader environmental concerns that go beyond the nation-state. Films like those on Minamata disease illustrate this vital interchange between the local and the planetary. Tsuchimoto's cinematic responses to a local instance of industrial pollution are not simply case studies in Japanese ecocinema; rather, they were instrumental in gaining worldwide recognition for the toxicity of methylmercury and the tragic suffering of its victims. The chapters in this volume seek neither to essentialize and isolate Japan, nor to generalize it as a case of modernity's excesses.

Many critics define "ecocinema" in activist terms, a "conscious film practice" arising from a desire to bring political practice back into cinema through ecofilm.[12] Films like Tsuchimoto Noriaki's documentaries on Minamata disease are clearly political acts meant to expose the slow violence of industrial pollution that decimated a poor, marginalized class of fisherfolk dependent on the ocean for their livelihood. While he may not have described himself as an eco-activist, we can, in retrospect, label him as such, given his anti-state, anti-capitalist stance and his identification with activist documentary directors. Similarly, documentarian Kamanaka Hitomi screens her films in smaller venues, where she is present and actively in conversation with viewers. She aspires to educate her audience through her cinematic political interventions so as to give rise to a new consciousness that will inspire viewers to intervene in environmental struggles.[13]

While recognizing the import of these openly political documentary films, *Eco-Disasters in Japanese Cinema* takes a wider approach to defining ecocinema in order to include genres beyond the documentary, or films without an explicit problem consciousness. The films in this volume do not all necessarily arise from or seek to promote an ecological consciousness, and some only address eco-disasters indirectly or peripherally. We agree with Rust, Monani, and Cubitt, who argue in *Ecocinema Theory and Practice*: "*all* films present productive ecocritical exploration and careful analysis can unearth engaging and intriguing perspectives on cinema's various relationships with the world around us."[14]

This approach allows us to see the original *Godzilla* (1954) as an early eco-disaster film, a response to the atomic bombings and Japan's third nuclear exposure. We discuss *Godzilla versus the Smog Monster* (1971) and *Nausicaä of the Valley of the Wind* (1984) alongside the evolution of the environmental movement in Japan that started in the 1960s. We analyze the concerns with atomic bombs, radiation, and nuclear power in *The Man Who Stole the Sun* (1979), *Nuclear Gypsies* (1985), and *Rhapsody in August* (1991).[15] Works like *Space Battleship Yamato* (1974–1975), *Evangelion* (1995–2021), and *BLAME!* (2017) are set in contaminated, apocalyptic futures as a way to address the precarity of our environmental present. Regardless of whether a film is intentional or obvious in its treatment of environmental disaster, we recognize the critical work these films do, especially given the stakes of making open political commentary or claiming the label of environmentalist in a country that waged war on the environment for decades while demanding personal sacrifice to rebuild the national economy, and where the nuclear industry's financial and political capital silences dissent. The films analyzed in this volume give voice to many different stories of environmental harm and speak to and beyond the eras in which they were produced.

Structure of the Book

This book is organized into four sections that mix genres and eras to address interrelated ecological issues: toxicscapes, contaminated futures and childhoods, nuclear anxiety and violence, and ruined and apocalyptic landscapes. Read collectively, these different thematic and genre explorations provide a multifaceted overview of how Japanese cinema has addressed environmental disaster. The films in this book range from realistic documentaries to monster and futuristic science fiction films that depict disaster through both live action and animation. While monster films often eschew realism, their depictions of pollution index real-world problems. The vast majority of films made after the Fukushima Daiichi disaster were documentaries, but *Eco-Disasters in Japanese Cinema* also references rare and controversial fiction films that were criticized for their on-location realism, which encouraged voyeurism. Some films seek an objective truth behind the eco-disasters they expose, while others rely on the escapist solutions of the happy ending. The mood of these disaster films also varies from the contemplative and investigative to the adventurous, farcical, and melodramatic.

"Toxicscapes" deals with pollution events in Japan both real and fictional. It opens with Christine L. Marran's chapter, which examines the ecocritical temporality captured in Tsuchimoto's *Minamata Diaries* (2004) and critiques the manipulation of realism in Levitas's *Minamata* (2020) that erases the history of suffering and struggle. Jonathan Abel's chapter on Banno Yoshimitsu's *Godzilla versus the Smog Monster* (1971) addresses the industrial pollution that plagued Japan in the 1960s and 1970s and concludes that the Smog Monster film provides a more useful framework for dealing with systemic environmental problems than

Timothy Morton's concept of the "hyperobject." Rachel DiNitto's chapter brings attention to the rare rural setting in the films of Kurosawa Kiyoshi in order to examine the toxicity of wild landscapes in *Charisma* (1991) via a comparison with irradiated zones. Last, Davinder L. Bhowmik's chapter on *Air Doll* (2009) argues that Kore-eda Hirokazu's use of a plastic doll in place of a human is a cautionary tale of impending ecological catastrophe and a critique of Japan's throwaway culture.

"Contaminated Futures and Childhoods" imagines the possible future of our current environmental harm and features young protagonists left to deal with this destruction. It opens with Kaoru Tamura's analysis of the *Space Battleship Yamato* series, not for its war themes but for the environmental anxiety of the era, symbolized by the recurring image of an uninhabitable orange-brown marble that signaled the end of planet earth. Roman Rosenbaum's chapter on Miyazaki Hayao's *Nausicaä of the Valley of the Wind* (1984) depicts the young eponymous princess trying to combat the degradation from an elaborate future conflict for scarce environmental resources. The film is layered with Miyazaki's personal experience of war and pacifism and his struggles to own the label "environmentalist." Christopher Smith's exploration of Anno Hideaki's *Evangelion* franchise reveals the increasingly prominent disaster story of intergenerational ecological conflict, in which children must repair the damage of the older generation in order to restore earth's ecological health. Lastly, Laura Lee's chapter takes up international artist Murakami Takashi's *Jellyfish Eyes* (2013), which also focuses on children of a scarred society. In *Jellyfish Eyes*, they are being tricked by a sinister and secret government research lab, but their play represents the value of a reenchantment necessary to avoid environmental annihilation.

"Nuclear Anxiety and Violence" addresses nuclear victims in Japan and the Pacific. This section opens with Shan Ren's comparison of the original *Godzilla* (1954) with Anno Hideaki's 2016 Japanese *Shin Godzilla* and the American *Godzilla* (Legendary Picture, 2018), two remakes that conceal, to the point of erasure, both radiation victims and nuclear violence in Japan and the Pacific. Eugenio De Angelis analyzes the domestically legendary yet internationally understudied film, Hasegawa Kazuhiko's *The Man Who Stole the Sun* (1979). The film takes a farcical approach to nuclear terrorism and turns the slow violence linked to nuclear power into an absurdist yet critically astute spectacle that problematizes the nuclear in Japan. Adam Bingham analyzes Kurosawa Akira's attempts to represent the unrepresentable—namely, the bombing of Nagasaki—not as a past event but as living history in his penultimate film, *Rhapsody in August* (1991). Jeffrey DuBois introduces Morisaki Azuma's *Nuclear Gypsies* (1985), a film not well known outside Japan, which extends the definition of nuclear victim beyond those who suffered from the atomic bombs, as it depicts the violence done to nuclear power plant workers and the community of outcasts who live in its shadow. Andrea Gevurtz Arai's chapter on Kamanaka Hitomi's *Ashes to Honey* (2010) and *Little Voices from Fukushima* (2015) continues this focus on nuclear harm, demonstrating how Kamanaka's nuclear visuality exposes the complex forms of nuclear eco-disaster with regard to local communities fighting to sustain their lives and livelihoods around nuclear power plants.

"Ruined and Apocalyptic Landscapes" depicts different scales of environmental destruction, from the apocalyptic to the personal. It opens with an analysis of the *Japan Sinks* franchise, a series known for its blockbuster images of destruction. Hideaki Fujiki analyzes the imagination of planetary change as it evolves through the 1973, 2006, and 2020 versions, shifting from a national fate to the material conditions necessary for a new, contingent, techno-utopian Japan that is able to survive environmental collapse. Amrita S. Iyer's chapter explores the relationship between humans and technology in Seshita Hiroyuki's animated film *BLAME!* (2017), where humans have become nearly extinct as a result of apocalyptic urban sprawl caused by sentient machines. Aidana Bolatbekkyzy's chapter examines Sono Sion's Fukushima trilogy—*Himizu* (2011), *Land of Hope* (2012), and *The Whispering Star* (2015)—tracking disasters and homelessness as they unfold across time and a series of ruined landscapes that engage the realism of the actual 2011 disaster and the fiction of an off-world, machine-dominated future. Lastly, Dong Hoon Kim's chapter on Hamaguchi Ryūsuke's *Asako I & II* (2018) reconsiders disaster as an emerging genre trope of Japanese melodrama and reveals the external and internal ruined landscapes of the disaster area and its residents as it shifts attention to the emotional and affective aspects of disasters.

The films analyzed in *Eco-Disasters in Japanese Cinema* depict potent critiques and tell stories of environmental harm through a wide range of genres and approaches. Key events of nuclear and industrial toxicity are powerfully retold regardless of whether they are monster films, animation, live action, or documentary. Many escape the specific frame of national identity and open up to a planetary perspective, as they illustrate the profound diversity of Japanese cinema and express the crisis of our broader ecological condition.

Notes

[1] For environmental messages in monster movies, see Rhoads and McCorkle, *Japan's Green Monsters*.

[2] For more on films made following the 1923 earthquake, see Lewis, *Powers of the Real*.

[3] For a short overview of the postwar environmental damage from the war and economic miracle, see chapter 7 of Rhoads and McCorkle, *Japan's Green Monsters*. For a detailed study of industrial pollution, see Walker, *Toxic Archipelago*.

⁴ Zwigenberg, "'The Coming of a Second Sun': The 1956 Atoms for Peace Exhibit in Hiroshima and Japan's Embrace of Nuclear Power."

⁵ Murray and Heumann, *Film and Everyday Eco-Disasters*.

⁶ Nixon, *Slow Violence and the Environmentalism of the Poor*.

⁷ Yuki, "Introduction"; Walker, "Preface."

⁸ See, for example, Fujiki and Phillips, *The Japanese Cinema Book*.

⁹ Lu and Mi, *Chinese Ecocinema*; Lu and Gong, *Ecology and Chinese-Language Cinema*; Wake, Suga, and Yuki, *Ecocriticism in Japan*.

¹⁰ Past, *Italian Ecocinema beyond the Human*, 8.

¹¹ Marran, *Ecology without Culture*, 6–8.

¹² Kääpä and Gustafsson, "Transnational Ecocinema," 3. For more on environmentalist films versus ecocinema, see Willoquet-Maricondi, "Shifting Paradigms."

¹³ For more political documentary films, see Ogawa Shinsuke's film series about violent protests by farmers in the 1960s and 1970s against eviction, resettlement, and the expropriation of their land for the construction of Narita Airport, and *The Wages of Resistance: Narita Stories* (Sanruizuka ni ikiru, 2014), codirected by Daishima Haruhiko and Ogawa's cinematographer, Ōtsu Kōshirō. Hara Kazuo's *Sennan Asbestos Disaster* (Nippon koku vs Sennan ishiwata son, 2017) follows the legal battles of citizen groups suffering from asbestos poisoning in Osaka. Nornes, *Forest of Pressure*; Nornes, "Wages of Resistance"; Anderson, "Sennan Asbestos Disaster."

¹⁴ Rust and Monani, "Introduction: Cuts to Dissolves—Defining and Situating Ecocinema Studies," 3.

¹⁵ The term "nuclear gypsy" is commonly used in Japan to refer to subcontracted, low-level nuclear workers. Horie, *Genpatsu jipushī*.

Bibliography

Anderson, Joel Neville. "'Sennan Asbestos Disaster': Kazuo Hara Discusses His First Film in 10 Years." MUBI, November 21, 2017. https://mubi.com/notebook/posts/sennan-asbestos-disaster-kazuo-hara-discusses-his-first-film-in-10-years.

Fujiki, Hideaki, and Alastair Phillips, eds. *The Japanese Cinema Book*. London: The British Film Institute, Bloomsbury Publishing, 2020.

Horie, Kunio. *Genpatsu jipushī*. Tokyo: Kodansha, 1984.

Kääpä, Pietari, and Tommy Gustafsson. "Introduction:Transnational Ecocinema in an Age of Ecological Transformation." In *Transnational Ecocinema: Film Culture in an Era of Ecological Transformation*, edited by Pietari Kääpä and Tommy Gustafsson, 3–20. Bristol: Intellect, 2013.

Lewis, Diane Wei. *Powers of the Real: Cinema, Gender, and Emotion in Interwar Japan*. Harvard East Asian Monographs 424. Cambridge: Harvard University Asia Center, 2019.

Lu, Sheldon H., and Haomin Gong, eds. *Ecology and Chinese-Language Cinema: Reimagining a Field*. Routledge Contemporary China Series 208. Abingdon: Routledge, 2020.

Lu, Sheldon H., and Jiayan Mi, eds. *Chinese Ecocinema: In the Age of Environmental Challenge*. Hong Kong: Hong Kong University Press, 2009.

Marran, Christine L. *Ecology without Culture: Aesthetics for a Toxic World*. Minneapolis: University of Minnesota Press, 2017.

Murray, Robin L., and Joseph K. Heumann. *Film and Everyday Eco-Disasters*. Lincoln: University of Nebraska Press, 2014.

Nixon, Rob. *Slow Violence and the Environmentalism of the Poor*. Cambridge: Harvard University Press, 2013.

Nornes, Markus. *Forest of Pressure: Ogawa Shinsuke and Postwar Japanese Documentary*. Minneapolis: University of Minnesota Press, 2007.

Nornes, Markus. "Wages of Resistance and the Spiritual Problem of Sanrizuka." *Senses of Cinema* (blog), September 2015. https://www.sensesofcinema.com/2015/documentary-in-asia/wages-of-resistance-documentary/.

Past, Elena. *Italian Ecocinema beyond the Human*. Bloomington: Indiana University Press, 2019.

Rhoads, Sean, and Brooke McCorkle. *Japan's Green Monsters: Environmental Commentary in Kaiju Cinema*. Jefferson, NC: McFarland & Company, Inc., 2018.

Rust, Stephen, and Salma Monani. "Introduction: Cuts to Dissolves—Defining and Situating Ecocinema Studies." In *Ecocinema Theory and Practice*, edited by Stephen Rust, Salma Monani, and Sean Cubitt, 1–13. Hoboken: Taylor and Francis, 2012.

Wake, Hisaaki, Keijiro Suga, and Masami Yuki, eds. *Ecocriticism in Japan*. Lanham, MD: Lexington Books, 2018.

Walker, Brett L. "Preface." In *Japan at Nature's Edge: The Environmental Context of a Global Power*, edited by Ian Jared Miller, Julia Adeney Thomas, and Brett L. Walker, xi–xiv. Honolulu: University of Hawai'i Press, 2016.

Walker, Brett L. *Toxic Archipelago: A History of Industrial Disease in Japan*. Seattle: University of Washington Press, 2011.

Willoquet-Maricondi, Paula. "Shifting Paradigms: From Environmentalist Films to Ecocinema." In *Framing the World: Explorations in Ecocriticism and Film*, edited by Paula Willoquet-Maricondi, 43–61. Charlottesville: University of Virginia Press, 2010.

Yuki, Masami. "Introduction." In *Ecocriticism in Japan*, edited by Hisaaki Wake, Keijiro Suga, and Masami Yuki, 1–19. Lanham, MD: Lexington Books, 2018.

Zwigenberg, Ran. "'The Coming of a Second Sun': The 1956 Atoms for Peace Exhibit in Hiroshima and Japan's Embrace of Nuclear Power." *Asia-Pacific Journal* 10, no. 6.1 (February 4, 2012). http://apjjf.org/2012/10/6/Ran-Zwigenberg/3685/article.html.

Toxicscapes

1

Temporality and Landscapes of Reclamation: Johnny Depp Goes to Minamata

Christine L. Marran

When cinema addresses the impacts of toxins in an environment, it will inevitably need to commit to a sense of time and place. The sense of temporality created in the film will make all the difference in terms of who and what become the subject of the film. Some films focus on a specific toxic event. Others offer a temporal framework that expresses long-term impacts.[1] Noriaki Tsuchimoto's documentary *Minamata Diary: Visiting Resurrected Souls* (Minamata nikki: Yomigaeru tamashii o tazunete, 2004) was the final film of over a dozen he made about the poisoning of the inland Shiranui Sea and its fisherfolk by toxic methylmercury. In *Minamata Diary*, he creates an expansive temporality in describing how hundreds of tons of toxic effluent released into Minamata bay by the Chisso Corporation, located in the corporate-castle town of Minamata, caused mortal damage to people, animals, fish, and the sea. This toxic methylmercury, which was used in the process of making plastics, varnishes, photographic chemicals, and other chemical-based products, was carried by the tides and currents thirty or more kilometers from the source. It entered the ecosystem through the fatty tissues of fish and bioaccumulated up the food chain. Those who ate these fish became severely debilitated with an incurable disease. Thousands of others died.[2]

Tsuchimoto's *Minamata Diary* and the more recent *Minamata* (2020) by Andrew Levitas both use photographs to tell this story of the poisoning of an inland sea and its denizens. Both films juxtapose still and moving images to depict the tragic damage visited on this place and its people. Yet only Tsuchimoto provides us with an *ecocritical temporality* that visually attends to the slow violence of industrial pollution and the longterm impacts on environment. While Tsuchimoto provides an ecocritical temporality, Levitas's film collapses time, erasing the nearly seventy years since the original outbreak. This chapter shows how, in contrast to Levitas' film, Tsuchimoto's approach produces an ecocritical temporality through photographs and shots of reclamation landscapes as his primary cinematic tableau. In doing so, he stages a visual allegoresis of living on a damaged planet.[3]

Exhibitions of Exposure

The idea for *Minamata Diary* began with a photographic installation in 1996 in Shinagawa, Tokyo, of five hundred home shrine portraits (*iei*) that Tsuchimoto had taken while traveling the Shiranui Sea area for a year with his wife, Motoko.[4] The photographs featured those who had succumbed to mercury poisoning. They included the young and the old, the recently deceased and those who had been enshrined for decades. A memo in the Tsuchimoto Papers archive indicates this project of Tsuchimoto's had been inspired by Christian Boltanski's 1989 Paris exhibit of enclosed walls covered in portraits of Jewish victims of the Nazi regime.[5] The Minamata Tokyo installation resembled Boltanski's arrangement of large-scale photos displayed in rows on the walls of an enclosed space illuminated with sharp white lighting.

Unlike Boltanski, however, Tsuchimoto provided the name of each deceased person. His goal was to memorialize these victims of corporate violence just as victims of war are memorialized. He felt that the thousands who had been forced to sacrifice their lives for the economic health of the corporate state should be memorialized just as those sacrificed in imperial battles had been memorialized. Arguing that victims of environmental poisoning should be known as names and faces rather than numbers and data, Tsuchimoto requested a list of the deceased from Chisso, who, by law, had to retain the records of those who died as a result of their criminal release of mercury into Minamata Bay.[6] Chisso, however, would not release the list, citing "privacy" concerns. Tsuchimoto Noriaki and his wife Motoko felt they had no other recourse but to travel across two prefectures and an inland sea to create a photographic record of the victims because "to pray for the repose of a soul (*shinkon*) you must first have a record (*kiroku*)."[7] It took one year.

In visiting families to take photos of their enshrined kin, the Tsuchimotos would first pray at the family shrine. If they received permission from the family to film the photographs of the deceased at the family altar, photographs called "iei," they would gently remove the framed photograph from the shrine for filming. Not all families agreed for the *iei* to be filmed. Many families had experienced years of

Figure 1.1. Footage used by Tsuchimoto in making his photography exhibit and, later, in making *Minamata Diary: Visiting Resurrected Souls* (Minamata nikki: Yomigaeru tamashii o tazunete, 2004). Tsuchimoto Noriaki, 2004, Cine Associé.

abuse in petitioning for certification to afford hospital bills and daily necessities, and they were afraid of the inevitable bullying, discrimination, and insults that could result if they participated. The Tsuchimotos were refused 160 photographs.[8] In *Minamata Diary*, the photos are displayed in separate groups, arranged atop tatami mats according to the subjects' town of origin and filmed from above in seconds-long shots (figure 1.1).[9]

Surprisingly, the photographs comprise only a few minutes of the total one-hundred-minute film. The bulk of *Minamata Diary* is the casual filming Tsuchimoto did with a video camera on the days he was refused access to photos.[10] Those shots of surrounding landscapes and local activities became the core of *Minamata Diary*. Tsuchimoto spent many hours filming the reclamation land that had once been a beautiful, sparkling bay, rich with sea life until it had been poisoned by Chisso and filled in with earth when the methyl mercury effluent reached twenty parts per million. The tragic burying of the sea (in Japanese, *umetatechi*, or "bury-and-build land") took many years. Locals watched in horror as huge metal drums were hammered into the bay's sea floor and filled with earth. They spoke of the suffocation of the sea creatures and mourned their deaths. While Tsuchimoto's early films depict this reclamation project, *Minamata Diary* creates a time-scape of the victims but also the survivors of slow violence who have come to terms with this site of unspeakable damage and who now practice "the art of living on a damaged planet."[11] This temporality is created through the juxtaposition of the still photographs of the deceased with long shots of the current daily lives and rituals of those living on or near this reclamation land. In the juxtaposition of still and moving images, Tsuchimoto builds an expansive ecocritical temporality.

The Aura of Immediacy

Andrew Levitas's *Minamata* is far less concerned with longterm health of the region, favoring instead an aura of immediacy. The film features Johnny Depp as *Life* photojournalist Eugene Smith, who traveled to Minamata in 1971 to photograph patients with Minamata disease. The film opens with a mother singing quietly to her achingly thin daughter as she holds her in awkward repose in the bath. This shot is a reference to the famed photograph taken by Smith in Minamata in 1972, and is the touchstone for Levitas's narrative.[12] The opening sequence attempts to build a vital reality through the animation of Smith's photograph. The photograph is used along with others to create a privileged connection with real history.[13] While this feature film depends on Smith's black-and-white photographs to produce an aura of veracity, it also dramatizes them with colorful animation for a dramatic aura of immediacy. Those not familiar with the long-term activism, legal battles, and suffering in Minamata will imagine that *Vanity Fair's* description of this film might be true: it is about "an intrepid journalist tries to expose a cover-up."[14] But Eugene Smith was not an investigative reporter, and the so-called cover-up had been exposed long before his arrival in Minamata, as described by both Eugene Smith and his collaborator, photographic partner, translator, and wife Aileen Smith in their 1975 book, *Minamata*, on which this film is based. In a recent interview, Aileen Smith confirmed, "We knew that they [Chisso] were giving us a completely false picture. We already knew what had really happened."[15]

Colorful scenes produced through the remediation and animation of the original grayscale photographs create a sense of immediacy and reality that collapses the time that has elapsed between the past—the moment the original photograph was taken—and our viewing present. The red hues of the dark room, the warm tones of daylight, the greens of Eugene's apartment effectively produce a sense of immediacy. At the same time, the film is sutured together through original photographs that insist in their solemn presence that this ecological drama is a "true story." Their animation brings history to life as an "actuality"— the Deleuzian film image that produces a sense of the present. At the same time, ironically, animation and colorization unmoor the film from the conditions of time and space that originally governed the photographs. It is perhaps instructive to bring up Smith's warning of the perils of artistic license:

The majority of photographic stories require a certain amount of setting up, rearranging and stage direction, to bring pictorial and editorial coherency to the pictures. . . . Whenever this is done for the purpose of a better translation of the spirit of the actuality, then it is completely ethical. If the changes become a perversion of the actuality for the sole purpose of making a "more dramatic" or "saleable" picture, the photographer has indulged in "artistic license" that should not be. This is a very common type of distortion.[16]

Smith acknowledged that he arranged photographs toward aesthetic value, but he also warned against sensationalism. Yet Levitas, perhaps unfamiliar with his subject's artistic philosophy, added multiple false events for drama. One fabricated scene features the torching of Eugene's darkroom by Chisso-backed arsonists. Another features Eugene and Aileen hotly pursued by Chisso staff after sneaking into the Chisso hospital with their cameras and discovering bloodied knives on tables and hidden documents attesting to the company's knowledge of their toxic emissions. Another depicts the offer of a large bribe by Chisso to Eugene. Another depicts the return of Eugene's photographs after the arson.

Meanwhile, photographer Aileen Smith's impactful role in representing the denizens of Minamata Bay and the Shiranui Sea as a photographer in her own right—particularly from a gendered point of view—is ignored in this film. One explanation might be because the white savior trope common to Hollywood cinema requires the diminishing of collaborative work. In the film, Aileen is treated as an adoring muse, assistant, and translator. Although Eugene in the film seems to acknowledge Aileen's potential contribution to his photographic endeavors, he ultimately treats her like a pupil. In real life, Aileen Smith points out this discrepancy between the film and her life with her partner: "The darkroom work was mainly Gene and I—I had already been in the darkroom tons and tons of hours over that year, but I never even one split second thought Gene was my teacher."[17] When the two photographers later collaborated to publish the famed book *Minamata*, they wrote the essays in such an intertwined way that it is hard to tell who is speaking at times.[18] Despite using the *Minamata* book as the basis for the film, this collaboration is not represented in the film.[19]

The iconicity of the opening photograph in *Minamata* serves to collapse time, making those who fell ill with Minamata disease seem to exist outside of time. The opening scene of Levitas's *Minamata* is expanded upon when Eugene, with Aileen's aid, shoots what became Smith's widely circulated, prizewinning photograph of congenital disease patient Tomoko (called "Akiko" in the film) being held by her mother in the bath. The mother in the film looks down at "Akiko" with loving eyes. The photograph has been endlessly described as a Michelangelo *Pietà*-like image.[20] This scene is the apex of Levitas's film, not only because the film highlights

Figure 1.2. *Pietà* image based on original photograph of "Tomoko and Mother in Bath" (1972) by W. Eugene Smith. Johnny Depp plays Eugene, holding the Minamata disease victim "Akiko" in a similar pose in Levitas's *Minamata*. Andrew Levitas, 2020, Minamata Film LLC.

this sequence multiple times but also because the film replicates the arrangement of bodies in a later scene, in which Eugene assumes a maternal pose as he holds "Akiko" while sitting outside on a wooden deck, looking down at her and singing like her mother (figure 1.2). The outsider, Eugene, becomes the insider in this arrangement of bodies.

The original photograph, generally known as "Tomoko and Mother in the Bath," caused consternation for Tomoko's family, the Kamimuras, for decades, such that Aileen Smith passed the rights of the photograph to the Kamimuras in 1998 after Eugene Smith's death. Miyo Inoue suggests that the 1996 Tokyo-Minamata exhibit, discussed above, likely sparked the family's desire to take the photograph out of circulation. The bath photo had been used in the exhibit's advertising without the family's permission. Dr. Masazumi Harada, who dedicated his work to understanding the impacts of Minamata disease, describes his stress at seeing Tomoko's image on posters and flyers, subjected to weather and blowing about the streets.[21]

The photograph had been used even earlier in flyers disseminated by the Canadian Association in Support of Native Peoples in advertising the visit of Minamata disease patients and filmmaker Tsuchimoto in 1975 to visit those in the Wabigoon River area who had been poisoned with methylmercury by Dryden Chemical. What this complicated situation reveals is that when this photograph of Tomoko is resuscitated, the conditions under which it was created are not insignificant to the present. Events held in Tokyo and Kenora, Ontario, were meaningful, well-intentioned events organized to support survivors and build policies toward eradicating mercury from Indigenous populations' waterways and food sources. Yet, as Harada noted, the mass distribution of the photograph meant that it had lost its "aura" in the Benjaminian sense. Furthermore, the photograph as flyer was flimsy and vulnerable in its materiality. Its exposure to the elements feels closely linked with the public exposure of the subject herself.

This was not the only debate involving the Tomoko photograph. Local artists, including Tsuchimoto, were appalled that Eugene Smith took photos of Tomoko's naked body without her permission. By contrast, known for his philosophy of only filming with the permission of the subject (*torasetemorau*), Tsuchimoto believed that while Tomoko could not speak, her stiff body language in the photo showed her discomfort with being photographed naked. Tsuchimoto, who was also in Minamata, criticized the photograph for "exposing an unconsenting subject to the gaze of the camera."[22] In making this photograph the crowning achievement for Eugene in his film, Levitas erases the controversy and historicity of the photograph and treats it as a timeless aesthetic object.[23] In fact, historically Eugene Smith was not unaware of the ethical issues involved in filming people who, in some cases as a result of their disability, could not directly give their permission to be photographed. He expressed the difficulties of photographing those afflicted with Minamata disease in a direct address to young Jitsuko, a girl afflicted with congenital Minamata disease who he often filmed: "Trying to photograph you, Jitsuko-chan, is to reach towards a mind that shades its passages so rapidly, I am frightened I am making grievous mistakes of perception. I do know that to me, every photograph I have made of you is a failure."[24] In this sensitive remark, Smith acknowledges the limits of photographic representation in the face of the determined aestheticism for which his images are known. He explicitly questions his ability to capture the devastating impact this invisible material has had on patients. This contextualizing language in the book *Minamata* acknowledges the subjectivity of the photographed. Ariella Azoulay has described this as a "civil contractual" relationship in photography. The "civil contract" acknowledges the subjectivity that exists beyond the photographic frame and beyond the photographer, and beyond the lens. In contextualizing the photographs with their essays in the original book *Minamata*, the Smiths are able to attend to that "contract" more explicitly even if the photograph does not.

In the case of Levitas's film, however, the photograph seems freely available for use. A few scenes suggest that Tomoko's mother enthusiastically gave permission to take the photograph. The ensuing decades-long history of the photograph and the controversy surrounding the photograph is erased in the process of collapsing the time that transpired between the snapshot of the original photograph, the present, and the controversies in-between. The personal life is made iconic, and it is made iconic to symbolize the pain produced by industrial pollution.[25] In other words, in remediating this controversial image, its ecopolitical symbolism is deemed meaningful enough by the filmmaker to ignore the controversial history of the photograph and Tomoko's privacy. The end roll, in fact, asks us to see Minamata disease as one among a long list of twenty-nine industrial pollution events around the globe at different points during the twentieth century, each represented by a photograph. Tomoko is made to be reborn as an iconic symbol of the problem of industrial pollution in capitalist modernity among a host of others from various decades and regions around the world. In this way, the vulnerable Tomoko and her mother, Ryoko, are made to exist *out of time*. The photograph remediated in the film preserves the body as if it had been embalmed in time. In Bazinian terms, it is "the preservation of life by a representation of life," accomplished by snatching it "from the flow of time."[26] The long-term consequences of Chisso's original sin, and the thousands of actions and responses of patients and families over the ensuing fifty years, are relegated to a single photograph. The aestheticism of the remediated *Pietà* photograph and its potential to move the audience in a melodramatic David and Goliath story of activism ignore the intervening complexities that have occurred between 1972, when the photographs were published in *Life* magazine, and the present. Eight Minamata disease sufferers were seeking justice in the courts as recently as 2020, which they were denied.[27] When the photograph is brought to life through digital effects, the impact is a powerful sense of reality, *as if* it were yesterday. Clearly, the commercial drama has limitations when it comes to representing the long-term impacts, or slow violence, of environmental pollution. Not only does the film collapse the historical specificity to which it aspires; it ultimately renders invisible the ongoing trials of the environment and people. As one fifty-year-old male audience member from Minamata put it upon watching the film, "For decades we have tried to come to grips with various positions involving Minamata. I wanted those to be represented in the film, but it just concluded by making us rewind to the past."[28] Instead of accounting for those intervening fifty-plus years of activism and adjustments, the film offers conventional motifs that become the stuff of an eco-noir: incriminating photographs are burned in an arsonist attack, bribes are rejected, and truths are locked in nearly inaccessible rooms haunted by the ghosts of dead cats. The remediated photographs in this commercial film represent a slice of an industrial pollution event but not the temporality under which the slow violence of industrial toxins unfolds.

Memento Mori that Smelled of the Sea

It might seem that Tsuchimoto's documentary film using photographic portraits of the deceased could not possibly be about anything other than the past. Yet a temporality that sutures the "then" and "now" is produced in how he builds a structural tension through moving images of life on the reclamation site punctuated by regular frontal shots of the shrine photographs. One feels the slight movement of the camera when it captures the *iei* in a frontal shot. These *iei* shots in his early work have been described by Miyo Inoue as establishing shots, describing their function in his first long documentary of Minamata patients, *Minamata: Victims and Their World* (1972):

> Tsuchimoto's visits to the diseased patients' homes often begin with the scene that contains the image of *iei* in different shot lengths. . . . It also sets up the narrative pattern which Tsuchimoto often turns to for the rest of scenes that involve *iei*: the establishing long shot of the altar; the zoom-in to *iei* and the face of the deceased; the intercutting between *iei*, the family member talking about the deceased, and Minamata Bay. Each establishing shot of the altar and *iei* gestures Tsuchimoto's, and in extension the viewers', entrance into a deceased patient's personal space and story. And while it is the remaining family member that tells the life story of the deceased on his/her behalf, the zoom-in to and close-up of the face on the *iei*, sometimes more than once in one scene, connects the story of struggle with the person who struggled.[29]

As Inoue describes it, the *iei* as establishing shot becomes the visual mode for establishing relations and creating a "lingering presence" of the deceased in this early film.[30]

In *Minamata Diary*, however, *iei* shots are not establishing shots. Rather, in terms of the overall structure of the film, they serve to punctuate long shot sequences of daily life as well as ritual, often on the reclamation land. They are shown to have been carefully selected by families who, in choosing the photograph for the 1996 installation, look for images that capture the liveliness and familiar facial features of the deceased. The kin also want the deceased to have an opportunity to *return the gaze of the viewer*. Tsuchimoto created this effect in the Tokyo installation as film scholar Kenji Ishizaka attested: "Facing the innumerable *iei* hanging on all four walls, I felt that I was conversely overtaken by a feeling of being looked at and I was speechless."[31] In the film, the mayor of Ashikita Town makes a plea at a town event, saying that Minamata patients will not be the *object* of the photographs: "This request [from Tsuchimoto] was emotionally moving because we [as viewers] will look at the photographs; but we will also, conversely, be seen by the photographs. To *change the perspective* is the big job of this initiative" (italics mine). This changed perspective is highlighting that all people living in this area, not just Minamata disease patients, are subjected to environmental toxins as a result of corporate greed and malfeasance. Capitalist modernity has made everyone a citizen of a damaged planet. Tsuchimoto's final remark in the film hints at the struggles of the living when they are not joined by all citizens as mutually impacted by environmental toxins: "It is only in recent years that Minamata patients speak in front of others."

As Ishizaka has pointed out, this film is like no other among Tsuchimoto's many Minamata films.[32] When asked by Ishizaka what he had found to be true overall in filming seventeen documentary films on the same subject, Tsuchimoto replied:

> *Minamata's salvation will be to see it over the long term because when you do, you see things that you normally cannot see.* In filming seventeen films about Minamata disease, I have witnessed Minamata and the Shiranui Sea over the long term. If we look at Minamata for two or three years, we end up with "Minamata as tragedy." But if we consider it over the long term, we can't make such a declarative statement.[33] (italics mine)

Minamata Diary maintains this sense of the long term. Watching the tides, Tsuchimoto had come to believe that the seas and living creatures will resuscitate: "Making a film about revival was not a mistake. There seem to be those activist types associated with Minamata who say there's no 'battle' or 'sharp critique' so they don't really get the film. But Minamata people or people from outside Minamata who plan to bury their bones here seem to understand this sense of the *everyday* in this film."[34] Tsuchimoto references temporality in this statement to refer to daily lives that exist outside of demonstrations, court battles, and other more spectacular events that appear in his earlier films. Revival amid loss of life sets the tone of *Minamata Diary* from the very start, and this is depicted by showing growth on the reclamation land.

The reclamation site where highly toxic waters and fish were buried in fresh soil is a symbolic location for *Minamata Diary*. The film records the evening of November 6, 1994, when the first-ever fire festival was held on this site. A Minamata patient from a multigeneration fishing family, Eiko Sugimoto, robed in white, stands on the earth surrounded by 1,200 torches lit for repose of the souls. She is a *miko*, a medium, relaying the message of a fish-being in a poem she wrote for this occasion. The film shows her performance in local dialect in its entirety and sets a tone of regret. Here is an excerpt of her poem that adds temporal layers to the cinematic location of the reclaimed site (*umetatechi*):

> *This is a story of when I was a fish*
> *Long ago, this [reclaimed land] was the sea.*
> *Fish brothers and sisters were born among the seaweed fronds*
> *And raised in the shallows.*
> *Every day these friends played here ...*
> *This place was like the womb of the mother*
> *It was a good sea. It was a good sea ...*

Suddenly . . . the fish brothers and sisters here, there, and everywhere
floated to the surface.
Something must have happened. We fish had no idea what might have
happened.
We try to flee but we cannot flee.
We had nowhere to flee to.
There was no one to tell our problem to and it was impossible to complain. . .

. . .

The land on which you are standing right there, there under your feet
Is where the fish brothers and sisters were buried.
Did you know that
I need you to know that!
We will become of the earth
When we are ready, we will become of the earth.[35]

This haunting performance ends with the fish, through Sugimoto, thanking the people for remembering their sacrifice on this day. Her performance concludes with what Tsuchimoto called an "ad lib": "All of you born in Minamata, come home! Come home to Minamata!" In the next sequences, Tsuchimoto explains how this land had been considered a graveyard of fish.

The film spends time on long shots of Masato Ogata, an activist and Minamata disease patient who had formerly argued vociferously for years against holding a concert on the reclamation land. Ogata's speech announces that this reclaimed land is a battleground (*senjō*), just like Okinawa, Hiroshima, and Nagasaki. He falls prostrate with an invited guest, the Okinawan singer Shokichi Kino, for a full minute in silent prayer to the fish and other creatures who were poisoned and then suffocated to death in the making of this park. He is now ready for this land to belong to the dead and to the living. The scene that likely encouraged the film's subtitle, "Visiting Resurrected Souls," comes from a sequence depicting a pencil-thin man in a bright yellow shirt who hops giddily from rock to rock, overturning heavy stones at the shore near the harbor where Chisso loads its ships (figure 1.3). He points to the curlicue shells called "*bina*" living among the empty shells of the past. In a voice-over, Tsuchimoto explains that "in this barren landscape" (*nandemonai fūkei*), this man is showing him evidence that the sea is reviving and that the periwinkle-like *bina* are returning because "nature has forgiven us humans."

The Temporality of the Reclamation Landscape

How should we commemorate the activism and the losses, the past and the future of a place that has experienced the devastating, long-term impacts of environmental pollution? Tsuchimoto made his first film on Minamata disease

Figure 1.3. The return of bina to a damaged landscape in Minamata Diary:
Visiting Resurrected Souls. Tsuchimoto Noriaki, 2004, Cine Associé.

in 1965; by that time, the middle-aged patients had been living with the damaged landscape for decades. The presence of the *iei* in *Minamata Diary* clearly shows the difficulty of a revival that takes place on top of the crushed, fragile bones of fish, the hardened shells of crustaceans, and the soft fleshy bodies of octopuses. The ongoing condition of this reclamation land is one of living in, and on, a damaged world. The fisherfolk and patients live in a temporality they know is dystopic, always subjected to physical challenges, and always threatened by another loss in the quest for justice. But, as Tsuchimoto puts it, thanks to the tides moving in and out twice a day, the future is not foreclosed. The sea lives on, and they live on, not redeemed, not resurrected, but perhaps renewed each time the tide reverses itself. The notion that the future is not foreclosed is found in an earlier film by Tsuchimoto, *Shiranui Sea*. He wrote: "In talking of Minamata, we are prone to see a 'dead sea.' But I created a structure for the film in which my opening scene starts with the voice of a fisherman who has returned from Minamata Bay and is surprised that oysters have returned to the bay, and the last scene is of a *fugu* in a lively catch. The revival of the Shiranui Sea and the [life] cycle, which is absent of death, is the topic of this film."[36] If photographs are about death, the film is about slow revival, but it is the juxtaposition of the two that creates the *ecocritical temporality* for this film.

Minamata Diary is not absent of death. The photographs, always shown in groups, produce a tension between individual experience and the large-scale poisoning of the Shiranui Sea, which was the life source for all those fishing its waters. As Tsuchimoto put it, "Memory can be weapons for the people. . . . I am not a *believer*, but with this journey, this group of the dead will bind us to something in the future."[37] That future is the reclamation land itself. It encapsulates and allegorizes the destruction and slow revival of life. As Sasaki insisted in speaking to local citizens, living through environmental damage is something we are all experiencing, not just the Minamata disease survivors. Tsuchimoto makes reclamation land the primary film location for shot sequences and punctuates these shots with the returned gazes of the deceased. The reclamation site with its sedimentary palimpsest combined with portraits invoke the toxic past, the damaged present, and lively present, producing a cinematic landscape that is multitemporal.

Acknowledgment

I thank the MacMillan Center at Yale University for their support while writing this essay, Aaron Gerow for providing access to the Tsuchimoto Papers archive, and Amit Baishya for his helpful comments.

Notes

[1] For a discussion of temporality in films on the environment, see Blasi, *The Work of Terrence Malick.*

[2] The cause of the first deaths in Minamata in 1956 was initially unknown, but a decade later, it was discovered that methyl mercury dumped by Chisso was the source. During the same time period, mercury effluent caused severe illness along Niigata Japan's Agano River and other watersheds in Kyushu; the Wabigoon watershed of the Asubpeeschoseewagong First Nation (also known as Grassy Narrows) Ontario, Canada; and elsewhere in the world. Unsurprisingly, mercury poisoning was a focus in the very first environmental conference at the United Nations in 1972, which had global environmental governance as its goal.

[3] My essay examines how Tsuchimoto's final work emphasizes multispecies survival in the wake of industrial violence in modernity. Other examples are found in Tsing, et al., *Arts of Living on a Damaged Planet.*

[4] It was organized by the Minamata Forum, led by the longtime Minamata disease activist Yūta Jitsukawa.

[5] Tsuchimoto's attached memo reads: "The world's MINAMATA is the first volume in environmental pollution. In the contemporary world, we mourn those sacrificed in war and we put our efforts into preserving their photographic portraits (*iei shashin*)," "Minamata-byō gisei-sha o tazuneru tabi" (NHK Kokusai hōsō genkō, 1995). The exhibit was attended by 140,000 people and went on to twenty-four more venues.

6 The Chisso Corporation was also obligated by law to hold and attend funerals for confirmed patients.

7 Tsuchimoto, "Minamata-byō giseisha no iei o tazunete / Watashi no Minamata-byō / Sono 40-nen."

8 Tsuchimoto explained why people were hesitant to be known as petitioners. He wrote that antagonistic people would abuse patients by accusing them of being greedy for compensation. If patients were denied confirmation, they'd be treated as if they had faked illness. Tsuchimoto explained further, "When they *were* confirmed, they would be pestered and intimidated with no moment's peace, and so they would utter to me and Motoko, 'Can you just forget us on this one?'" "Minamata-byō giseisha o tazuneru tabi" (NHK Kokusai jōsō genkō, 1995).

9 Some of the *iei* are familiar, having appeared in Tsuchimoto's previous documentaries in establishing shots inside homes or of family members carrying them through demonstrations, to sit-ins, and at court battles as they resolutely fought to prove that the powerful Chisso Corporation had caused fathomless sickness and death by emitting toxic methylmercury into their fishing waters.

10 Tsuchimoto, "Minamata-byō wasuresasenai 'kao' 452 mai."

11 Tsing, et al., *Arts of Living on a Damaged Planet*.

12 In this paper, when first names "Eugene" and "Aileen" appear without surnames, they refer to the film figures..

13 In her discussion of documentary film in *Immediations*, Pooja Rangan argues that in documentary, "disenfranchised humanity is repeatedly enlisted and commodified to corroborate documentary's privileged connection with the real. . . . The word immediate derives from the Latin immediātus, meaning 'without anything between,'" Rangan, *Immediations: The Humanitarian Impulse in Documentary*, 2.

14 https://andrewlevitas.com/about-andrew-levitas/. *Kyoto Journal* treats it as a "true story drama thriller," https://www.kyotojournal.org/conversations/aileen-mioko-smith-pt1/.

15 Teeter and Rodgers, "An Interview with Kyoto Activist Aileen Mioko Smith," *Kyoto Journal*. On July 4, 1970, Dr. Hajime Hosokawa testified that Chisso was aware of the toxicity of their wastewater and confirmed it in testimony on his deathbed.

16 Smith, "Photographic Journalism," *Photo Notes*, 4–5.

17 Teeter and Rodgers, "An Interview with Kyoto Activist Aileen Mioko Smith."

18 Smith and Smith, *Minamata*.

19 A. Smith addressed the film's disregard for the collaborative work: "It feels like your life is kind of ripped off of you. Gene and I were partners in this work. It was a unique partnership—he as a veteran photojournalist doing his final work, me doing my first— the two of us were one. We took a similar number of rolls of film. Both our photographs are in the book. It's seamless. I cherish that reality. The movie doesn't show any of my photographs. The reality that a lot of people who see the movie are going to think [happened] is not necessarily the reality that happened to me or us." Teeter and Rodgers, "An Interview with Kyoto Activist Aileen Mioko Smith."

[20] Inoue, "Exhibition, Document, Bodies: The (Re)presentation of the Minamata Disease."

[21] With appreciation, I use Inoue's translation of Harada with a few minor changes. Also, according to Inoue, Harada's brother-in-law, Kamimura Yoshio, saw the posters being stepped on by passersby when he was working as a cab driver in Nagoya and the exhibit went there. See Inoue, "Exhibition, Document, Bodies," 51; and Yamaguchi, *Sumisu: Minamata ni sasageta shashinka no 1100 nichi*, 197.

[22] Azoulay, *The Civil Contract of Photography*.

[23] Sand, "Latent Image: W. Eugene Smith's Controversial Minamata Photograph," 14. The debate around the photograph regarded the legal and ethical rights the subject of a photograph should have "once it enters public consciousness."

[24] Smith and Smith, *Minamata*, 74.

[25] Azoulay, the author of multiple books on photography of women and the stateless, argues that by placing a photograph about violence in a remediated context, it should be toward reconstructing the situation toward civic understanding and not aesthetics: "When and where the subject of the photograph is a person who has suffered some form of injury, a viewing of the photograph that reconstructs the photographic situation and allows a reading of the injury inflicted upon others becomes a civic skill, not an exercise in aesthetic appreciation," 14.

[26] Bazin, "The Ontology of a Photographic Image," 34.

[27] "Minamata Disease Claims Rejected by Japan High Court."

[28] Keita, "Minamata eigaka no Jo-ni- Deppu to kantoku Jimoto no 'sottoshite' e no kotae."

[29] Inoue, "Exhibition, Document, Bodies," 67.

[30] Inoue, "Exhibition, Document, Bodies," 76.

[31] Noriaki and Kenji, *Dokyumentari- no umi e*, 317.

[32] Tsuchimoto had been making films about Minamata disease since 1968. His 1971 film *Minamata—The Victims and Their World* won the Grand Prize in Montreal for the First International Film Festival on Human Environment. The film was shown at the first United Nations Human Environmental Conference in Geneva in 1972, supported by a delegation of sixteen people from Minamata, including sufferers.

[33] Tsuchimoto and Ishizaka, *Dokyumentari- no umi e*, 319.

[34] Tsuchimoto and Ishizaka, *Dokyumentari- no umi e*, 319–320, italics mine.

[35] Sugimoto is part of a group called Hongan no kai, who, as Miyamoto shows in her book *A World Otherwise: Environmental Praxis in Minamata*, seeks an alternative approach to the ways in which Minamata sufferers had sought justice. The book covers years that footage for this film was taken, especially 1994.

[36] Tsuchimoto, "Eiga 'Shiranuikai' no haikei," pamphlet (Suginami Kiroku Eiga o Miru Kai, 1990).

[37] Tsuchimoto, "Minamata-byō gisei-sha o tazuneru tabi" (NHK Kokusai hōsō genkō, 1995).

Bibliography

Azoulay, Ariella. *The Civil Contract of Photography*. New York: Zone Books, 2012.

Bazin, André. *What is Cinema?*, Vol. 1. Translated by Hugh Gray. Berkeley: University of California Press, 2004.

Blasi, Gabriella. *The Work of Terrence Malick*. Amsterdam: Amsterdam University Press, 2019.

Inoue, Miyo. Dissertation. "Exhibition, Document, Bodies: The (Re)presentation of the Minamata Disease." UC Berkeley, 2018.

Miyamoto Yuki. *A World Otherwise: Environmental Praxis in Minamata*. Lanham, MD: Lexington Books, 2021.

Rangan, Pooja. *Immediations: The Humanitarian Impulse in Documentary*. Durham: Duke University Press, 2017.

Shinno, Keita. "Minamata eigaka no Jo-ni- Deppu to kantoku Jimoto no 'sottoshite' e no kotae." *Asahi Shinbun* (September 23, 2021).

Smith, W. Eugene, and Aileen Mioko Smith, *Minamata*. New York: Holt, Rinehart, and Winston, 1975.

Teeter, Jennifer, and Ken Rodgers, "An Interview with Kyoto Activist Aileen Mioko Smith." *Kyoto Journal* (May 2021).

Tsing, Anna, et al., eds. *Arts of Living on a Damaged Planet*. Minneapolis: University of Minnesota Press, 2017.

Tsuchimoto Noriaki. "Minamata-byō gisei-sha o tazuneru tabi." NHK Kokusai hōusō genkō, 1995. https://tutimoto.inaba.ws/honbun.php?bunsyo_id=515.

Tsuchimoto Noriaki. "Minamata-byō wasuresasenai 'kao' 452 mai." *Asahi Shinbun* (October 26, 1995). https://tutimoto.inaba.ws/honbun_s.php?bunsyo_id=580&word =%27%E6%B0%B4%E4%BF%A3%27.

Tsuchimoto Noriaki. "Minamata-byō giseisha no iei o tazunete / Watashi no Minamata-byō / Sono 40-nen." *Komei Shinbun* (May 12, 1996).

Tsuchimoto Noriaki and Ishizaka Kenji, *Dokyumentari- no umi e*. Tokyo: Gendai Shokan, 2000.

Yūjin Yamaguchi, *Sumisu: Minamata ni sasageta shashinka no 1100 nichi*. Tokyo: Shogakukan, 2013.

2

Hedorah vs. Hyperobject; or Why Smog Monsters Are Real and We Must Object to Object-Oriented Ontologies

Jonathan Abel

The scariest film is *Godzilla versus the Smog Monster* (*Gojira tai Hedorah*, 1971, hereafter *Hedorah*), or so I thought as I first watched the film as a child on a black-and-white, thirteen-inch television screen as a "Late Late Movie" on WWOR-TV, broadcast out of Secaucus, New Jersey. As an asthmatic kid born the same year the film was released, growing up in the Jersey suburbs of Newark and New York City, I had a visceral feeling from the movie about the foibles of what we then simply called "air pollution," or "smog" when it was denser. The film had such a deep impact on my young mind that I instantly recalled my fear when I read Timothy Morton's books *Dark Ecology* and *Hyperobjects* last year—treatises ruminating about our impending ruination—the ideas of which have managed to crossover from academia to mainstream and pop culture.[1] At first glance, Morton's concept of "hyperobject" (which is already something of a meme) seems like the perfect lens through which to engage not only global eco-disasters but also their Japanese fictional manifestations, *kaijū* (giant monsters); and yet, the more I thought about it, the more I understood that Hedorah beats hyperobjects every time.

Hedorah is one of the sillier *kaijū* films, and yet it burned a place in my memory because it provided such vivid and clear images of what pollution does to

people and how inexorable the problem may be. At base, the film tells the story of a
monster who consumes pollution and emits (even vomits) worse pollution, which
kills humans indiscriminately, until Gojira and his human compatriots conspire to
"dry up" and vanquish the creature, but not before many humans have died and
Gojira is severely injured. Though most of us who experienced the Cold War—that
era of pollution, and, indeed, its allegorization as *kaijū* films—have been living for
a very long time under the awareness that the days for humanity are numbered, I
realized while reading Morton that the sublime dread of witnessing the end of the
world had clearly yet to settle in for some. Otherwise, how could Morton's ideas
appear new and valuable to readers? The more I began to consider it, the more
I realized that *Hedorah* provides a more useful framework for engagement with
the intractable "bigger than big" systemic environmental problems we face than
does the concept of hyperobjects, which was developed precisely for naming such
issues.[2]

Monster as Hyperobject

As whimsical a children's film as they come, *Hedorah* presents a dynamic of
hyperobject and object relations in clear terms. The *kaijū* (giant monster) Hedorah
is at once a hyperobject (that which exceeds our wildest imaginations) as well as
an exemplar of the inversion of the concept—an object that stands as an objection
to hyperobjects writ large. Comporting with the definition of hyperobjects that
considers them beyond human grasp, throughout the film, Hedorah is shrouded
in mystery. There are several scenes in which characters want to understand what
is happening and what Hedorah is (doing), only to be confounded with a lack of
information or cognitive ability. For example, early in the film, while the Yano
family eats dinner while watching news coverage of the recent mysterious events
at Suruga Bay, a newscaster's voice-over says, "What is this creature that appeared
after the ships collided in Suruga Bay? Some sort of sea monster? Or some nation's
secret weapon? Whatever it was, its terrible force heaved the ships apart in an
instant" (5:00). Or when the mother of the Yano family, Toshie, is asking her
husband about the possibility of a "tadpole creature" wreaking havoc on land, Dr.
Yano responds, "Hard to say. These things aren't in zoology textbooks" (18:00).
Or after one of the early battles, the news report on the radio in Yukio's car raises
a number of questions: "Is this terrestrial Hedorah the same monster that sank
the tankers? Where did Hedorah come from? Why was Godzilla here? There's a
mountain of unresolved questions about this baffling case" (31:00). Here, with
the naturalistic metaphor of the mountain, we have a description of the human
inability to understand (不可解).

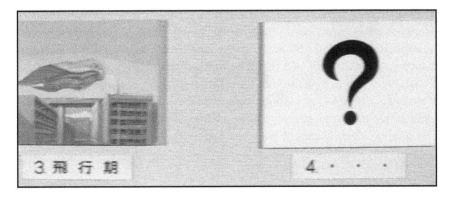

Figure 2.1. A newscast listing the known phases of Hedorah's growth asks what will come next (46:00). Yoshimitsu Banno, 1971, Tōhō.

But more than simply being a mystery that lies beyond human knowledge, what we do find out about Hedorah seems to fulfill all of Morton's five characteristics for a hyperobject:

1.   the monster is "viscous," sticking to other objects and other hyperobjects (like Gojira), oozing black toxic sludge.

2.   the monster is "molten," transcending time and space by hearkening from out of this world (a "shooting star" (流れ星), according to the film's poster) and continuing beyond its own death, as we shall see at the often neglected end of the film.

3.   the monster is "nonlocal"; Hedorah is massively distributed and able to travel through space, sea, land, and air environments and media (he appears in animated form as well, as in the sludge he spews).

4.   the monster is "phased" in two ways: appearing to come and go in three dimensions but inhabiting other worlds (animation) and literally taking four morphological stages of transformation that baffle the humans (see figure 2.1): a) the aquatic habitat stage in a tadpole shape; b) the early terrestrial stage, like a slimy caddis fly with legs and a tail; c) the airborne stage, in which it flies by means of a gelatinous thrust; and d) the late terrestrial stage.[3]

5.   the monster is "interobjective," both the sum of the measurements of himself but at the same time exceeding all such measurements because of his various transformational phases.

More than all this, the abject fear instilled by the monster on the nightmares of my youth attests to its bigger-than-big, hyperbolic shadow. Certainly, it would be easier to just label the black-sludge spewing, emetic monster a hyperobject, a complex, unwieldy mishmash that is beyond our ability to grasp or fight. But the film does not only present the monster in this way. It both stages and resists taking a sublime, decisionist, or nihilistic approach when dealing with the intractable, ineluctable, and ultimately unknowable.[4] Instead, the film allows for various and sundry culturally created categories and ontologies with which to break the problem down into manageable units.

Hyperobject Hype

At first glance, Timothy Morton's notion of hyperobjects (a putatively new approach to philosophical definitions of objects to account for massively distributed, ill-defined, yet ominously extant objects in the universe), which they use to discuss the unwieldy topic of global warming, seems perfectly appropriate for discussing the human impact on the environment and for helping us understand the monster film *Hedorah*. Yet even though hyperobjects seem appropriate to the hyperscales of the problems of the world and the film, ultimately, the film resists simply presenting them as hyperobjects alone.

This article uses *Hedorah* in an attempt to explicate what is so inherently problematic about Morton's use of object-oriented ontologies (OOO) in relation to climate change, not because the descriptive usage is wrong or misapplied but because the prescriptive line of thinking down which it leads is not particularly useful and is potentially detrimental. OOO is a branch of philosophical thought that rejects the human being as the ground or center for philosophical thought. OOO pushes us to step outside of ourselves and acknowledge the world, universe—indeed, everything—as all things that exist in relation to each other. Although the value in this approach is undeniable (for making us think more ethically about the planet and nonhuman, and even inanimate, objects), it is simultaneously true that OOO is internally contradictory, a useful philosophical oxymoron. Morton calls hyperobjects "real yet inaccessible."[5] In other words, OOO presents a Kantian antinomy: on one hand, *we* must entertain the use-value of thinking beyond the human-centered philosophy (the inaccessible); on the other hand, we must acknowledge the impossibility of doing so because the "we" of the previous sentence recenters that very human "we" seek to transcend.

The idea of "hyperobjects," then, is necessarily contradictory. Though Morton tries to move beyond the limitations of the (humanly) relative term by arguing that "the hyperobject is not a function of our [human] knowledge: it's hyper relative to worms, lemons, and ultraviolet rays, as well as humans," to take this theorization at its word presumes the kind of human knowledge or will to knowledge—that we can understand the position of worms and lemons; that we can understand completely the "hyper"-ness of a hyperobject in relation to the other (the worms)— that itself bespeaks the worst kind of violent tendencies to colonize, seize, and control the knowledge of the other, that which is at the limits of human-bound comprehension.[6]

Anticipating this critique, Morton writes that OOO is "an emerging philosophical movement committed to a unique form of realism and nonanthropocentric thinking. Least of all, then, would it be right to say that hyperobjects are figments of the (human) imagination."[7] Even if we take this tautological claim to be valuable in getting us beyond the self-centered hermeneutical circle, the sentence itself works as a talisman against human-centered thought without transcending it. Morton claims that their own strategy "is to awaken us from the dream that the world is about to end, because action on Earth (the real Earth) depends on it," but in the end, it simply reifies the notions that there are two worlds: the human-constructed, Anthropocene-ic one, which is, indeed, about to end, and the "real earth" (Gaia) which, per definition, will survive us.[8] This call to wake up is a call to hear yet another humanist bedtime story or lullaby, that of the hyperobject that potentially can lull us all back into a state of complacency. Morton's urge to get beyond the human-world interface of correlationalism may be a useful one for transforming philosophy, but it is not necessary for spurring change in the human-world interface required to stop human-caused changes to the climate.[9] Indeed, engaging with that human-world interface is necessary if humans are to take actions to mitigate their harm on the world. Understanding climate change as a hyperobject, we might as well throw our hands up in despair because the enormous sublime of the hyperobject makes easily accomplished incremental change seem inconsequential.

Of course, Morton understands my objections here, but I'm not sure they resolve them. So, Morton is at pains to distinguish hyperobject from the infinitude of the sublime: "hyperobjects are not forever. What they offer instead is *very large finitude*. . . . There is a real sense in which it is far easier to conceive of 'forever' than very large finitude."[10] We know the problem is huge, but it is measurable.[11] Morton acknowledges the problems with responding to the immense problem with incrementalism through a series of examples—"the poor fools who are trying to recycle" or "drive a Prius."[12] In the end, Morton rightly recognizes this cynical critique of incrementalism as consonant and complicit with neoliberal and conservative approaches that would argue it is "better to do nothing."[13] They respond:

> Doing nothing evidently won't do at all. Drive a Prius? . . . It won't solve the problem in the long run. Sit around criticizing Prius drivers? Won't help at all. Form a people's army and seize control of the state? . . . Every

> position is "wrong": every position, including and especially the know-it-
> all cynicism that thinks that it knows better than anything else.[14]

Ending with "every position is 'wrong,'" Morton buries what should be the lede—incrementalism is the only solution we have toward very big yet not infinite objects. Of course, driving a Prius causes other problems (hybrids continue to burn carbon, draw inordinately on rare earth materials, and encourage more driving by giving a false sense to owners of being above guilt), and yet it is one of the many contentious modes of being in the world that lessens or slows the poisoning of the environment infinitesimally (though not infinitely). Incrementalism is doing some(little)thing.

The Kantian transcendental critique has a long trail through recent critical theory. OOO, and along with it Morton's derivative theory of "hyperobjects," want us to not only understand that there is something that transcends human knowledge but also that concepts like "hyperobject" grasp it well. But other, more powerful critical theories of recent decades provide more nuanced positions to the always already moving target of the transcendent. What cultural critics Karatani Kōjin and Gayatri Chakravorty Spivak have right about colonialism and phallocentric power structures, Morton has wrong about the use value of hyperobjects.[15] In other words, we must respond to the objects of climate change while understanding the hyperobject will always elude our response.

Here Be Monsters: The Use Value of Object over Hyperobject

Medieval European maps figured the limits of the imagination as specifically monstrous by placing "here be dragons" in areas of the world at the limits of the known. Such concrete objects as dragons (symbols for the unknown and gestures toward the unknowable) are useful. Morton has a sense of this when he returns to the subject of hyperobjects, arguing:

> We are faced with the task of thinking at temporal and spatial scales
> that are unfamiliar, even monstrously gigantic. Perhaps this is why we
> imagine such horrors as nuclear radiation in mythological terms. Take
> Godzilla, who appears to have grown as awareness of hyperobjects such
> as global warming has taken hold.[16]

Here, Morton acknowledges that we need myths to help us think when confronting problems that are exceedingly huge and otherwise incomprehensible to human beings. But rather than embracing such tangible imaginative cultural responses that allow us to conceive of the otherwise inconceivable, Morton instead wants us simply to try harder to apprehend hyperobjects.

In short, Morton wants us to become like Tilda Swinton in the short video for Orbital's "The Box." In the video, the featured character/protagonist moves through our world at a seemingly normal pace while the city races around her. This effect, of course, is achieved through stop-motion photography of Swinton painstakingly walking extremely slowly through her environment. As the Swinton figure moves on her own timescale, we move with her and are able to apprehend as she does the secret messages of climate change—the slow violence of it— which is here (for Morton) represented on a television screen flashing words that Swinton and the audience stare at while others in the world whiz by and cannot see. For Morton, the victory of the film is that it can show us and Swinton the hidden words: "MONSTERS EXIST."[17] But to posit that we should simply walk like Swinton's character is an elitist and heroic view of the world. The point of the film is clearly the inverse of Morton's analysis—that we cannot ever take the place of Swinton and have the superhuman skill to walk the world like her (or, for that matter, dodge bullets like Neo in *The Matrix*). What such heroic myths stage is our inability to be superheroes. This experience of cultural products that stage the transcendent can be transcendental as long as we don't think we ever can transcend or become super. It can make us aware of other ways of seeing. This is why the video for "The Box" and *Hedorah* too are important.

On rewatching *Hedorah* as a grown-up, I noticed that the makers had in mind something more than stealing the scarce breath of an asthmatic kid; above all, the film seeks to spur a movement toward a world in which problems like Yokkaichi asthma and the sulfuric sludge (*hedoro*) at Suruga Bay or Tagonoura Bay are seen, anticipated, and avoided rather than seen as inevitable, a world in which human beings work with nature (Gojira) to overcome the worst tendencies of the human being and technology entanglement, a world in which taking aim at a monster matters, even as we recognize there will always be yet another monster on the horizon, even recognizing that all living creatures will not be affected in equal ways by environmental degradation.[18] But "hyperobject" names the monster as beyond the human ability to adequately engage; and, in so naming, it enables us to bracket off and neglect as much as engage with the dire problems we face. In short, we need tangible visions of climate change like *Hedorah* more than we need concepts like the hyperobject to help us overcome the challenges ahead. We can take objection to objects, not so much to hyperobjects.

Monster as Object—Hedorah as Moving Target

Hedorah is both a stand-in for all pollution and its attendant effects (a hyperobject) as well as a specific representation of the historical sludge and air pollution that accrued as an "epiphenomenon" or "externality" of Japan's rapid economic growth of the 1950s and 1960s (an object). As such, the film raises the tension between an object and a hyperobject, taking the overwhelming sublimity of the task of responding to pollution and balancing it with an achievable task. And it does so by making clear and visible the difficult to comprehend effects of environmental pollution.

Like the previously mentioned Orbital video, in which time is sped up to reveal hidden messages, *Hedorah* features a few scenes that vividly depict the effects of pollution. First, about thirteen minutes into the film, Dr. Yano is snorkeling under the sludge to try to find the secrets of this new life-form, when an underwater shot of a seafloor littered with the waste of human consumerism suddenly clouds over with a black, ink-like substance. Soon after, we have a sublime image of Ken calling "Papa" to the open sea. Second, at about thirty-eight minutes, as Hedorah—in airborne mode—soars overhead releasing his toxic fumes, we see not only girls collapse as they are doing their morning calisthenics (an image based on true news stories at the time) but also a quick shot of leaves shriveling on the vine.[19] Finally, at fifty-one minutes, we have an enjambment of these two kinds of water and air pollution presented: Hedorah flies overhead as the chrysanthemums (symbols of the nation and emperor) in front of the Yano house wilt within seconds, followed by a cut to the fish tank inside the Yano house clouding over with sludge as the fish die.

In his formulation of the "slow violence" of multiform destruction over long time spans, Rob Nixon acknowledges the problem of perceptibility and suggests precisely this increase of timescale as a possible remedy for activist artists: "to render slow violence visible entails, among other things, redefining speed."[20] Yet ultimately, Nixon recognizes that the challenge for the activist cultural producer is to "make slow violence visible" while not reifying the "privileging of the visible."[21] If the speeding up of the effects of pollution for the film in the dying of flora and fauna reify the importance of the visual, they also render perceptible that which might otherwise lie beyond human perception. In this sense, Hedorah (the monster) and *Hedorah* (the film) are the opposite of hyperobjects. They are tangible metaphorical stand-ins for the amorphous hyperobjective issue of man's harm to the environment; the monster (like the film) is localizable, trackable on radar, targetable—in short, finite.

One important scene presents the compound effects of pollution at the verbal (not visual) level. After Uncle Yukio (the brother of Toshie) and his girlfriend, Miki, return to Dr. Yano's lab to discuss newly discovered facts about the creature, Miki wonders aloud, "If Hedorah breathes in factory fumes, wouldn't that solve our air pollution?"[22] Here, she plays the role of the hopeful audience who, scenes before, witnessed Hedorah sucking smokestack pollution from a factory. The logic of the film seems to break down at this moment. As a pollution-eating monster, we might think the monster would be a savior of humankind. And yet the film deals with this would-be contradiction elegantly. Dr. Yano admonishes Miki (and us) by revealing the inner logic of the film and the law of entropy: "Absolutely not. Hedorah is far more dangerous. . . . If Hedorah consumes factory fumes and releases sulfuric acid mist . . . it won't clean our air. We'll be smothered in toxic smog" (35:00). The monster only eats pollution to weaponize it, rendering the slow suffocation by pollution into a more quickly killing sulfuric acid sludge. This confrontation with the hyperobject enables a kind of complacency in the film as we shall see, suggesting that rather than a solution, wrestling with hyperobjects may be part of the problem.

Film as Object of Hyperobject

So Hedorah is both indicative of an object and a hyperobject. This appears in the film as a tension between those who simply want to attack the monster and those who appear more complacent with the threat. From the boy Ken Yano and his father, Dr. Yano, to the media and military and even Gojira, we have examples of those who react to Hedorah as though it were an object, something to target and attack. But in the guise of Uncle Yukio and Miki (and the crowd of dancing hippies they hang out with), the film presents a reaction to Hedorah as though it were a hyperobject. Yukio and Miki's gang dance as the city is destroyed in one scene. The scene has echoes of *The Blob*'s movie theater scene; as the black and gray abject oozing sludge descends the stairs of the dance hall, the psychedelic lava lamp-like oil slide projections on the walls visually evoke the viscous nature of the beast. The dancers stop and scream long enough to watch the sludge spare a cat, but the general mood is more of a mad Nero playing his fiddle as Rome burns than of activist youth madly searching for a solution (24:00).

And in another series of scenes, the youth plan and hold an antipollution dance party and bonfire at the base of Fuji. Standing in front of a manga image of Hedorah devouring Mt. Fuji, Yukio lectures to his comrades. Someone in the crowd starts the scene, saying, "So Hedorah has won?" To which Yukio responds, "We reap what we sow. Hedorah is a monster of our own making. A million people. . . . Party a go-go! Pretty cool, huh? Let's gather the youth of Japan for a big party at Mt. Fuji before Hedorah gets there." This is the theory of the "go-go" dance party (figure 2.2), while in practice, only a few people attend as bewildered local farmers look on. They have given up hope: "It's no use grumbling. The green earth only exists in our hearts now. Everyone, let's sing! Let's dance! Let's send our energy out into the universe!" In short, the youth are being shown neither taking incremental action against pollution nor staging a revolution; when confronting a Hedorah as hyperobject, they neither tune in nor turn on; they simply drop out. As Nixon's work reminds us to think about the inequities of climate change, we should note here that the farmers suffer differently from the students from the metropole and those who sell and buy gas masks.

Figure 2.2. Yukio takes a marker to a poster that says "Fight Against Pollution!! A Million Person Movement, All Japan Youth Union" and changes the "movement" into a "go-go party" (45:00). Yoshimitsu Banno, 1971, Tōhō.

Perhaps the starkest figuration of the tension between action and complicity, object and hyperobject, was visible to at least the thirty-eight thousand consumers at the metalevel outside of the film who purchased the forty-five single of the film's theme song, "Return the Sun," which is sung by Miki (played by Mari Keiko) in the film.[23] While the B-side of the record has the bleak theme song inspired by the aesthetics of Rachel Carson's *Silent Spring* (translated and published in Japan in 1964), the A-side of the record has a song that was not featured in the film.[24] The A-side is a much more upbeat children's tune about defeating Hedorah, entitled "Beat Hedorah." The two songs begin as follows:

Side B—"Return the Sun"	**Side A—"Get Hedorah"**
Mercury Cobalt Cadmium	Hedorah, Hedorah, Hedorah
Lead Sulfuric acid oxidants	Hedorah, born of sludge
Cyanide Manganese Vanadium	Kills all the dragonflies and the birds
Chromium, Potassium, Strontium.	Wipes out the sky, wipes out the fields.
Dirty ocean, dirty sky	
	Flying saucer, Hedorah the monster.
All the living things are gone.	Sulfuric acid mist raining down.
The fields and the mountains have gone silent.	Hedorah's glowing heat gun.
	Run Gojira with your radioactivity.
No one on earth.	C'mon (*ganbare*) Gojira.
No one left to even cry.	Hang in there, fight, you have this.
	Our Godzilla

The two sides of the record replay the inherent duality of the film and the monster as both hyperobject that exceeds our human powers of comprehension and an object that we can destroy: the dance while Tokyo suffocates, the hippie-dippy groovy, "let's all go-go rather than protest" B-side; and the childishly naive but action-packed A-side. The B-side is too close to the neoliberal position of doing nothing or selling gas masks to profit from disaster or buying them to temporally preserve oneself, as we see in one of the film's several animations (42:00). The naive side *at least* works to eradicate the monster in its most tangibly threatening form. Both sides are somehow wrong as Morton might emphasize, but this tension between them is precisely what the film writ large explores (making it akin to the work of Rob Nixon's activist writers). We are overwhelmed by the enormity of the problem, and yet we must try something. It is in the tension between these two positions that the film succeeds where Morton's hyperobjects fail.

When Godzilla Flies

Of all the zany antics the film perpetrates on its viewers (from non sequitur-like animated shorts to multiscreen visualizations of televised reactions to the monster), the one that most animates Godzilla fans is a scene where the atomic creature reveals a heretofore unknown ability—the ability to fly. The sheer ridiculousness of the otherwise earthbound fictional creature flying highlights the contradictions and tensions at the heart of the film—between the plausible or imaginable object and the beyond-expectations quality of the hyperobject.

The final shots of the film present the tension between the object and hyperobject in a stark way. After Hedorah is defeated in the final minutes of the film, we get confirmation of our unease, which was first raised by Ken early on when he innocently suggests to a reporter that there might be more than one Hedorah: "There isn't just one Hedorah" (11:00). In the final sequence (figure 2.3), a frame of Ken and Miki waving goodbye to Gojira cuts to the heroic beast walking toward the horizon (and the next film in the series perhaps). Then, in rapid succession, we have a cut to the famous print of *The Great Wave off Kanagawa* by Hokusai, renowned as a depiction of the sublime human (in the form of a boat) confrontation with the elements of nature, then a black screen with white lettering reading "will there be another?", and finally, an answer to that question—an image of (another?) Hedorah's eyes surfacing in the sea and the character for "the end."

Just when we might expect the film to celebrate overcoming the object of Hedorah, it toggles back to the hyperobject view of the beast. The duality of Hedorah is that there is one now, but there always may be one more creature. The notion we are left with is that Hedorah is one and many; Hedorah needs to be killed, and Hedorah will live on. Even as we know—and the film knows—Hedorah (and by proxy, pollution) exceeds the time frame of the film, it presents the problem as one

Figure 2.3. Montage: When the object is destroyed, the
hyperobject remains. Yoshimitsu Banno, 1971, Tōhō.

with a hard target and definable beginning, middle, and end, with a gesture to the
transcendental task (the one that always escapes in our incessant game of Whac-
A-Mole with pollution). In this way, the film states the problem perfectly: Because
we can never completely transcend, we must be oriented toward the transcendent,
we must be transcendental; or to put it another way, we must be vigilant.

Hedorah is, in fact, a better figure for acknowledging and taking account of
pollution than the concept of hyperobject (which leaves little space for human
action but instead simply replays the paralyzing aesthetics of the sublime when

HEDORAH VS. HYPEROBJECT : JONATHAN ABEL : 41

thought of as a transcendent rather than a transcendental category). In short, *Hedorah* makes visible the hard-to-picture slow violence, even while recognizing that which will forever remain beyond the visible. It allows us to strategically essentialize, breaking off but one area of humankind's degradation of the environment and putting a target between its red eyes.

Notes

[1] Hudson, "At the End of the World, It's Hyperobjects All the Way Down"; Meis, "Timothy Morton's Hyper-Pandemic"; Staff, "World Waystar Entertainment: Vince McMahon, Hyperobject."

[2] Where its Japanese theme song emphasizes the dual use of technology (whoever is behind the remote control determines the goodness or badness of the robot), the American pop cultural appropriation of the Japanese anime *Tetsujin 28* as *Gigantor* came with a theme song that tried to express the unfathomable bigness of the robot: "Bigger than big, / taller than tall, / Quicker than quick, stronger than strong. / Ready to fight for right, against wrong."

[3] "Gojira tai Hedorah," n52.

[4] Agamben, *State of Exception*; Schmitt, *Political Theology: Four Chapters on the Concept of Sovereignty*; Schmitt, *Dictatorship*.

[5] Morton, *Dark Ecology*, 25.

[6] Morton, *Hyperobjects*, 2.

[7] Morton, *Hyperobjects*, 2.

[8] Morton, *Hyperobjects*, 7.

[9] Morton, *Hyperobjects*, 9

[10] Morton, *Hyperobjects*, 60.

[11] Morton, *Being Ecological*, 76–77.

[12] Morton, *Hyperobjects*, 156.

[13] Morton, *Hyperobjects*, 157.

[14] Morton, *Hyperobjects*, 136.

[15] Karatani. *Nation and Aesthetics: On Kant and Freud*; Spivak, *A Critique of Postcolonial Reason*.

[16] Morton, *Dark Ecology*, 25.

[17] Morton, *Dark Ecology*, 41.

[18] In the 1960s and early 1970s, people downwind from petrochemical facilities in Yokkaichi City in Mie Prefecture began to suffer from a grouping of bronchial and pulmonary diseases that came to be referred to as "Yokkaichi asthma," the result of sulfuric dioxide poisoning. See, for instance, Avenell, *Transnational Japan in the Global Environmental Movement*, 29–51. The dumping of sulfuric sludge (known as *hedoro*) from the paper industries into the bays of Suruga or Tagonoura became internationally known

ecological problems in 1970, reported for instance in the *New York Times*. See Oka, "Sato Plans Action to Meet Pollution Crisis in Japan"; and Oka, "Japan Urged to Save Polluted Harbor."

[19] See, for instance, "Kōtei no kōkōsei-ra 40 sū-ri ga taoreru Suginami shinkenzai yaita gasu ka" and "Kōkagaku sumoggu sakkā taikai o osou chūgakusei, tsugitsugi taoreru Urawa." See also "Tōhō tokusatsu eiga sakuhin-shi: Gojira tai Hedora," 356–357, and "Supesharu intabyū: Sakano Yoshimitsu," 94–95.

[20] Nixon, *Slow Violence and the Environmentalism of the Poor*, 13.

[21] Nixon, *Slow Violence and the Environmentalism of the Poor*, 15.

[22] The scene is also discussed in Rhoads and McCorkle, *Japan's Green Monsters: Environmental Commentary in Kaiju Cinema*, 124.

[23] "Gojira tai Hedorah: Kaesu taiyō wo" and "Hedora wo yattsukero."

[24] Carson, *Sei to shi no myōyaku: Shizen kinkō no hakai-sha kagaku yakuhin*. "Return the Sun" is also translated as "Bring Back Nature." See Ryfle, *Japan's Favorite Mon-Star: The Unauthorized Biography of "The Big G."* 164; "Sutaffu intabyū 11: Manabe Riichirō sairoku," 121.

Bibliography

Agamben, Giorgio. *State of Exception*. Chicago: University of Chicago Press, 2008.

Avenell, Simon. *Transnational Japan in the Global Environmental Movement*. Honolulu: University of Hawai'i Press, 2017.

Carson, Rachel. *Sei to shi no myōyaku: Shizen kinkō no hakai-sha kagaku yakuhin*. trans. Aoki Ryōichi. Tokyo: Shinchōsha, 1964.

"Gojira tai Hedorah," *Tōhō Stadjio mēru* n52 (1971).

"Gojira tai Hedorah: Kaesu taiyō wo" (Lyricist: Sakano Yoshimitsu; Composition: Manabe Riichiro; Arrangement: Takada Hiroshi; Performed by Mari Keiko and Honey Nights Moon Drops).

"Hedora wo yattsukero" (Composition: Koichi Sugiyama; Performed by Mari Keiko and Honey Nights Moon Drops) *Gojira tai Hedora* (Tokyo: Victor, 1971) BX-88.

Hudson, Laura. "At the End of the World, It's Hyperobjects All the Way Down." *Wired*. November 16, 2021. Accessed July 25, 2023. https://www.wired.com/story/timothy-morton-hyperobjects-all-the-way-down/.

Karatani, Kōjin. *Nation and Aesthetics: On Kant and Freud*. London: Oxford University Press, 2017.

"Kōkagaku sumoggu sakkā taikai o osou chūgakusei, tsugitsugi taoreru Urawa." *Asahi Shinbun*. August 17, 1971.

"Kōtei no kōkōsei-ra 40 sū-ri ga taoreru Suginami shinkenzai yaita gasu ka." *Asahi Shinbun*. July 18, 1970.

Meis, Morgan. "Timothy Morton's Hyper-Pandemic." *New Yorker*, June 8, 2021.

Morton, Timothy. *Being Ecological*. New York: Penguin Books, 2018.

Morton, Timothy. *Dark Ecology: For a Logic of Future Coexistence.* New York: Columbia University Press, 2016.

Morton, Timothy. *Hyperobjects: Philosophy and Ecology after the End of the World.* Minneapolis: University of Minnesota Press, 2013.

Nixon, Rob. *Slow Violence and the Environmentalism of the Poor.* Harvard University Press, 2011.

Oka, Takashi. "Japan Urged to Save Polluted Harbor." *New York Times*, August 17, 1970.

Oka, Takashi. "Sato Plans Action to Meet Pollution Crisis in Japan." *New York Times*, July 29, 1970.

Rhoads, Sean and McCorkle, Brooke. *Japan's Green Monsters: Environmental Commentary in Kaiju Cinema.* Jefferson, NC: McFarland, 2018.

Ryfle, Steve. *Japan's Favorite Mon-Star: The Unauthorized Biography of "The Big G."* New York: ECW Press, 1998.

Schmitt, Carl. *Dictatorship.* New York: John Wiley & Sons, 2015.

Schmitt, Carl. *Political Theology: Four Chapters on the Concept of Sovereignty.* Chicago: University of Chicago Press, 2010.

Spivak, Gayatri Chakravorty. *A Critique of Postcolonial Reason: Toward a History of the Vanishing Present.* Cambridge: Harvard University Press, 1999.

Staff. "World Waystar Entertainment: Vince McMahon, Hyperobject." *POST Wrestling*, March 28, 2023. Accessed July 25, 2023. https://www.postwrestling.com/2023/03/28/world-waystar-entertainment-vince-mcmahon-hyperobject-essay/.

"Supesharu intabyū: Sakano Yoshimitsu." *Gojira Tōhō chanpion matsuri pāfekushon.* eds. Dengeki hobīmagajin henshū-bu. Tokyo: Kadokawa, 2014.

"Sutaffu intabyū 11: Manabe Riichirō sairoku." *Gojira Tōhō chanpion matsuri pāfekushon,* eds. Dengeki hobīmagajin henshū-bu. Tokyo: Kadokawa, 2014.

"Tōhō tokusatsu eiga sakuhin-shi: Gojira tai Hedora." *Tōhō tokusatsu eiga zenshi.* eds. Tanaka Tomoyuki, and Tōhō kabushikigaisha. Tokyo: Tōhō kabushikigaisha shuppan jigyō-shitsu, 1983.

3

The Toxic Vitality of Kiyoshi Kurosawa's *Charisma*

Rachel DiNitto

Japanese classic cinema of the early postwar era garnered international accolades and shaped the image of Japan through alluring visuals of a garden paradise. By contrast, directors in the 1990s reveled in the dystopian. Film scholar Tim Palmer argues that representations of the environment are crucial to the global identity of Japanese cinema. In the 1950s, Akira Kurosawa and Kenji Mizoguchi crafted a cinematic "garden aesthetic," representing "Japan as a source of natural abundance, beautiful and untarnished wilderness, a limitless milieu of diverse organic splendor."[1] By contrast, Palmer asserts that in the 1990s, directors like Kiyoshi Kurosawa presented Japan as an eco-horror landscape in decline. Kiyoshi Kurosawa's *Charisma* (1999) is set in the rural landscapes of wooded forests and open meadows, but it depicts the natural world as neither the pure, untouched counterpart to human folly seen in classic cinema, nor the bleak, industrial wasteland of the 1990s.[2] *Charisma* centers on Yabuike, a policeman caught amid the struggle over the sickly, eponymous tree that is supposedly killing the surrounding forest by means of a virulent toxin. Yabuike attempts in vain to negotiate among the human factions trying to enact their will on nature by attempting to save or kill the Charisma tree. Critics have analyzed *Charisma* as a commentary on the modern Japanese struggle between the individual and society.[3] This chapter argues for the materiality of the forest as more than a backdrop for human struggle; rather than focus solely on the actions of the humans, nature is acting and interacting with the humans as part of an enmeshed web of toxic ecology.

Using Palmer as a departure point, this chapter similarly pairs 1950s films with *Charisma* in order to dig deeper into the divide between "untarnished wilderness"/environment in decline and active human/passive nature. I argue that *Charisma* is more than a "reversal of the garden aesthetic" achieved through depictions of a post-1990s Japan in ruins.[4] Rather, I read *Charisma* through and against the themes and *mise-en-scènes* of these earlier films and environmental theories to demonstrate how Kurosawa complicates binaries and depicts what I term a "landscape of toxic vitality." The film focuses on the sickly yet supposedly deadly Charisma tree that we are told is killing off the surrounding forest. But the pitched battles over the tree obscure the large-scale industrial poisoning of the landscape by the botanist Jinbo, and the fact that while some trees are dying, the majority of the natural landscape is thriving in spite of Jinbo's chemicals. Nature in *Charisma* is complex, contradictory, alive, and it is not simply a metaphor for human society. Yabuike is unable to successfully read the environment or navigate the battles over it. The vitality of the landscape in *Charisma* is similar to that of contaminated environments, and hence, I term it "toxic vitality," meaning that such zones are neither fully barren wastelands nor lush biodiverse havens. I argue that the landscapes in *Charisma* are symbolic of nature's toxic vitality, in which the environment is far from dead, even if it is deadly. By emphasizing the vitality of nature, I am not dismissing the contaminated state of these areas. Rather, I seek to break down binaries in order to decode the contaminated nature in the film.

As a means of addressing these conflicting images of nature and *Charisma*'s toxic landscapes, I turn to research on irradiated landscapes like the wildlife refuges at Cold War-era nuclear production sites in the US—for example, the Rocky Flats National Wildlife Refuge that was created out of the contaminated security buffer zone for the secret Rocky Flats plutonium production plant in Colorado. Shiloh Krupar dismisses the divide of pure/impure or nature/waste used by the government to distinguish wildlife preserves from the nuclear sites that house them. Krupar argues, "Rocky Flats is natural *and* contaminated; these are not mutually exclusive conditions of existence."[5] Krupar's conceptualization allows us to escape the binary of the "virgin" forests of the 1950s silver screen versus the decrepit landscapes of 1990s films in order to think more about how toxicity and nature function in *Charisma*, and the reality of contaminated environments that do not adhere to easy binaries.

Unlike environmental critiques that tend to "make nature the passive victim of contamination," or containment myths about a human ability to remain separate and unaffected by industrial chemicals, in *Charisma*, nature has the agency to enact its will regardless of human desires, and there is no indication that the chemicals are harmless to humans.[6] Rather, everything in the film is "enmeshed in a dense network of relations."[7] To examine nature's active role, my concept of toxic vitality draws on Jane Bennett's *Vibrant Matter*, specifically her definition of "vitality": "the capacity of things—edibles, commodities, storms, metals—not only to impede or block the will and designs of humans but also to act as quasi agents or forces with trajectories, propensities, or tendencies of their own."[8] Bennett's conception of nonhuman agency is germane to the depiction of nature in *Charisma*, where both the human and nonhuman are reacting to the toxic environment. When asked about the "forests, poisoned pastures, apocalyptic pollen drifts, fossil-filled quarries, and blood-soaked golf courses" in his films, Kurosawa answered, "For many people, plant life is generally seen to be quiet and beautiful and tame. But the way that trees survive over several centuries is by decimating everything around them, in a very cruel and beautiful way. It's the contradiction between plants being very still, and yet so voracious and devastating, that interests me."[9] Kurosawa's attention to the materiality and agency of the plants should not be lost in our analysis.

The emphasis in *Charisma* is on the contrast between the toxins of the Charisma tree and the forest that is struggling to live. But Charisma is not the only source of poison in the film. Parts of the forest are dying, and human health is at risk, but the connected ecological web in *Charisma* makes it impossible to distinguish the source of the contaminants or to definitively identify a particular landscape as pure or contaminated. Is the forest dying because of Charisma's natural toxins or Jinbo's industrially produced toxicants (the chemicals she adds to the water table to kill the tree)? The film does not allow for the division of safe/ toxic or pure/impure. Instead, Kurosawa creates a landscape of toxic vitality in *Charisma*, a space where nature lives and dies amid natural toxins and industrial toxicity, much like the wildlife refuges on irradiated land. The humans are not separate from the landscape or immune from the harm they cause, for as Bennett argues, "to harm one section of the web may very well be to harm oneself."[10] Rather than see the landscapes in *Charisma* as either safe or contaminated, I argue, as does Krupar, that the landscape is both "natural *and* contaminated." This means that while there are scenes of dead and dying trees, there are also scenes of vibrant natural splendor; unspoiled, virgin nature can and does exist within contaminated zones, especially when the contamination is not visible to the naked eye. Below, I begin with a brief description of the films and their use of natural imagery.

The Garden Aesthetic of *Rashomon* and *Ugetsu*

As mentioned above, Tim Palmer argues that the Western celebration of Japanese film in the 1950s and 1960s hinged on the *mise-en-scene* of the "lush garden paradise" of an "unspoiled, verdant, natural preserve" as exemplified by Akira Kurosawa's *Rashomon* (1950) and Kenji Mizoguchi's *Ugetsu* (1953).[11] Both movies received high honors at the Venice International Film Festival and indelibly shaped the international reception and reputation of classic Japanese cinema.[12] Both films also depict a preindustrial nature; the land supports its human inhabitants through logging and farming but remains relatively unspoiled. Importantly, the temporal settings of the films predate the era of industrial chemical poisoning. The famous establishing shot for *Rashomon*, a period piece set in the twelfth century, is set at the giant ruined Rasho gate, where a priest, woodcutter, and commoner seek shelter from the driving rain. The woodcutter tells the enigmatic story of a murder, and the film unfolds as a series of flashbacks set in the woods, where a nobleman and his wife encounter the notorious criminal Tajomaru. The story— the same diegetic event—is told serially from the perspective of these three and the woodcutter, who found the corpse. Set in a wooded area outside Nara, the camerawork emphasizes both the natural setting and *Rashomon*'s cinematic virtuosity; the filming techniques far outweigh the narrative needs of the plot. The camera is constantly in motion—low angle tracks, downward tilts, pans, close-ups, extreme long shots, swipes—in the four-minute sequence when the woodcutter walks through the forest, and also in the scenes when the husband, wife, and thief face off in the woods. The constantly shifting cinematic point-of-view emphasizes the instability of a multi-viewpoint narrative in which the wife, thief, and dead nobleman all admit to the crime. While the plot revolves around the intrigue and deception of this deadly love triangle, the setting is one of untouched nature. Lush leaves and brush, giant logs, and towering trees enclose the characters in a space set off from the outside world. This wilderness contrasts sharply with the decrepitude of the man-made Rasho gate, the entryway to a city now in ruins from warfare, earthquakes, whirlwinds, fires, famine, plague, crime, and death. While some of these threats are human-made, they differ significantly from the harm produced by the toxic chemicals in *Charisma*.

Nature in *Rashomon* oscillates between the driving rain at the city gate and the undisturbed woodlands. By contrast, Mizoguchi's *Ugetsu* shifts from the farmed countryside to the eerily wild Lake Biwa to the curated nature of Japanese gardens, painted folding screens, and kimono patterns. Mizoguchi also shot on location in the rural areas of western Japan, namely outside Kyoto. *Ugetsu* is also a period film set in a medieval era of warfare. The husband Genjūrō, his wife, and young son live in a farming village subject to the raids of marauding soldiers who force the villagers to retreat to the surrounding hills for safety while the settlements are pillaged. Genjūrō goes to town to sell his wares and is entranced by a young noblewoman, Lady Wakasa, who turns out to be a ghost in search of the love she was denied in her short time on earth. The scenes on and around Lake Biwa function as an uncanny bridge connecting the farmland of daily toil to the phantom world of elegance and beauty. The lake is surrounded by reeds, a liminal setting known for traditional ghostly sightings, and the mist that encompasses the lake adds an ominous, spectral threat. Lake Biwa also borders Lady Wakasa's palace, which magically transforms as Genjūrō walks through it on his way to deliver his wares. The run-down, weed-choked, overgrown ruins transform into an impeccably maintained, traditional Japanese house replete with a manicured courtyard garden. The curated nature at Wakasa's house is referenced in the opening title sequence of the film as stylized paintings of trees, flowers, waves, and hills. These designs are echoed in the kimono and folding screens that adorn Lady Wakasa and her home. However, in the end, this stylized nature is only an illusion, as Genjūrō awakens from the enchantment with the ruins of Wakasa's manor lost in the grasses and reeds behind him. The film ends with the widowed Genjūrō back home crafting pottery, and the camera rises above the cultivated landscape to emphasize the constancy of nature in one of the many crane shots that dominate *Ugetsu*. Unlike the incessant motion of the camera in *Rashomon*, *Ugetsu* relies on "long shots of natural harmony," described as the "flowing scroll," "one shot—one scene" style of static, long-duration takes.[13]

Charisma's Toxic Vitality

The protagonist of *Charisma*, Yabuike Goro, is a policeman on forced leave after a botched hostage negotiation where both hostage and hostage-taker ended up dead. He heads out of town and enters a forest, where he unwittingly walks into a pitched battle over the eponymous tree, a decidedly uncharismatic, sickly species fanatically cared for by Kiriyama, a former inmate at a now abandoned sanitarium. Kiriyama guards the tree against human threats and feeds it elixirs through IV tubes. Forest rangers try in vain to save the surrounding trees that are dying by planting seedlings, and they are under orders to retrieve the Charisma tree for further research. The botanist Jinbo regards Charisma as an invasive species and claims that while Charisma appears weak, it thrives at the cost of the surrounding forest. Jinbo is willing to kill the entire forest by poisoning the water table in order to destroy Charisma and restore the woods to their original state. Toward the end of the film, Nekojima arrives at the forestry base to retrieve the tree for a wealthy collector. Yabuike is caught in the crosshairs of these battles, befriending Kiriyama and his enemies only to find himself at the center of the confrontation. The film comes to a climax as the rangers dig up Charisma, but Jinbo steals it and sets it on fire. Yabuike then finds another tree—from all appearances, an old, dead snag—and proclaims it another Charisma. He fights Jinbo and Nekojima for the tree and ends up in a quasi-hostage showdown when Nekojima threatens to kill Jinbo. Yabuike destroys the tree but leaves behind a small shoot. He abandons the woods with a wounded Nekojima, and the film ends with Yabuike looking into the distance at the city in flames, as sirens ring and helicopters fly overhead. He calls his boss, who asks, "What the hell have you done?"

In order to see the toxic vitality in *Charisma*, we need to look beyond the eponymous tree and the human intervention to the other representations of nature in the film. Just as the title of the film is a misnomer for the sickly, unappealing tree, the Charisma tree is not a synecdoche for nature in the film. It only represents one aspect of the natural environment. Charisma is killing other plants, but in the process, it is dying itself. In *Charisma*, human attempts to contain or control the environment are in vain, and the surrounding nature thrives in its toxic vitality; the organic splendor is a site of both natural beauty and deadly battles as some plants die and others live. The sections below examine depictions of nature in *Charisma* as thriving and toxic, as well as the anthropogenic attempts to control it. The *Rashomon* effect in *Charisma*, where the truth is elusive, frustrates Yabuike's attempts to read the landscape and demonstrates how the concept of toxic vitality itself defies binaries that attempt to differentiate safe from dangerous or pure from contaminated, or to separate nature from the fate of the humans within it.

Thriving Nature

Kurosawa is famous for the obstructed vision of his cinematic frames, namely the walls, bars, doorways, and windows that separate his characters from the camera. In *Charisma*, thriving nature also acts to obstruct the cinematic vision. This obstructed vision is also utilized in *Rashomon* in the aforementioned, four-minute woodcutter sequence, where the dazzling display of camera angles often places branches, leaves, and trees between the camera and the woodcutter. *Charisma* similarly employs an obstructed vision to showcase the vitality of nature: lush trees and leafy shadows intervene between the camera and its subjects, and the forest canopy reflects off car windshields, impeding the transparency of the glass. In multiple shots, branches and leaves invade the building through windows and doors. In one scene, in which Nekojima and his men are scouting the forest, the camera tracks the men through the woods as they pass behind and amid the intervening trees. Similarly, trees partially obscure the view as Kiriyama and Yabuike spy on the forest rangers. In *Rashomon*, the camerawork emphasizes the abundant natural splendor and places the viewer within it, but in *Charisma*, the obstructed vision at times turns the woods into a maze, hindering the character's ability to navigate it. Toward the end of the film, Nakasone and Tsuboi—men whose jobs require them to work in forests—get lost in the woods, something that never happens in *Rashomon*.

There are many shots of thick underbrush, moss, grasses, plants, and streams in *Charisma*. In one scene, Yabuike sits with the sanitarium director's widow on the balcony of the facility (figure 3.1). In contrast to the dark, decrepit interior of the building, a classic feature of Kurosawa's films, this full shot frames them at a table on the veranda and keeps the focus on the lush natural background: the yellow leaves of a large deciduous tree on the right, green pine trees and meadow grasses in the background, and rain dripping off the building. Kurosawa's stable camera, the long take, and the extremely minimal actor movement emphasize the overwhelming presence of nature in this scene, highlighting the vitality of the natural surroundings. The other important landscape in *Charisma* is the high meadow where the Charisma tree grows in an area apart from the woods. Kurosawa uses extreme long shots, aerial shots, and deep focus to emphasize the vastness of this meadow landscape and the surrounding foothills (figure 3.2).

Figure 3.1. Yabuike and the sanitarium director's widow on the balcony. Kurosawa Kiyoshi, 1999, Nikkatsu.

Figure 3.2. The Charisma tree in the high meadow. Kurosawa Kiyoshi, 1999, Nikkatsu.

Despite the shots of the ailing Charisma tree and its purported harm to the forest, the vast majority of scenes are outdoors amid a vital, pervasive natural landscape. Yabuike enters the woods five minutes into the film and only leaves at the very end of the movie; like its classic predecessors, *Charisma* was primarily shot outdoors on location—in this case, near Mt. Fuji.

Toxic Nature

The forest in *Charisma* is a place of danger and harm, but the threat is not the same as in the older films. In *Rashomon* and *Ugetsu*, the woods are perilous because of the presence of bandits and rogue soldiers. In *Charisma*, the menace is multifold—human and more-than-human—and at times invisible. Kiriyama shoots at and stabs others, Jinbo is poisoning the water, and Yabuike is caught in bear traps, indicating the presence of large, wild animals. But the film's plot primarily focuses on the danger from the Charisma tree as something foreign and external to the ecosystem. Jinbo tells Yabuike that the tree is an invasive species brought from the continent, a monster that produces a virulent toxin that will eventually kill the whole forest. But the forest is already a toxic zone, as evidenced by Jinbo's warning that Yabuike should not eat the wild greens or fruits he finds by the stream because they contain powerful carcinogens that over time may be lethal. But is this stream poisonous because of Charisma, Jinbo's industrial chemicals, or some other source? The answer is unclear because the woods are a place of both natural and anthropogenic harm, as evidenced by the complaint Chizuru, Jinbo's sister, makes to Yabuike: "This is a horrible place. Foul-smelling ozone, ultraviolet rays. Then there are poisonous weeds, snakes, and bugs. Poison everywhere." Chizuru does not distinguish the anthropogenic harm to the ozone from the naturally occurring toxins of weeds and venomous snakes, their own attempts at survival.

As evidenced in Jinbo and Chizuru's comments, nature is not a passive victim of human action, and neither is the environment deadened. Rather, it is powerful and deadly. Jinbo tells Yabuike that the young plants are being drawn to Charisma as if they are drugged. Her ideas about Charisma's agency mirror Kurosawa's theory about plants. To return to Bennet's argument, nature in *Charisma* works "not only to impede or block the will and designs of humans but also to act as quasi agents or forces with trajectories, propensities, or tendencies of their own." The Charisma tree, and the "poisonous weeds, snakes, and bugs," are agents of harm, but their toxins lack the large scale and production, the long temporalities, and the violence of Jinbo's chemicals.

This combination of the lush natural environment and toxicity is reminiscent of the wildlife refuges around highly contaminated former nuclear facilities. These zones, which were created as an environmental barrier separating the facilities from residential communities, are teeming with animals and plants. However, as Joseph Masco argues, the flora and fauna in these preserves are "unusually radioactive," and these "new forms of nuclear nature" are not limited to the US.[14]

> The global effects of nuclear production have transformed the global environment, making the biosphere itself a postnuclear formation. Because the trace elements of atmospheric fallout are now ubiquitous in soils and waterways, flora and fauna, the "nature" of wildlife as a concept has changed in the nuclear age.[15]

The Charisma tree is barely surviving in this contaminated environment, but other trees and grasses are thriving without Kiriyama's scaffolding, elixirs, and balms, and seemingly in spite of Jinbo's chemicals—just as the flora and fauna thrive at nuclear wildlife reserves. Yet the anthropogenic harm should not be overlooked. Like radiation, modern industrial chemicals are "ubiquitous in soils and waterways, flora and fauna," and in human bodies. Nature in *Charisma* is thriving, but that does not mean it is not contaminated or that Jinbo's chemicals are benign. As evidenced in sites of "nuclear nature," the divided labels of pure/polluted, nature/waste, and wilderness/wasteland are not easily applied.

Nature and Anthropogenic Harm

Jinbo seeks to return the forest to an "original state," before the sanitarium director introduced the Charisma tree. Christine Marran argues that Jinbo's "forest is a nostalgic one that would harken to a pure forest of the past—a fraught notion given that definitions of what constitutes an 'invasive species' can vary for ecologies and peoples."[16] Jinbo's characterizations of the Charisma tree provide her the rationale she needs to poison the entire forest, a scale only possible with industrial chemicals. At first, Yabuike aids her because he thinks she is adding chemicals to improve the soil. Jinbo's true intent is revealed to him by Chizuru later in the film, but in the earlier scenes, Kurosawa visually tricks the audience into believing Jinbo. In a film in which all other interior shots adhere to Kurosawa's dark, decrepit aesthetic, Jinbo's home stands out for its light and transparency; the camera emphasizes the clean lines and neat and orderly rooms of the open, glass-enclosed structure, as well as the presence of her scientific instruments (figure 3.3). When she lectures Yabuike on the ecosystem and the dangers of Charisma, the scene is not shot outdoors near the tree, as are many others, but inside her home. Kurosawa uses a shot-reverse shot sequence of close-ups on Jinbo's and Yabuike's faces that is extremely rare in *Charisma*, and one that is not used for other scenes of emotionally important dialogue. The transparency of Jinbo's dwelling and the camerawork enhance her credibility. But in this scene, the close-ups and *mise-en-scène* conceal rather than reveal. Jinbo deceives Yabuike. Despite her professed care for the forest, she is actively killing it.

Figure 3.3. Jinbo at her home. Kurosawa Kiyoshi, 1999, Nikkatsu.

Jinbo seeks a natural purity not possible in contaminated environments; she keeps trees and plants in large glass boxes inside her house, separated from their natural habitat. Yabuike is arguably as much under Jinbo's spell as Genjūrō was under Wakasa's in *Ugetsu*. Jinbo's desire to control nature is akin to the curated and ultimately illusory nature at Wakasa's palace. Jinbo tries to bend nature to her will. However, she is not the only character to use nature for her own purposes. The forest rangers plan to profit from Charisma by selling the tree to a wealthy collector. At the beginning of the film, Tsuboi asks Yabuike if he is trying to rediscover himself in the great outdoors, implying Yabuike is using nature to restore himself, but Kiriyama is skeptical of such endeavors. He says, if you save the forest, you are only doing it for yourself so you can take walks. Kiriyama argues that the "forest is a battlefield where plants live and die. If only Charisma survives, that's the way it works." Yet he too intervenes with the elixirs and balms in an attempt to keep Charisma alive.

Palmer argues that Kurosawa only uses extreme long shots of natural vistas when "his films confirm that all prospects of saving the world, its potential to withstand humanity, have gone," and that nature in Kurosawa's films is "no match for the unthinking machinations of mankind."[17] This comment implies that the film is a parable about anthropogenic harm to an untouched and helpless nature. But in *Charisma*, nature impedes human will, acts on its own purposes, and thrives amid contamination. It is possible that the Charisma forest will survive even the apocalypse in the distant city.

The Riddle of Toxic Vitality

Film critic Tom Mes argued that *Charisma* is "masquerading as a detective film," and I would emphasize the "masquerading" part, since the mystery of the dying forest is never solved.[18] Neither Yabuike nor the audience can truly tell if the forest is being harmed by naturally occurring toxins, an invasive species, or industrial chemicals. Is Charisma killing off other trees or is Jinbo's poison to blame? Is the forest truly dying? In this regard, *Charisma* echoes the conundrums of *Rashomon* and *Ugetsu*. But unlike the relatively happy endings of those films, *Charisma* ends with a dead tree, an injured man, an impending apocalypse, and no resolution.

Kosuke Kinoshita argues that *Rashomon* "maintains the credibility of each [character] to some degree," but in *Charisma*, Yabuike is surrounded by a cast of completely untrustworthy, unhinged characters capable of violence and deception, showing the humans to be as deadly as the nonhuman world.[19] Kiriyama warns him not to trust Jinbo, as does her sister Chizuru, who then proceeds to guide Yabuike straight into a bear trap. Chizuru claims she dragged Yabuike to safety from a burning car at the beginning of the film, but she may have set the fire in the first place to kill him. Jinbo presents herself as an objective scientist caring for the forest, but she purposely poisons the water and lies to Yabuike about it. Tsuboi's job is environmental protection, yet he is driven by the temptation of profit and tips off Nekojima, enabling him to sell Charisma. The characters are using Yabuike for their own purposes, trapping him in a maze of lies and deception. Chizuru alludes to this when she comments to Yabuike that the "whole thing is starting to seem a little ridiculous" and "anyone who spends time in the forest will go nuts." The enigmatic nature of *Charisma* is echoed in the human actions of the earlier classic films. Yabuike is no better able to solve the mystery in *Charisma* than the bystanders or court officials in *Rashomon*, or than Genjūrō is able to see through the blinding enchantment of his phantom lover, Wakasa, in *Ugetsu*.

All three films share depictions of human avarice, pride, and lust. But in the earlier films, nature does not drive the characters' motivations; nor do they attempt to enact their will upon it. In *Charisma*, the battle is not just among the human factions or between Charisma and the other trees. The forest itself plays tricks on the characters, primarily through its hallucinogenic mushrooms. When Yabuike consumes them, the line between the real and the illusory becomes impossible to gauge. Rather than the mythical spirits of *Ugetsu*, in *Charisma*, the forest's botanicals entrance and entrap the human characters. Yabuike's name, literally "pond in the grove," is an oblique reference to "In a Bamboo Grove" ("Yabu no naka"), the short story Akira Kurosawa used as a basis for the *Rashomon* scenes that take place in the woods.[20] His name implies that Yabuike is also lost in this vital yet deadly sylvan maze. The *Rashomon* effect in *Charisma* similarly complicates the viewer's ability to rely on binaries like pure/impure, natural/contaminated, and passive nature/active humans in order to make sense of the film.

Conclusion

What is the eco-disaster in *Charisma*? Is it the loss of the eponymous tree? The apocalypse of the city that echoes the recurring scenes of conflagration in Kurosawa's films? The dying forest? Or human blindness to our role in creating this contaminated nature? *Charisma* presents no answers. In general, Kurosawa's films are a "rejection of the primacy of narrative clarity" and explanation, and *Charisma* is representative in that regard.[21] *Charisma* is simultaneously a parable about the risks of anthropogenic harm, a critique of myopic conservationism, a testimony to nonhuman agency, and a Suzuki Seijun-esque campy, mushroom-induced hallucination that leaves viewers guessing.[22] But it is also an important commentary on the state of nature in our contaminated world. Images of a pure, untouched, safe nature persist, as do the opposite. *Charisma* visualizes a space where these two landscapes—the natural *and* contaminated—meet, the space of toxic vitality. The film does not allow us to forget our presence within that space.

Notes

[1] Palmer, "The Rules of the World," 212.

[2] *Charisma (Karisuma)*. To avoid confusion between the two Kurosawas, I refer to Kiyoshi as Kurosawa and his predecessor as Akira Kurosawa.

[3] Mes, "Review: Charisma (Karisuma, 1999, Kiyoshi KUROSAWA)"; Gerow, "Young Kurosawa Thrives in Uncertain Times."

[4] Palmer, "The Rules of the World," 220.

[5] Krupar, "Transnatural Ethics," 307.

[6] Krupar, *Hot Spotter's Report*, 12–13.

[7] Bennettt, *Vibrant Matter*, 13.

[8] Bennettt, *Vibrant Matter*, viii.

[9] Stephens, "Another Green World," 72.

[10] Bennettt, *Vibrant Matter*, 13.

[11] Palmer, "The Rules of the World," 210.

[12] *Rashomon* took the top prize, the Golden Lion, and *Ugetsu* took the Silver Lion, the secondary honor. Mizoguchi won awards at Venice three years in a row. Both films depict a traditional, medieval Japan and are based on premodern stories.

[13] Palmer, "The Rules of the World," 215; Lopate, "From the Other Shore."

[14] Masco, "Mutant Ecologies," 532, 533.

[15] Masco, 531. The Hanford Reach National Monument, created from the buffer zone around the Hanford Nuclear Reservation, America's most contaminated nuclear site, is home to "over 800 species considered rare, threatened, endangered, and/or new to science." See Cram, "Wild and Scenic Wasteland," 91.

[16] Marran, "Arboreal Unicorns and Other Megaflora: On Kurosawa Kiyoshi's Film Charisma," 274.

[17] Palmer, "The Rules of the World," 220–221.

[18] Mes, "Review: Charisma (Karisuma, 1999, Kiyoshi KUROSAWA)."

[19] Kinoshita, "Multi-Viewpoint Narrative: From *Rashomon* (1950) to *Confessions* (2010)," 82.

[20] The story was originally published in Japanese in 1921. For the English translation, see Akutagawa, "In a Bamboo Grove."

[21] Posadas, "Fantasies of the End of the World," 454. Posadas cites Aaron Gerow on trends in Kurosawa's generation of filmmakers: Gerow, "Recognizing 'Others' in a New Japanese Cinema," 6.

[22] Marran, "Arboreal Unicorns and Other Megaflora: On Kurosawa Kiyoshi's Film Charisma." Stephens says Suzuki Seijun is "the only Japanese filmmaker to whom Kurosawa is willing to profess a strong devotion." See Stephens, "Another Green World," 68. Like Suzuki, Kurosawa also worked for Nikkatsu and similarly battled with the film company for not conforming to genre conventions.

Bibliography

Akutagawa, Ryūnosuke. "In a Bamboo Grove." In *Rashōmon and Seventeen Other Stories*, translated by Jay Rubin, 10–19. London: Penguin Books, 2006.

Bennett, Jane. *Vibrant Matter: A Political Ecology of Things*. Durham: Duke University Press, 2010.

Charisma (Karisuma). Drama, Mystery. Nikkatsu, 2000.

Cram, Shannon. "Wild and Scenic Wasteland: Conservation Politics in the Nuclear Wilderness." *Environmental Humanities* 7 (2015): 89–105.

Gerow, Aaron. "Recognizing 'Others' in a New Japanese Cinema." *Japan Foundation Newsletter* 39, no. 2 (2002): 1–6.

Gerow, Aaron. "Young Kurosawa Thrives in Uncertain Times." *Daily Yomiuri*, February 24, 2000.

Kinoshita, Kosuke. "Multi-Viewpoint Narrative: From *Rashomon* (1950) to *Confessions* (2010)." In *The Japanese Cinema Book*, edited by Hideaki Fujiki and Alastair Phillips, 81–93. London: British Film Institute/Bloomsbury Publishing Pic, 2020.

Krupar, Shiloh R. *Hot Spotter's Report: Military Fables of Toxic Waste*. Minneapolis: University of Minnesota Press, 2013.

Krupar, Shiloh R. "Transnatural Ethics: Revisiting the Nuclear Cleanup of Rocky Flats, Colorado, through the Queer Ecology of Nuclia Waste." *Cultural Geographies* 19, no. 3 (2012): 303–327.

Lopate, Phillip. "From the Other Shore." In *Charisma (Karisuma)*. Nikkatsu, 2000.

Marran, Christine L. "Arboreal Unicorns and Other Megaflora: On Kurosawa Kiyoshi's Film Charisma." In *Ecocriticism in Japan*, edited by Hisaaki Wake, Keijiro Suga, and Yuki Masami, 267–278. Lanham: Lexington Books, 2017.

Masco, Joseph. "Mutant Ecologies: Radioactive Life in Post-Cold War New Mexico." *Cultural Anthropology* 19, no. 4 (2004): 517–550.

Mes, Tom. "Review: Charisma (Karisuma, 1999, Kiyoshi KUROSAWA)." Midnight Eye: Visions of Japanese Cinema, March 20, 2001. http://www.midnighteye.com/reviews/charisma/.

Palmer, Tim. "The Rules of the World: Japanese Ecocinema and Kiyoshi Kurosawa." In *Framing the World: Explorations in Ecocriticism and Film*, edited by Paula Wiloquet-Maricondi, 209–224. Charlottesville: University of Virginia Press, 2010.

Posadas, Baryon Tensor. "Fantasies of the End of the World: The Politics of Repetition in the Films of Kurosawa Kiyoshi." *Positions* 22, no. 2 (2014): 429–460.

Stephens, Chuck. "Another Green World." *Film Comment* 37, no. 5 (October 2001): 64–66, 68, 71–72.

4

Plastic Garbage in Kore-eda Hirokazu's *Air Doll*

Davinder L. Bhowmik

Viewers familiar with Kore-eda Hirokazu (b. 1962) invariably associate his feature films with the workings of memory, a theme the director first established in *Maboroshi no hikari* (1995), solidified in *After Life* (1998), and made part and parcel of his cinema thereafter. But as with any auteur, Kore-eda's filmography is comprised of more than a single, albeit salient, characteristic. In Linda Ehrlich's book-length study, *The Films of Kore-eda Hirokazu*, for example, she analyzes Kore-eda's films in terms of the natural elements featured therein, such as water, fire, and metal. Critics such as Akira Mizuta Lippit have noted the documentary impulse in the director's works, such as in *Distance* (2001), which tells the aftermath of the 1995 sarin gas attack by the Aum Shinrikyō cult.[1] And since his winning the Palme d'Or in Cannes for *Shoplifters* (2018), essays on the nature of family bonds that pair Kore-eda with Yasujiro Ozu have appeared in succession.[2] Far less scholarly attention has been paid to Kore-eda and the environment, a social concern that has occupied the director from very early in his career.

The ravishing, long rural landscape scene at the end of *Maboroshi*, which serves as a counterpoint to the dense, dark urbanity of the film's opening, underscores the costs that attend modernization. The only bits of nature one sees in *Nobody Knows* (2004) are the fledgling plants the film's abandoned children put in used noodle cups and later transplant at the far edge of a barren parking lot. This concrete lot is but one of countless ugly vistas shown of Tokyo. In *I Wish* (2011), an abandoned lot the camera lingers on is filled with swaying pink and white cosmos in the countryside, where children from both city and country explore to their hearts' delight. Attention to nature in the form of seasonal and other elements, such as those Ehrlich writes of, fills Kore-eda's oeuvre.

Kore-eda films also point to a wide range of the director's social concerns, which include the AIDS epidemic (*Kare no inai hachigatsu—August Without Him*, 1994), child welfare (*Nobody Knows*), the judicial system (*The Third Murder*, 2017), and the family unit (*Still Walking*, 2008; *I Wish*, 2013; *Like Father, Like Son*, 2013; *Our Little Sister*, 2015). Less overt, but critical for fully understanding Kore-eda's worldview is the way his films speak to the issue of the environment. *Distance* is an early film that addresses the physical and psychological impact of the Aum Shinrikyō cult's release of sarin gas in the Tokyo underground. The adverse effect of poison gas in the environs is a clear theme. *Air Doll*, on the other hand, is a film whose connection to the environment is far subtler and, thus, what I aim to explicate in this essay. I argue that Kore-eda's use of a plastic doll that serves to console her owner, who himself occupies a precarious position as a restaurant worker, shows how the human and more-than-human are both threatened in a moment marked by climate change and impending ecological catastrophe. The doll, a market commodity, will soon become obsolete, and the restaurant worker, a neoliberal subject, knows how expendable he is. It is the film's planetary dimension that offers relief from these grim conditions and hope for a new form of community.

Air Doll: Reception

Air Doll is a film about a plastic blow-up doll that is purchased by an emasculated restaurant employee to assist in his sexual needs and to ameliorate his loneliness. One day, the doll, named Nozomi (Hope), discovers she has a heart, which effects in her an ontological change from doll to human. This shift also leads her to explore the world around her. She settles into a part-time job at a video rental store, where she falls for a fellow employee, Jun'ichi. One day, Nozomi falls and punctures herself, whereupon she begins to deflate. In an erotically charged scene, Jun'ichi blows air back into Nozomi and repairs the puncture. On another occasion, Nozomi tries to reciprocate, only to learn Jun'ichi has no air plug. Nozomi's creation of a plug results in tragedy. Bereft of Jun'ichi, Nozomi places herself in the trash, surrounded by hollow objects that resemble herself and which she has collected during her wanderings.

If Kore-eda's filmography has generated scholarship on issues that include the Japanese family, the judicial system, and human memory, how then have critics responded to *Air Doll*? Diane Wei Lewis explains how Kore-eda adapts the film from manga and focuses on issues of gender and precarity. She writes,

"In Koreeda's film, the innocent and childlike Nozomi's plight symbolizes the fraying of human relationships and the failure of the heterosexual family, a crisis that threatens Japan's future by endangering the child."[3] Indeed, the failure of the heterosexual family can be seen in the fact that air dolls are the only form of companionship Nozomi's owner can manage in his circumscribed life. And true enough, in the film's poignant final scene, Moe, a child who lives nearby, places her doll in Nozomi's arms, forming only a simulacrum of mother and child.

Kristopher Cannon interrogates how *Air Doll* "positions spectators to follow the life of a thing by upsetting normative orientation toward inanimate objects." He does this by showing how the film reframes subject-object relations and discloses the autonomy of things.[4] Like Cannon, Michelle Cho also focuses on the object in *Air Doll*—namely, the doll as a hollow, fantastic object. Cho analyzes the fantastic in two ways: first, as an example of a global "fantastic" cinema, and second, as a privatized fantasy that is "a survival strategy against hostile and depersonalized social relations and a key to the social forces of atomization that result in the absence of community in the lived spaces of late capital."[5] Cho's analysis shows how Nozomi is an object in two senses: the first is the commodity fetish, and the second is the "other of the self" that exists independently and cannot be objectified. Cannon and Cho's focus on Nozomi's agency is both instructive and welcome.

Eunjung Kim considers the doll as an embodiment of disability for a variety of reasons, including the suggestion made by a rehabilitation worker in 1980 that disabled men and women use dolls for their sexual needs. Kim's innovative analysis focuses on the passivity in, and the death of, dolls. Je Choel Park observes similarities in *Distance* and *Air Doll*, but rather than focusing on the respective film's relation to the environment, Park explores the formation of community— the survivors in *Distance* and the postnational Nozomi in *Air Doll*. Kim's attention to disability and Park's attention to community expand viewers' knowledge of the uncanny figure of the doll.[6]

In her essay on *Air Doll*, Barbara Hartley describes the film's complexity in its depiction of the type of hollow life that hyper-capitalism creates. She takes pains to find a way to understand *Air Doll* not as a work that fixates the gaze on a naked body but rather as a film in which Nozomi does the gazing outward. Hartley writes, "she gazes to learn, to become, and to be like, rather than to possess, colonize, or control."[7] While I concede Hartley's point about Nozomi's agency, given that Korean actor Doona Bae plays the air doll's part, the doll's learning of language with which to enunciate everyday Japanese expressions such as "*itte kimasu*" ("I'm off") or "*tadaima*" ("I'm back") cannot but recall the manner in which Koreans were colonized by the Japanese during the Asia-Pacific War.[8] The objectionable scene of the video store owner's rape of Nozomi also serves to remind the viewer of the wartime period in which the Japanese military employed euphemistically called "comfort women" (*ianfu*) to serve the sexual needs of its soldiers. And finally, the tragic scene of Nozomi first cutting Jun'ichi, who spurts blood, and then wandering the city cannot but call to mind poison woman Abe Sada, who, out of love, severed her lover's penis and testicles and carefully wrapped the organs in her kimono before leaving the inn where the couple had spent their last night.[9] Like many critics, Hartley does not touch on these scenes' evocation of Japan's colonial past; instead, her focus is squarely on contemporary Japan in the moment of late capitalism, when neoliberal reforms such as the casualization of labor deplete individuals of their vitality, and environmental degradation fills the earth with contaminants.

An Ecocritical Reading of *Air Doll*

Anyone who has lived in Japan knows how much single-use plastic exists. In fact, Japan is second only to the United States in the generation of plastic packaging waste per capita. And while Japan is second behind Germany in its management of plastic through a successful disciplining of the citizenry to recycle 85 percent of it, only a fraction of this is meaningfully recycled; the remainder is either incinerated or exported. Scientists have painstakingly shown how residual matter in the form of microplastics accumulates in the ocean, and they have forecasted that these plastics will quadruple by 2050, resulting in toxicity, inflammation, cancer, and a myriad of other health issues. That Kore-eda's *Air Doll* has a plastic blow-up sex toy as its titular character, a clear departure for a director best known for his examination of human memory, begs for an analysis of the film that focuses on plasticity and waste. In the reading that follows, I argue that Kore-eda's use of a plastic doll rather than a human makes *Air Doll* a cautionary tale in its critique of Japan's throwaway culture.

Two scenes that serve as bookends in *Air Doll* are an early scene in which Nozomi, enticed by a bird cry, sets out to discover the broader world outside her owner's squalid apartment, whereupon she observes a neighbor bidding farewell to his daughter, Moe, before disposing of his trash. Nozomi's language formation, mimicking Moe's phraseology (*itte kimasu*), is what stands out in the scene, making the trash disposal a rather trivial, albeit realistic, detail. However, the fact that the final and most memorable scene is of Nozomi placed atop a *noncombustible* trash heap after she has separately placed Jun'ichi in the combustible trash pile underscores the importance of garbage and its management in *Air Doll*. And if these scenes do not announce the subject of trash clearly enough, certainly the choice of the child's name, Moe, the verbal root of *moeru* (to burn) surely does![10]

When Nozomi visits her birthplace to learn how she ended up with a heart, a roomful of newly manufactured plastic dolls lies in wait. After some speculation of the matter by the dolls' creator, he leads Nozomi upstairs, where she is saddened to see a room full of used dolls. In response to her question about what will happen to them, her creator explains that he disposes of them once a year in spring. "Regrettably, they are noncombustible," he says. This sequence is important for reasons of plot, since Nozomi will go on to place herself with other noncombustible garbage, and Jun'ichi with combustible garbage, precisely because she learns the distinction between plastic objects and humans from her creator in these scenes. To be sure, the myriad of new and used air dolls we see also serve to emphasize the proliferation and disposal of plastic goods in Japan.

Yet another indication that waste and its disposal are central concerns in *Air Doll* can be seen in the film's most painful scene: Nozomi's rape. After successfully dodging her owner, Hideo, who comes into the video rental store, the manager, noticing Nozomi's behavior, puts two and two together and outs her for pursuing her fellow employee, Jun'ichi, while being in a relationship with Hideo. The next horrendous scene, in which the camera pans toward the manager raping Nozomi in a back room, is so saturated with the sound of penetration, the manager's heavy breathing, and Nozomi's dissociative humming, it is easy to overlook the visual elements. Affixed to the wall are two pieces of paper, one above a bin for combustible trash such as newspapers and the other for noncombustible trash such as plastic. To the right of these signs is a third piece of paper on which is written "Tidy up what's dirty" (*kitanai mono wa kichinto*). A final sheet of paper implores employees to "conserve energy" (*setsuden*). Although these signs might simply add to the film's realism by including verbiage commonly used in the storeroom of a business, they also serve to highlight the issue of waste, an aspect of *Air Doll* that is easy to overlook.

The Planetary in *Air Doll*

One of the curious features of the otherwise cramped and gloomy apartment the lowly restaurant worker Hideo lives in is a telescope, and a ceiling from which planets are suspended. Taking a cue from Christophe Thouny, who draws on Gilles Deleuze and Félix Guattari's geophilosophy and recent debates on the Anthropocene to argue that *Air Doll* is a radical critique of neoliberal societies as they transition into a posthuman planetary world, I would like to consider next how Kore-eda makes the move from the local to the planetary in the film.[11]

The film clearly marks Hideo, a restaurant worker whose superior tells him he is infinitely replaceable, as a neoliberal subject. As such, he is not dissimilar to his doll, a consumer product. Occupying an equally bleak home and workplace, Hideo takes refuge in companionship with Nozomi, his air doll, an object that sexually pleases without the bother a human relationship would entail. That Hideo lives in Tsukishima, a man-made island in Tokyo Bay, is noteworthy, for he is not a denizen of Tokyo proper but rather makes his home in an in-between space that is itself equipped with a telescope and festooned with plastic planets. It is these objects that quite literally give *Air Doll* a planetary dimension. And like Spike Jonze's science fiction film *Her* (2013), which Jeroen Boom and Anneke Smelik analyze through a posthuman framework, the planetary in *Air Doll* indicates a postanthropomorphic shift, or a process of becoming-earth, central to a posthumanism that defines subjectivity as based on the inclusion of relations to a myriad of more-than-human others.[12] In short, the human is decentered.[13]

In addition to the telescope and planets—of which the winter triangle, Sirius, Procyon, and Betelgeuse, adorn the apartment ceiling—the holiday decor in the video rental store and Hideo's apartment feature twinkling lights, spherical ornaments, and cut-out stars. Even the wind chime, a stock feature in Kore-eda's films, is, in *Air Doll*, decorated with the celestial bodies of a crescent moon and stars (figure 4.1). On one hand, the film depicts Tokyo as an urban space populated by alienated, lonely individuals similar to Hideo: a hoarder/bulimic young woman, an ailing elderly man, and an aging office worker. On the other, the film is chock-full of objects that gesture to the planetary, which offers lines of flight for the city's most beleaguered. The absence of community in the film's urban space is an effect of neoliberal capitalism and is indeed grim. The planetary, though, offers the viewer a futurity in which a new type of community, embodied by the human and the more-than-human, arises. The planetary is a force that injects life into the deadened, alienated humans that people *Air Doll* and awakens them to the beauty and fragility of the more-than-human that surrounds them.[14]

Figure 4.1. Celestial wind chime. Kore-eda Hirokazu, 2009, TV Man Union, Inc., Bandai Visual, Asmik Ace, Engine Film Inc., Eisei Gekijo.

Upon realizing she has a heart, echoing *The Wizard of Oz*, Nozomi begins to exhibit humanlike behavior: walking, speaking, even working part-time. The fantastic mode Kore-eda deliberately urges cinematographer Ping Bin Li to employ mitigates somewhat the temptation to read Nozomi as a representation of a wartime sex slave.[15] In a key scene, Nozomi engages in a planetary dance in which she appears to elongate as she leaps and jumps among the apartment's suspended planets. In a later dream sequence, Nozomi lies perpendicular in a column of water, where bubbles gurgle out of her mouth. This visually gorgeous scene, a nod to Hans Christian Andersen's *The Little Mermaid*, encapsulates the idea of a material body dissolving into foam. Whereas Andersen's mermaid is tasked with obtaining an immortal soul, Nozomi's celestial dance and oceanic submersion hint at her movement toward the planetary.

The interpretation of the posthuman condition as vital-materialist—that is, that the entirety of the world is made up of the same matter—is helpful for understanding Nozomi's trajectory from the earth to the cosmos. As a philosophy of becoming that emphasizes the materiality of all living things, vital materialism transcends the logic of binary oppositions such as organic and inorganic, or human and machine.[16] According to Rosi Braidotti and Maria Hlavajova, "the world and humans themselves are not dualistic entities structured according to dialectical principles of internal or external opposition, but rather materially embedded subjects-in-process circulating within webs of relation with forces, entities and encounters."[17]

By emphasizing common matter between Nozomi and the air and water in the scenes described above, *Air Doll* engages with broader discussions on ecological issues today and prompts the move from anthropocentrism toward a more geophilosophical perspective on the precariousness of the earth. Despite the attention paid to materiality in the film, the reason that Nozomi and Jun'ichi's love ultimately fails is revealed when, to Nozomi's consternation, Jun'ichi leaks blood, not air, after she cuts him. The gap between human and more-than-human seems to be unbridgeable. Had the film ended with Jun'ichi's death, the film would reinforce the duality I argue it ultimately eschews.

Rather than reifying binary oppositions, Kore-eda allows for an openness to the possibility of community in the form of something larger than this world: the planetary. He does this by making Nozomi a hollow body whose dying breath forges connections between the human and more-than-human. The cinematic language by which *Air Doll* attempts this bold move is through the spores of a dandelion that represent Nozomi's birthday wish, conveyed near the end of the film. As Nozomi lies in a noncombustible garbage heap, she appears to be just another throwaway plastic doll, but the air that leaves her bodily form becomes the air that blows out her birthday candle in a postfilm scene the entire cast populates

Figure 4.2. Nozomi in the garbage heap. Kore-eda Hirokazu, 2009, TV Man
Union, Inc., Bandai Visual, Asmik Ace, Engine Film Inc., Eisei Gekijo.

(figure 4.2). This same air sends the dandelion spores to several of the individuals
previously shown to be part of the alienated urban landscape. In short, Nozomi
cannot die because she is not human. Instead, she is, as Gilles Deleuze and Félix
Guattari put it, becoming-imperceptible, "the last horizon and immanent end of
all becomings, where one leaves the former self behind and radically fuses with the
environment. It is a process of blurring former distinctions between self and others,
of becoming cosmic, interconnected, and collective, beyond established notions of
individuality. To become-imperceptible is not to dissolve into nothingness, but
to radically dissolve into and merge with the world in an ultimate unfolding of
potentials."[18]

In the spectacle of Nozomi's "death" at the end of the film, a spore drifts into
the hoarder-bulimic's apartment, impelling her, as it did Nozomi earlier in the
film, to look out the window and exclaim, "How pretty!" (kirei). This seemingly
simple repetition only transpires after a lengthy process in which Nozomi goes
from inanimate form to animate form when drops of water touch her hand early
in the film; Nozomi, constrained by her embodied humanism, is subjected to
rape; and Nozomi, accepting the potential of disembodied posthumanism, finally
merges into a planetary dimension. At the end of the film, Nozomi has found a
line of flight in which Nozomi's planetary consciousness ever so slightly touches
the alienated lives around her, creating a new community.

In his reflections on *Air Doll*, Kore-eda cryptically alludes to the possibility
that exists in emptiness (*kûkyo wa kannô de aru*), but it is Yoshino Hiroshi's poem

"Life is," narrated over a montage late in the film, that is its metalanguage and that makes explicit the view of life *Air Doll* offers:

> Life is
> Life is
> Made, it seems, so no one of us is alone complete
> Flowers too
> Are insufficient
> Having only stamen and pistil
> Are insufficient
> An insect or breeze must come
> To matchmake between pistil and stamen
> In life,
> Everything
> Contains within itself a void
> That is filled by another.
> The world is probably
> The sum of others
> However
> No one knows
> Nor are we told
> To fill the void in each other
> We are all of us scattered
> Indifference is our relation to each other
> Sometimes
> we cannot even bear the relation we are given
> A flower is blooming
> A horsefly bathed in sunshine until just now
> Alights
> I too, once was a horsefly for someone
> And you too once were the wind for me
> Why is it
> The world is created
> So delicately?[19]

Herein lies the reason why it is critical to understand *Air Doll* through a fantastic mode rather than a realistic one. Focusing on Nozomi's ontological disposition as posthuman results in a positive formation of community, which Kore-eda acknowledges the film manifests.[20] This reading is counter to one in which Nozomi rather simply functions as an objectified sex tool for a male in crisis.

If, as I argue, *Air Doll* must be considered through the fantastic mode like the didactic tales that are its literary predecessors—*The Little Mermaid, The Wizard of*

Oz, or *Pinocchio*—what is the film's message? An examination of the final scene, in which the hoarder-bulimic awakens, is telling. The scene breaks the fantastic mode. Gone are the spores and anything related to the cosmos. The young girl pushes away the curtains, opens the window, and takes a deep breath. Looking down below at the spectacle of Nozomi in the trash heap surrounded by the hollow items Nozomi had carefully collected, the young woman echoes the first words Nozomi ever uttered: "How pretty!"

Air Doll begins and ends with scenes of garbage, and nods to waste are littered throughout the film. The last scene, which shows the hoarder-bulimic's garbage-strewn apartment and the young woman moved by the sight of Nozomi in the trash, recalls one of the signs scrawled in the back room of the video rental store: "Tidy up what's dirty." Contextually, this admonishment surely implores employees to wash their soiled dishes. On a planetary scale, it suggests, as does Yoshino's poem, respect for all forms of life, organic and nonorganic, combustible or noncombustible, human or plastic.

Notes

[1] Lippit, "Between Disaster, Medium 3.11."

[2] Choi, "Ozuesque as a Sensibility"; and Risker, "Questioning the Nature of Family Bonds."

[3] Lewis, "From Manga to Film: Gender, Precarity, and the Textual Transformation of *Air Doll*," 119.

[4] Cannon, "Ec-Static Air," 266.

[5] Cho, "A Disenchanted Fantastic," 224.

[6] Kim, "Why Do Dolls Die?"; Park, "Envisioning a Community of Survivors in 'Distance' and 'Air Doll.'"

[7] Hartley, "Intertextuality, Sex, and the Hollow Life in Kore'eda Hirokazu's *Air Doll*," 44.

[8] When I raised this issue with Kore-eda, he emphasized that he simply wanted to have critically acclaimed Doona Bae star in his film (personal conversation, May 18, 2017). The rape scene is difficult precisely because it is a graphic depiction of sexual violation. And while there is no doubt that those who know Japan's colonial history may be doubly troubled by the scene because it is a Japanese man who rapes a Korean female (playing a Japanese human) it is also true that *Air Doll* is a character-driven film in which Doona Bae dazzles. Finally, and fortunately, Kore-eda's move from the local to the planetary effectively eschews the problematic frame of the nation-state.

[9] Marran, *Poison Woman: Figuring Female Transgression in Modern Japanese Culture.*

[10] Even a casual visitor to Japan will see how ubiquitous it is to see garbage separated into combustible and noncombustible waste.

[11] Thouny, "Living as If We Were Air Dolls." I would like thank Christophe Thouny for sharing his essay on *Air Doll* with me in draft form. Posthumanism is the attempt to

challenge humanist assumptions that undergird the concept of the human. Posthuman thought eschews the human/nonhuman divide foundational since the Enlightenment and seeks to understand "the shifting ground on which new, diverse, and even contradictory understandings of the human are currently being generated, from a variety of sources, cultures, and traditions." See Bradoitti, *Posthuman Knowledge*, 11.

[12] Interestingly, when I asked Kore-eda what his favorite recent films were, he mentioned Jonze's *Her* (personal conversation, May 16, 2017.) Given how Kore-eda has a stated preference for *Air Doll*, his version of a love story between an animate and inanimate object, his admiration for Jonze's *Her* is not surprising. See Kore-eda, *Eiga o torinagara kangaeta koto*.

[13] Boom and Smelik, "Paradoxical (Post)Humanism," 1.

[14] I am inspired by Mary Louise Pratt, who writes about the planetary as a force and not a structure in the introduction of her recent book, *Planetary Longings*.

[15] Kore-eda, *Eiga o torinagara kangaeta koto*, 224.

[16] Vital materialism is one of the ideas by which the divide between human/nonhuman is bridged. This version of new materialism, as theorized by Jane Bennett, assumes that matter must be regarded as an active part of the political processes that heretofore have been governed by human subjectivity. Bennett seeks to rethink traditional distinctions between matter and life to establish that agency is not solely attributable to humans. See Bennett, *Vibrant Matter*.

[17] Braidotti and Hlavajova, *Posthuman Glossary*, 40.

[18] Braidotti and Hlavajova, *Posthuman Glossary*, 213.

[19] Kore-eda, *Eiga o torinagara kangaeta koto*, 231.

[20] Kore-eda, *Eiga o torinagara kangaeta koto*, 231.

Bibliography

Bennett, Jane. *Vibrant Matter: A Political Ecology of Things*. Durham: Duke University Press, 2010.

Boom, Jeroen, and Anneke Smelik. "Paradoxical (Post)Humanism: Disembodiment and Becoming-Earth in Her." *Journal of Posthuman Studies* 3, no. 2 (2019): 202–218.

Braidotti, Rosi. *Posthuman Knowledge*. Cambridge: Polity Press, 2019.

Braidotti, Rosi, and Maria Hlavajova, eds.. *Posthuman Glossary*. London: Bloomsbury Academic, 2018.

Cannon, Kristopher L. "Ec-Static Air: The Unseeable Sounds of Being Beside Oneself." *Discourse* 38, no. 2 (2016): 265–280.

Cho, Michelle. "A Disenchanted Fantastic: The Pathos of Objects in Hirokazu Kore-Eda's *Air Doll*." In *Simultaneous Worlds: Global Science Fiction Cinema*, edited by Jennifer L. Feeley and Sarah Ann Wells, 223. Minneapolis: University of Minnesota Press, 2015.

Choi, Jinhee. "Ozuesque as a Sensibility." In *Reorienting Ozu: A Master and His Influence*, edited by Jinhee Choi and Kosuke Fujiki. Oxford: Oxford University Press, 2018.

Ehrlich, Linda C. *The Films of Kore-Eda Hirokazu: An Elemental Cinema*. Cham: Springer International Publishing AG, 2020.

Hartley, Barbara. "Intertextuality, Sex, and the Hollow Life in Kore'eda Hirokazu's *Air Doll*." *Australasian Journal of Popular Culture* 10, no. 1–2 (2021): 39–50.

Kim, Eunjung. "Why Do Dolls Die? The Power of Passivity and the Embodied Interplay between Disability and Sex Dolls." *Review of Education/Pedagogy/Cultural Studies* 34, no. 3–4 (2012): 94–106.

Kore-eda, Hirokazu. *Eiga o torinagara kangaeta koto*. Shohan. Tokyo: Mishimasha, 2016.

Lewis, Diane Wei. "From Manga to Film: Gender, Precarity, and the Textual Transformation of *Air Doll*." *Screen (London)* 60, no. 1 (2019): 99–121.

Lippit, Akira Mizuta. "Between Disaster, Medium 3.11." *Mechademia* 10 (2015): 3–15.

Marran, Christine L. *Poison Woman: Figuring Female Transgression in Modern Japanese Culture*. Minneapolis: University of Minnesota Press, 2007.

Park, Je Cheol. "Envisioning a Community of Survivors in 'Distance' and 'Air Doll.'" *Film Criticism* 35, no. 2/3 (2011): 166–186.

Pratt, Mary Louise. *Planetary Longings*. Durham: Duke University Press, 2022.

Risker, Paul. "Questioning the Nature of Family Bonds: An Interview with Hirokazu Kore-Eda. *Cineaste: America's Leading Magazine on the Art and Politics of the Cinema* 44, no. 2 (2019): 42–43.

Thouny, Christophe. "Living as If We Were Air Dolls—Theory from the South/East." Unpublished conference paper.

Contaminated Futures
and Childhoods

5

Environmental Anxiety and the Toxic Earth of *Space Battleship Yamato*

Kaoru Tamura

In the darkest days of March 2011, just after reactor number one at the Fukushima Daichii nuclear power plant had exploded in a cloud of toxic smoke, Google detected a noticeable uptick in online references to "Yamato."[1] Bloggers, tweeters, and other netizens began furiously to discuss the parallels between the unfolding disaster and the beloved 1970s TV anime *Uchūsenkan Yamato* (*Space Battleship Yamato*, hereafter referred to as *SBY*), whose nuclear apocalyptic plot seemed suddenly more relevant than ever.[2] Watching the "Fukushima Fifty" on television, forty- and fifty-something-year-old Japanese could not help but remind people of Captain Okita Jūzō and his valiant crew, flying off to the Larger Magellanic Cloud Galaxy 148,000 light years away to retrieve the earth-saving "Cosmo Cleaner D" (*kosumo kurīnā* D).[3] One mournful blogger, observing the slow progress of the radiation cleanup, asked with more sadness than irony, "where, and what preparation is the contemporary *SBY* making for a sojourn in order to bring back 'a radiation-cleaning device?'"[4]

Why people were thinking such thoughts is not hard to understand. *SBY* offers a plainly antinuclear parable. It was also tremendously popular. Many consider it the single most influential anime of all time, including Hideaki Anno, the director of another antinuclear parable, *Shin Gojira* (2016).[5] Nevertheless, despite its starkly antinuclear message, scholarship has generally not approached *SBY* as an environmental commentary per se. Most scholars, especially before the triple disaster of 2011, have instead concentrated on its "nationalist flavor," to use Baryon Posadas's deliberate understatement, for the series can be interpreted as a virtual "restaging of the Second World War," where "Yamato" refers both to the famous imperial battleship and to the archaic name for Japan itself.[6] After the events of 2011, other analyses less focused on World War II have appeared, such as that of Ikuho Amano, who states that "in the post-3/11 context, renewed fan interest in *Space Battleship Yamato* suggests not only nostalgia for the romantic heroism which the anime elicits, but also their recognition of the anime's critical engagement with the issues of technology."[7] While there is certainly evidence for nationalist and technology-based readings of *SBY*, an environmental interpretation of the anime, especially one focused on apocalyptic pollution, stands out as even more compelling, since it is, as this paper will show, so thoroughly grounded in *SBY*'s plot, execution, and making-of story.

The following environmental reading of *SBY* starts with a brief overview of its grim, apocalyptic plot, which epitomizes both Sabine Höhler's conception of "spaceship Earth" and the "annihilative apocalypticism" Lawrence Buell identifies with the nuclear age.[8] It then offers a brief survey of the environmental anxiety of the seventies, an era when dire news of "red tides" filled the newspapers, and books like Ariyoshi Sawako's *Cumulative Pollution* (1974–1975) struck fear into the public.[9] *SBY*'s creator, Toyoda Aritsune, has spoken candidly about the effect of this pessimism on the development of *SBY*, especially with regard to nuclear power. Finally, the paper will turn to the anime itself and analyze the plot, script, and visual elements through the lens of the anxiety surrounding environmental destruction in Japan, especially *SBY*'s ubiquitous use of the iconic "blue marble" image of earth captured by *Apollo 17* and now famously associated with Earth Day.[10] However, in *SBY*, this blue-green marble, a universal symbol of life and nature, is not blue at all. Rather, it is "orange-brown," a sickly, irradiated, apocalyptic version of the original, symbolizing death and environmental destruction rampant in Japan's postwar, high-growth era.

SBY's Apocalyptic Plot

Scholars have noted the pervasive tendency of 1960s and 1970s environmentalist rhetoric to employ apocalyptic themes. Ursula Heise also remarks on the transfer of nuclear, Cold War language to environmentalist scenarios, as in the title of Paul Ehrlich's 1968 book, *The Population Bomb*.[11] Lawrence Buell traces environmental apocalypticism even further back to the nineteenth century, identifying a number of different themes that will be referred to in the final section of this paper.[12] *SBY*'s plot fits perfectly in this trend. The story begins in the year 2199, when a technologically superior alien race called the Gamilas attack the earth with nuclear meteorite bombs, destroying all plant and animal life on the surface of the planet and forcing the remaining humans into underground cities. Even underground, however, the radiation slowly poisons people. Extinction seems assured since the human space fleet lacks the ability to fly interstellar distances and thus represents no match for the Gamilas. Hope comes in the form of a *deus ex machina*: humans recover a capsule from the wreckage of a mysterious craft on Mars. Inside are blueprints for a faster-than-light engine, called the "wave motion engine" (*hadō enjin*), as well as an invitation from a certain Queen Starsha to her distant planet, Iscandar, in the "Large Magellanic Cloud," where, she promises, she possesses a device called the "Cosmo Cleaner D" that can purge the earth of its radiation and restore the planet to its former blue-green condition. In order to make this long journey, humans install the wave-motion engine in the wreckage of the World War II battleship *Yamato*, found sitting on the bed of the dried-up ocean, exactly where it came to rest after being sunk 254 years earlier. So begins the voyage of the *SBY* and its crew of 114, captained by the valiant Okita Jūzō, which will last for twenty-six episodes in the original animation, bringing the crew to Iscandar and back to save the day. While the choice of the *Yamato* as the crew's craft has attracted considerable attention and bolstered the predominantly nationalistic interpretation of the anime, it is worth pointing out that the *SBY*'s voyage is undertaken for all humankind, not just the Japanese. After all, the *SBY*'s mission is to save the damaged earth, the common home of all.

1970s Environmental Anxiety and the Making of *SBY*

In order to appreciate *SBY* as a work of environmental anxiety, it is important to understand the deeply gloomy context of its genesis, a period of widespread environmental pessimism about everything from water pollution to nuclear power, not to mention the fact that in 1974, the year *SBY* was first televised, Japan was experiencing its first major economic downturn since the war, largely due to the oil shock.[13] Rhoads and McCorkle's chapter on the era's environmental challenges, aptly titled "1970s Japan: 'A Polluters' Paradise,'" makes clear the environmental situation was even more dire than the economic one. They pay particular attention to the sea, since "the importance of the sea to the Japanese people cannot be overstated . . . oceans and seas are literally the lifeblood of Japan."[14] Various prefectural governments declared that Tokyo Bay was a "dead" body of water, devoid of all marine life, as was the case in Osaka, where fishermen abandoned their fishing rights in 1969. Meanwhile, "red tides" of plankton, caused by pollution, swept through the Inland Sea. This coloration clearly has special resonance with *SBY*, even though its red-orange earth results from radiation rather than from chemical pollution. Is it any coincidence, furthermore, in this climate of marine devastation, that *SBY* features a ship that must sail through space rather than on the sea—a ship found sitting high and dry on a bomb-evaporated seabed?

Such connections between the dire environmental news of the day and the development of *SBY* is not an isolated incident for cultural production. After all, the *Gojira* and *Gamera* franchises of the same period explicitly addressed the desperate state of Japan's environment, especially its seas and sea life.[15] 1971's *Gojira vs. Hedora,* in which Gojira battles a monster produced from sludge (*hedoro*), serves as a wry example. One of the creators of *SBY*, Toyoda Aritsune, who was supervising director of all twenty-six episodes of the original 1974–1975 run, specifically discusses the environmental anxiety of the seventies when recalling the genesis of the series. Interestingly, he points his finger to one event in particular, 1970's Osaka International Exposition, which he regards as the turning point that signaled the end of public optimism about technological advancement, particularly with regard to nuclear power. "After the exposition," he wrote later, "it was as if the pendulum swung back the opposite direction, and people suddenly began to reflect more on high economic growth and to doubt its rosy future. Pollution became a serious social problem and science fiction writers were criticized for creating and promoting a bright, rosy future. We science fiction writers did not just write rosy futures."[16] Toyoda had particular reservations about nuclear power and its potential to create the ultimate, planet-killing *kōgai* (environmental pollution). For example, he published a book in 1980 entitled *A Challenge to Nuclear Power Plants: Personal Research of the Status and Problems of Fifteen Nuclear Power Plants.*[17] Likewise, his science fiction novel, *Atoms on the Frozen Soil (Tōdo no Kaku,* 1994), tells the story of a hero sneaking into North Korea to stop a catastrophic meltdown at a power plant. In contrast, his story "My Neighbor's Windmill" (*Tonari no Fūsha,* 1985), seems to support nuclear power, although some have interpreted it differently, such as Kawamura Minato, who believes that it could be read as a criticism of the nuclear power industry.[18] While Toyoda has never described himself as an opponent of nuclear power, and has indeed expressed qualified support for it at certain points, his overall view of the energy source remains unambiguously skeptical, if not outright fearful.

Where *SBY* stands with regard to Toyoda's nuclear fears is not hard to pinpoint. If the anime's nuclear apocalyptic plot alone were not enough in that regard, we also have his explicit statement on the matter:

> The concept [of *SBY*'s] setting arose first of all from the idea of an apocalypse caused by *kōgai* (environmental pollution). If *kōgai* were to happen on a global scale, science dictates that it would bring humanity to the edge of extinction. Let's say we use James Lovelock's Gaia theory. If I had used it, the story would have been pretty exciting, although I did not know it back then. So I created a plot in which the Earth has been contaminated by radiation. All the same, I did not want to stir up the anti-nuclear-power groups. I was aware that the current light-water

reactors were following all the safety regulations. I am proud to have studied science in college and didn't want to create an unscientific plot, where, for instance, the reactors all explode tomorrow. In my view, global radioactive contamination could only be caused by war. So I decided that the setting of SBY must be based on my belief that nuclear power and its military use cannot be separated.[19]

Toyoda clearly wishes to tread lightly around the controversial link between nuclear energy and weapons. While he recognizes the threat of the nuclear (both bombs and power plants), he is unwilling to credit the scientific possibility of a worldwide simultaneous meltdown. Still, even if Toyoda prefers not to see *SBY* as a polemical, anti-scientific, antinuclear parable of nuclear apocalypse, the imagery in the anime tends to indicate otherwise—the white flashes, the enormous explosions, and the hideous, burnt-orange aftermath, an ocean-less rock floating in space.

Environmental Themes in *SBY*

While Toyoda's comments on the subject of pollution and nuclear power plants is illuminating, it is the animation itself that provides the best basis for an environmental reading of the series. There is no shortage of material in that regard, so my analysis will focus on only the most outstanding examples. Before doing so, however, it is worthwhile to point out how innovative and revolutionary *SBY*'s animation was when it debuted, and how full of new ideas and images it was, such as the first ever space battle scenes. "A fully fledged space opera," as Amano calls it, *SBY* predates *Star Wars* by three years.[20] Much of the visual impact of the anime is the creation of Matsumoto Leiji, a manga writer who was hired for his superb ability to draw mechanical apparatuses, and his beautiful, sensual, imaginative renditions of the cosmos set the animation apart. Matsumoto has a particular affinity for outer space, and it shows throughout the series.[21] Such beauty is all the more impressive for the fact that animation of the period was hand-drawn into cell sheets, where the only way to convey picture depth was through color gradation. Given Matsumoto's tremendous skill and sensitivity, the following observations about color, image, and framing cannot be dismissed as accidental or unimportant.

One of the most iconic and ubiquitous shots of the series is an image laden with environmental anxiety, namely the aforementioned "orange-brown marble" of the opening sequence. We see the *Yamato* breaking free of the muddy seabed and rising into space, leaving behind in the distance a sickly, discolored planet that contrasts starkly with the beauty of the surrounding cosmos, drawn as a deep indigo beset with twinkling stars. Whereas the "blue marble" version of this image, famous from Earth Day posters, stands as a symbol of precious life, the grotesque, orange-brown planet of *SBY* suggests death, disease, and toxicity (figure 5.1).

Figure 5.1. Orange-brown earth. Matsumoto Leiji,
1974, Tohokushinsha Film Co.

The environmental anxiety this provoked in the Japanese was not unfounded, given the similarity of the color to the "red tide" of plankton poisoning Japan's Inland Sea in the 1960s and 1970s. Indeed, could there be any more potent image of environmental destruction than this iconic image of the whole earth viewed from space, humanity's home, scorched and rendered uninhabitable? As Robert Poole points out in his book on the similar "earthrise" picture captured by *Apollo 8*, this sight of earth from space can be deeply moving, including for the astronauts who first beheld it. Frank Borman, a member of the *Apollo 8* crew, recalled, "I happened to glance out of one of the still-clear windows just at the moment the Earth appeared over the lunar horizon. It was the most beautiful, heart-catching sight of my life, one that sent a torrent of nostalgia, of sheer homesickness, surging through me."[22] James Lovell, also on the crew, was struck by the earth's unique color. "Up there," he explained, "it's a black and white world. There's no color. In the whole universe, wherever we looked, the only bit of color was back on Earth. . . . People down there don't realize what they have."[23]

Illustrator Matsumoto and other *SBY* creators strove for a similar potency when they decided to strip the earth of its unique color and show it again and again as an orange-brown wasteland. The sense of loss and extinction is unavoidable, calling into question James Lovell's assessment that "people down there don't realize what they have." And yet Matsumoto and the creative team did not make the earth a white, colorless moonscape or a charred gray-black, both of which would reasonably be the outcome of a nuclear holocaust and would convey a similar sense of lifelessness. Instead, they selected orange-brown to show the result of the Gamilas' meteorite bombs, which exterminated all life on the earth's surface and evaporated the seas. This color was also reminiscent of the prevalent air pollution, a serious environmental threat for 1970s Japan. *SBY*'s orange-brown-red palette simultaneously evokes air pollution, red tide, and, as we observed in Toyoda's remarks about nuclear power, radioactive contamination, tapping into contemporary anxiety about *kōgai* in all its potential forms.

The sickly orange-brown marble is not limited to the opening sequence. Several crucial scenes feature it as an emotional backdrop that enhances anxiety, interacting with the drama of the characters almost in the manner of nondiegetic music. Indeed, sentimental music often also accompanies these scenes, as in the first episode, when Okita spots an earthbound nuclear meteorite whizzing past his ship and exclaims, "No. We can't do it now. We don't have the arms to prevent the nuclear bombs." He and the crew are forced to sit helplessly as the blue marble transforms into an orange-brown marble before their eyes, perhaps suggesting mankind's inability to stop the destruction caused by environmental contaminants. Captain Okita's love for Mother Earth shows with equal clarity in the final episode as well, when Okita succumbs to radiation poisoning, in effect sacrificing himself to save the earth. His painful passing receives suitably sentimental and dramatic treatment in the animation. Drawing his final breaths, Okita whispers a memorable and moving last line: "the earth . . . everything and everyone is dearly missed." Accompanying the voice-over of his last words, the orange-brown earth fills the screen, symbolizing his pain and bitter sacrifice (figure 5.2).

Toyoda's critics, who occasionally accused him and other sci-fi writers of painting too rosy a picture of the future, would be forced to admit that there is nothing rosy here. Rather, there is a clear critique of anthropocentric, planetary harm.

The orange-brown marble serves a similarly critical function in a pivotal, two-shot scene in the fourth episode, which features Yamato's departure from the earth on its long journey into space. Here again, we cannot help but feel a sense of grief as the earth slips away—both metaphorically through nuclear destruction, which renders it uninhabitable, and then literally as the crew abandons it on their mission, leaving it to recede smaller and smaller in their wake. In the first shot, as the ship leaves the earth's orbit, firing its powerful wave-motion engine, the planet appears in the background behind the silhouetted ship, orange, pockmarked, and alien except for a few wisps of swirling white clouds, clearly borrowed from the blue marble image. If not for these clouds, we would not recognize our ocean-less planet at all. In the second shot, immediately following the first, the scene cuts to

Figure 5.2. The dying Captain Okita and the orange-brown earth.
Matsumoto Leiji, 1975, Tohokushinsha Film Co.

the Yamato's control room, where the orange-brown marble looms in the front window, confronting the crew with the full enormity of the destruction for the first time (figure 5.3).

Mournful strings play in nondiegetic fashion as the officers grapple with the horrifying sight before them and try to keep hope for the planet's salvation. Their dialogue could be taken directly from the language of 1970s environmental advocacy:

Mori Yuki: *Look, the earth is getting smaller.*

Tokugawa Hikozaemon (chief engineer): *It's heartbreaking. I can't stand to look at it directly.*

Sanada Shirō (technician): *It's a terrible sight—more than I imagined on the earth's surface.*

Shima Daisuke (chief navigation officer): *Can we save the earth? The damaged earth?*

Kodai Susumu (combat leader): *Of course! We will save the earth at any cost!*

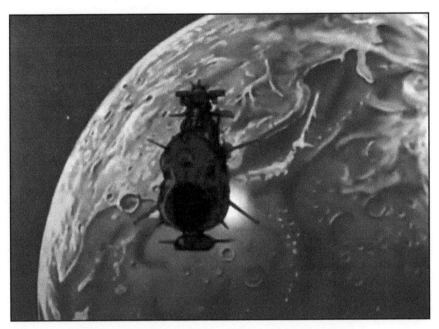

Figure 5.3. The alien-looking earth behind the *Yamato*.
Matsumoto Leiji, 1974, Tohokushinsha Film Co.

As the *SBY* creators no doubt intended in their illustrations and music, we struggle to share Kodai Susumu's optimism at this moment of horror. Indeed, in the previous shot, which shows the ship moving away from the earth, one cannot help but note that the planet moves slowly to the lower right as the dark silhouette of the ship remains fixed in the upper left of the frame. It is as though the earth is sinking, slipping away. Their respective directions of movement are also noteworthy. Given that Japanese is usually read right to left, this leftward drift of the *Yamato* represents advancement, progression, departure. The earth, meanwhile, is regressing, a thing of the past left in the dust, a piece of used-up garbage inevitably discarded. In a 1970s climate of environmental anxiety, when the oceans and skies seemed on the verge of being used up forever, the tension between "progress" and destructive consumption must have been particularly poignant.

At this moment of high visual pathos, it is difficult to avoid the sensation that the animation revels somewhat in the destruction, evoking the maximum emotional effect from viewers. Likewise, the shot in the opening sequence of the *Yamato* lying on the dry seabed, reflecting the orange-red evening light on its rusted hull, contains a solemn beauty that transcends mere destruction. The strong sense of nostalgia and loss connoted by this image of the sunken *Yamato* relates not only to a lost place, the precious blue-green planet destroyed by radiation bombs, but also unavoidably to a lost time, before the death and destruction of World War II. Comic writer Yamada Reiji has commented in his YouTube video series, *Yangu Sandē* (no. 207), that the battleship *Yamato* serves as a symbol of Japan's defeat in World War II. Indeed, the mood of these images of the ruined *Yamato* in *SBY* is overwhelmingly mournful, as sci-fi critic Fujita Naoya has also noted, remarking that "*SBY* possesses a particular temperament of 'mourning' for the battleship Yamato and its *eirei* (souls of the war dead)."[24] Yet, as many would agree, this sense of mourning and loss in *SBY* extends beyond the images of the ruined Yamato and imbues the entire series, including the departure scene described above. Such pervasive mournfulness naturally calls into question whether it is directed primarily at the battleship and its dead or instead envisages a larger, more general loss, for which the *Yamato* serves merely as a memento.

The best test of this question comes in a scene in episode three that should, if the former explanation is correct, be the height of sentimental nationalism. Instead, it proves to be quite the opposite. The episode features a three-minute *mise-en-scene* showing the original *Yamato's* doomed, one-way sortie and eventual sinking. The departing ship, depicted as a dark black silhouette, silently enters a fog bank, giving the flawless impression of a ghost ship until a fisherman looking on exclaims to his friend, "It's the *Yamato*. It's a Japanese battleship." Voice-over narration explains, "with fuel for only one way, the *Yamato's* sortie was advanced in the face of death, prepared not to return." Ominous martial music accompanies the subsequent shot of the ghostlike battleship as it burns and goes under, the narration announcing flatly that the "*Yamato* had sunk." As the ship slips under the surface, the crew of the nearby destroyer and the American pilot flying overhead salute the dying soldiers. There is no celebration of victory on the American side, no celebration of bravery or gallantry on the Japanese side, only mutual sadness. The voice-over concludes in a starkly anti-war tone, moralizing, "this is perhaps the sad destiny of any product created for the purpose of war. The *Yamato* finally went to solemn sleep with some three thousand solders." Despite the potentially patriotic subject matter of this episode, a simplistic, nationalistic reading of *SBY* has never seemed more untenable than it does here. The episode's meditation on loss feels bigger than that—bigger than a battleship, a nation, or even a single war, especially when considered in combination with the mournful tone that underlies the entire series. Indeed, as the *Yamato* sinks, it is hard not to sense that the loss *SBY* has in mind is planetary, the loss of everything and everybody, a feeling that stems more from environmental anxiety than from memories of World War II.[25]

Probably the most solemn scene of all, the final one in the series, also suggests a larger message than just war and heroic death. It offers up the conclusion the audience has been waiting for: after so much sacrifice and loss of life, including that of the beloved Captain Okita, the crew of the *Yamato* finally secures the

Cosmo Cleaner D, brings it back to earth, and cleanses the planet. At this moment of triumph, no background music plays. No sound can be heard at all, no words, just a reverential, almost holy silence as we witness the sickly orange-brown orb transform back into a gorgeous, cerulean blue, shining in the cosmos like a precious jewel. The names of the creators then appear, superimposed over the healed earth. The mission of the *Yamato* is complete. The earth has been saved. In this final vision of planetary catharsis, the victory feels larger than just the outcome of a battle with the evil Gamilas, whose almost secondary role in the plot underscores what 1970s viewers no doubt sensed from the outset: the real war to save the planet is not against alien invaders but against fellow humans, and we collectively must be earth's saviors.

The clearest distillation of this message comes not in this solemn finale, however, but rather in the recurring ending sequence of every episode, which, like the intro sequence, features a song and key images. Without delving too deeply into the plot of *SBY*, which can be quite convoluted even in the first season—to say nothing of its successors—we can observe in this ending sequence that the creators of *SBY* want us to take the theme of "Mother Earth" very seriously—even literally. What we see as the ending song plays is an image of Starsha superimposed over that of her beautiful, earth-like planet, Iscandar.[26] As mentioned earlier, Starsha is the Queen of Iscandar, the last survivor of her people, who offers her help to humanity by sending them the blueprints for the special engine and giving the crew of *SBY* the Cosmo Cleaner D. As a further plot twist, Starsha secretly rescues the older brother of Kodai Susumu, who appeared to die in a space battle in episode one. The pair fall in love and become a kind of Adam and Eve on Iscandar, repopulating the devasted planet. Thus, when we see Starsha's serene face superimposed over a verdant Iscandar in the ending sequence, we are left with little doubt that she personifies Iscandar and, by extension, stands in as a kind of Mother Earth, or at least a Mother Iscandar, a sister to Mother Earth. It is clearly not a direct personification—after all, she represents a different, earth-like planet and is herself not saved by the *Yamato*—but we are at least meant to imagine that a similar queen exists here on earth, a queen possibly forced underground, sickened with poison, robbed of her beauty. As Starsha says to the crew of the *Yamato* in the final episode, "ultimately, the savior of the earth is you. I am sorry to test your strength and courage by bringing you here, but it is only through your own strength that you can seize tomorrow's happiness." The environmental implications of these words could hardly be clearer. In this context, *SBY* serves not so much as a tale of war or heroism but as one of human redemption, where the pollution in need of cleaning is not alien but rather anthropogenic in the most literal sense. Quite rightly, if the earth is one day reduced to an orange-brown wasteland, it will not be because of the Gamilas' meteorite bombs.

Conclusion

My analysis in this chapter only skims the surface of the environmental content and messaging of *SBY*. There is ample material in support of an environmental reading of the series, especially if one includes later iterations of the anime and the spin-off manga of Matsumoto.[27] Even with the small selection of evidence presented here, however, it is obvious how dominant environmental themes are in the plot, script, and illustration of *SBY*, and how formative environmental anxieties were in the 1970s genesis of the series, as attested to by the specific recollections of *SBY* supervisor, Toyoda Aritsune. The prevailing mood of loss and mourning in *SBY*, noted by numerous critics as one of the defining characteristics of the show, stems directly from the environmental anxieties of Toyoda and his colleagues, not from memories of the historical Yamato or Japan's defeat in the war. Those anxieties, moreover, while particularly prominent in a 1970s Japan afflicted with smog and red tides, are unfortunately not just relics of the past, outdated by half a century of environmental progress, especially with regard to nuclear contamination. Indeed, during the 3/11 disaster, they proved more current than ever, as indicated by the uptick in online references to "Yamato." We certainly could have used a Cosmo Cleaner D then (and now). But as lamentable as the continued relevance of those anxieties is—as much as we would have hoped to have progressed further in the last fifty years—one element of *SBY*'s enduring message is worth celebrating: as Starsha says, we must all act as the saviors of the earth.

Notes

[1] Amano, "Mourning to Allegory," 325–326.

[2] This paper will focus only on the original first series, which debuted on October 6, 1974, and concluded on March 20, 1975, with the twenty-sixth episode. Although not very popular initially, the show was rebroadcasted in 1974–1975 and gained a wide audience, spawning a movie version in 1977 and second and third seasons in 1978 and 1980, respectively. A remake of the first season, set in the year 2199 (as opposed to 2201 and afterward for the second and third seasons), came out in 2013. Reportedly, *Mission Impossible* director Christopher McQuarrie plans to produce and direct a feature film adaptation of *SBY*'s American version, called *Star Blazers*, which was broadcast from 1979 to 1984.

[3] "The Fukushima Fifty" refers to a group of brave workers who remained on the site of the Fukushima Daiichi plant after the meltdown. Their story has since spawned a movie starring Ken Watanabe. It is an interesting fact that the initial fifty workers were replaced by another fifty, and so on, as their exposure rose beyond permitted levels and they could no longer remain on site.

[4] Amano, "Mourning to Allegory," 327.

[5] Eldred and Ito, "Yamato Discussion."

[6] Posadas, "Remaking Yamato," 320.

[7] Amano, "Mourning to Allegory," 335. Many other assessments are possible as well. *SBY* is a complex and multifaced work of art. For instance, the journey of the hero, Kodai Susumu, to Iscandar can easily be regarded as a *bildungsroman*.

[8] Höhler, "Envisioning Human Habitats." See also her book *Spaceship Earth*. Buell, *Environmental Imagination*.

[9] Marran, *Ecology without Culture*. She gives an analysis of Ariyoshi's work in the third chapter.

[10] Heise, *Sense of Place*, 23. She discusses the power of the *Apollo* images and their immediate appropriation by the environmental movement, most famously for the first Earth Day in 1970. See also Poole, *Earthrise*. Although he focuses on earlier image of the earth captured by *Apollo 8* in 1968, Poole analyzes the symbolism of the earth seen from space even more exhaustively, both tracing the concept backward in time to classical antiquity and cataloging its myriad uses and influences down to the present day.

[11] Heise, *Sense of Place*, 26.

[12] Buell, *Environmental Imagination*, 301f.

[13] Amano, "Mourning to Allegory," 329.

[14] Rhoads and McCorkle, *Japan's Green Monsters*, 108.

[15] Rhoads and McCorkle, *Japan's Green Monsters*, 111.

[16] Toyoda, *Uchūsenkan Yamato*, 69–71. According to Toyoda's claims, the producer, Nishizaki Yoshinobu, can be regarded as a historical revisionist. He insisted on playing the "Battleship March" (*Gunkan Māchi*) over a scene of the battleship *Yamato* in 1945. Toyoda opposed it because *SBY* was not a World War II anime, and he prevailed. The march was not played. Toyoda was also against using the battleship *Yamato* as a space vehicle. He believes it was the idea of Matsumoto Leiji, the series' director. Although the battleship was one of the most popular vehicles in boys' entertainment from the time of Oshikawa Shunrō's *Undersea Battleship* (1900), the flying battleship was introduced by Kajiwara Ikki in *Shin Senkan Yamato* in 1961.

[17] Toyoda, *Genpatsu no Chōsen*.

[18] Toyoda, "Tonari no Fūsha."

[19] Toyoda, "Genpatsu Saigai," 81.

[20] Amano, "Mourning to Allegory," 326.

[21] Arai, *Uchūsenkan Yamato*, 72–76.

[22] Poole, *Earthrise*, 1–2.

[23] Poole, *Earthrise*, 2.

[24] "Yamada Reiji no Yangu Sandē." See also Fujita, "Taidan," 353.

[25] The atmosphere of defeat and loss comes through also in the selection of character names. The names of Captain Okita Jōzō and the commander of the fleet, Hijikata Ryū, are taken from famous samurai of the Shinsengumi, a samurai group that fought and

died for the Tokugawa Shogunate at the end of the Edo period. Needless to say, the family name of Tokugawa Hikozaemon, chief engineer of the *SBY*, is from the shogun's family, the Tokugawa clan, which was also defeated in the Boshin War of 1867–1868. The name of the *SBY*'s technician, meanwhile, Sanada Shirō, comes from the Sanada clan, which fought for the Toyotomi clan and was defeated in the early seventeenth century. On the other hand, the name of the show's main character, Kodai Susumu, is a compound of *kodai*, "ancient times," and *susumu*, "to move forward," thus suggesting a return to a lost time or place rather than defeat.

[26] Toyoda got the idea for the journey to Iscandar from the sixteenth-century Chinese novel *Journey to the West*, which is about a priest, Tang Sanzang, who goes to India and brings back the Buddhist sutras for the sake of saving people. He came up with the name Iscandar because India was the furthest point that Alexander the Great reached in his conquests.

[27] Matsumoto, *Uchūsenkan Yamato*.

Bibliography

Amano, Ikuyo. "From Mourning to Allegory: Post-3/11 Space Battleship Yamato in Motion." *Japan Forum* 26, no. 3 (2014): 325–339.

Arai, Hiroyuki. *Uchūsenkan Yamato to 70nendai Nippon.* Tokyo: Shakai Hyōronsha, 2010.

Buell, Lawrence. *The Environmental Imagination: Thoreau, Nature Writing, and the Formation of American Culture.* Cambridge: Harvard University Press, 1995.

Eldred, Tim, and Michiko Ito. "Railway of Fantasy: A Yamato Discussion with Hideaki Anno, Leiji Matsumoto, and Hiroshi Miyagawa, translated from the 1988 Railway of Fantasy Concert Program." June 27, 2013. https://ourstarblazers.com/vault/252/.

Fujita, Naoya. "Taidan: 3/11 to SF teki Sōzōryoku." In *3.11 no Mirai: Nihon, SF, Sōzōryoku*, edited by Kasai Kiyoshi, Ebihara Yutaka, Fujita Naoya, and Tatsumi Takayuki. Tokyo: Sakuhinsha, 2011.

Heise, Ursula. *Sense of Place and Sense of Planet: The Environmental Imagination of the Global.* Oxford: Oxford University Press, 2008.

Höhler, Sabine. "'Spaceship Earth': Envisioning Human Habitats in the Environmental Age." *GHI Bulletin*, no. 42 (Spring 2008): 65–85.

Höhler, Sabine. *Spaceship Earth in the Environmental Age, 1960–1990.* London: Routledge, 2015.

Marran, Christine. *Ecology without Culture: Aesthetics for a Toxic World.* Minneapolis: University of Minnesota Press, 2017.

Matsumoto, Leiji. *Uchūsenkan Yamato.* Tokyo: Akita Shoten, 1975.

Poole, Robert. *Earthrise: How Man First Saw the Earth.* New Haven: Yale University Press, 2008.

Posadas, Baryon Tensor. "Remaking Yamato, Remaking Japan: Space Battleship Yamato and SF Anime." *Science Fiction Film and Television* 7, no. 3 (2014): 315–342.

Rhoads, Sean, and Brooke McCorkle. *Japan's Green Monsters: Environmental Commentary in Kaijū Cinema.* Jefferson, NC: McFarland & Company, Inc., 2018.

Toyoda, Aritsune. *Genpatsu no Chōsen: Ashi de Shirabeta Zen 15-kasho no Genjō to Mondaiten.* Tokyo: Shodensha, 1980.

Toyoda, Aritsune. "Genpatsu Saigai to Uchūsenkan Yamato." In *3.11 no Mirai: Nihon, SF, Sōzōryoku,* edited by Kasai Kiyoshi, Ebihara Yutaka, Fujita Naoya, and Tatsumi Takayuki, 75–92. Tokyo: Sakuhinsha, 2011.

Toyoda, Aritsune. "Tonari no Fūsha." In *Nihon Genpatsu Shōsetsu Shū,* edited by Kakitani Kōichi. Tokyo: Suiseisha, 2011.

Toyoda, Aritsune. *Uchūsenkan Yamato no Shinjitsu.* Tokyo: Shōdensha, 2017.

"Yamada Reiji no Yangu Sandē, No. 331, 'Yūreisen toshiteno Yamato Ron: Nihon Otaku Shoki OS, *Uchūsenkan Yamato* ga Hajimetamono, Owarasetamono, Motte Kaettekitamono.'" Accessed June 22, 2022. https://youtu.be/1DYkajBvC1E.

6

Miyazaki Hayao's Eco-Disasters in Japanese Cinema: Rereading *Nausicaä*[1]

Roman Rosenbaum

"I don't want to be considered an ecologist, so I puff away on my cigarettes."[2]

Miyazaki's animations have been called eco-sagas or eco-fables with an ecophilosophical message, wielding an ecological aesthetic that is "trying to save the planet."[3] Yet despite these accolades, the renowned animator steadfastly refuses to unambiguously embrace the role of the environmentalist. The ironic introductory epigraph hides an uncomfortable, somewhat idiosyncratic truth and has serious undertones in a country where the corporate culture of conformity and social group mentality override notions of political dissent and individualism. There is considerable risk to the individual who takes on large Japanese corporations, and Miyazaki is no exception.

Japan in the 1980s was considered an environmental pariah during the rapid bubble, economic growth period. It was renowned as the world's leading importer of tropical timber and as an ardent supporter of whaling, to name only two well-known examples. Many of Japan's domestic environmental issues can be attributed to the "construction state" (土建国家, *doken kokka*) ideology, where industrialization and economic growth were national priorities for postwar Japan.[4]

This sociopolitical environment was rampant when Miyazaki began his work on *Nausicaä of the Valley of the Wind* (hereafter, *Nausicaä*), and the story's narrative reflects the struggle of Japan's ecology movement from the 1970s onward.[5] Local environmental issues inspired Miyazaki's work on *Nausicaä*, including the bitter dispute surrounding the Sanrizuka (三里塚) district, where the local agricultural community fought the Japanese government to oppose the construction of Narita Airport. Other ecological struggles included egregious incidents like the Tsuruga nuclear power plant accident, where fifty-nine workers were exposed to radiation on March 9, 1981, and officials in charge endangered the public and nearby residents by failing to inform them immediately.[6] Despite Miyazaki's resistance to the label of "ecologist," his subtle, inconspicuous use of allegory has a long history of covert social criticism. Western audiences are accustomed to viewing the human-environment relationship in terms of the former being superior to the latter, which serves primarily as a source for raw materials or resources for consumption in our high-growth consumer societies. By contrast, Miyazaki's worldview highlights not only the animistic—the "alive" aspect of our natural environment—but also depicts humans as an inseparable dependent part of nature.[7]

Within the context of the current debates about climate change and global warming, Miyazaki's *Nausicaä* is a key text that combines the themes of pacifism and environmentalism, which are central to his trilogy of postapocalyptic works. Through a kaleidoscope of fictional characters, Miyazaki portrays how sociopolitics are the fulcrum on which the connections between the environment, politics, history, war, nuclear apocalypse, and environmental degradation are balanced precariously in the pursuit of an elusive ecotopian ideal. This notion of an "ecological utopia," where the environment can flourish amid social stability, was inspired by the eponymous 1975 novel by Ernest Callenbach, which influenced the countercultural and green movements in the 1970s. In this sense, *Nausicaä* is a turning point in the history of animated environmentalism, wherein Miyazaki enlarges local concerns to the global level by embedding his personal history into the legacy of war, the atomic destruction of Hiroshima and Nagasaki in 1945, and social issues like the Minamata poisoning. In this chapter, Miyazaki's postapocalyptic trilogy is discussed in relation to our twenty-first century, where advanced technologies and industrial societies are in competition, producing environmental degradation with global consequences for all.

Nausicaä as Part of Miyazaki's Postapocalyptic Trilogy

Hisaaki Wake has noted that it is common for Japanese artists to display ambivalence regarding their strategies for producing popular cultural works and their publicly stated position on nature and environmental issues, and Miyazaki is no exception.[8] In what has been referred to as his "postapocalyptic trilogy" (ポスト黙示録三連作, *posuto mokushiroku sanrensaku*): *Future Boy Conan* (1978),

Nausicaä (1984) and *Laputa: Castle in the Sky* (1986), Miyazaki deals with the devastating consequences of war. The narratives reject conflict and present the universal values of pacifism—including not only an anti-war stance but also nonviolence, passive resistance, and a strong sense of morality—as the only viable solution in a world degraded by human pollution. However, the settings are primarily fantasies that are far removed in space and time from the historical record of imperial Japan, albeit with the common focus on humanity's rampant destruction of the environment.[9] The first animation in this trilogy was *Future Boy Conan* (未来少年コナン, Mirai Shōnen Konan), a postapocalyptic science fiction anime series adapted from *The Incredible Tide*, the 1970 novel written by American science fiction writer Alexander Key, and broadcast by NHK in 1978. The animation follows a devastating conflict that is fought with "ultra-magnetic weapons" far greater than anything seen earlier, which brings about an apocalyptic world reminiscent of the atomic bomb landscapes of Hiroshima and Nagasaki. Through the resulting earthquakes and tsunamis, the earth is thrown off its axis, its crust rocked by massive tectonic movements, and the continents are torn completely apart and sink deep below the sea. The story essentially revolves around the protagonist, Conan, who was born into this postapocalyptic environment and, after many adventures, succeeds in destroying the superweapon, which the chief dictator, who is referred to as Director, was trying to deploy in order to maintain his hegemony over the world.

The image below, from Miyazaki's seminal animation *Nausicaä*, depicts the protagonist in her hazard suit, which protects her in a contaminated world (figure 6.1*). Nausicaä* was the second in this series of postapocalyptic works following in

Figure 6.1. In a contaminated landscape, *Nausicaä*'s suit is still relevant today. Miyazaki Hayao, 1984, Studio Ghibli.

the wake of the nuclearization of Japanese society triggered by the devastation of Hiroshima and Nagasaki in 1945. The first chapter of the manga *Nausicaä of the Valley of the Wind* was published in 1982, and it was later developed into a series that created one of the most iconic animation studios in film history. The manga follows the journey of Nausicaä, a princess who finds herself caught in another war as the world's remaining kingdoms fight over diminishing natural resources. The animation by the same title appeared in 1984. As insinuated by the heavy focus on environmental pollution in the manga and the animation, nuclear disasters the world over were a frequent occurrence. The first chapter of the manga appeared after several nuclear incidents—including the Three Mile Island nuclear power plant accident in 1979, the Tsuruga incident in 1981, and the furor created over the narrowly avoided catastrophe when the *K-314* Soviet nuclear submarine collided with the aircraft carrier *USS Kitty Hawk* in the Sea of Japan on March 21, 1984.[10]

Following the success of *Nausicaä*, a third work, *Laputa: Castle in the Sky*, was released on August 2, 1986, a little over three months after the Chernobyl nuclear disaster on April 26.[11] In his third postapocalyptic narrative, Miyazaki imagines a flying city in which nature and advanced technology live together in peace, an armistice that is only shattered by human interference. When the chief villain, Colonel Muska, demonstrates the source of Laputa's power via a secret weapon lying dormant in the castle, the explosion bears the unmistakable shape of an atomic cloud. As the last postapocalyptic work, the island in the sky depicted in the image above is a synergy of technology and nature, and it symbolizes an elusive ecotopia, where nature and technology exist in harmony—that is, until humanity arrives and "pollutes" this proverbial Garden of Eden (figure 6.2).

Figure 6.2. Laputa, the "ecological" castle in the sky.
Miyazaki Hayao, 1986, Studio Ghibli.

All three works display lost opportunities for potential ecotopias, wherein humanity fails to acknowledge its interdependence with nature amid the constant striving for resources and the conflict over territory. The trilogy distinctly displays Miyazaki's ecological message to a world where human technology is leading inexorably toward the abyss of environmental degradation. It is not until the release of *The Wind Rises* in 2013 that Miyazaki published his political manifesto in the online Ghibli magazine, *Neppu*, and confessed his sociopolitical agenda in relation to the environment. For Miyazaki, it was not until his first journey overseas to Sweden in his thirties that he realized how much he loved the natural environment of Japan. As he became conscious of the ever-increasing threat to the natural environment, his vision of Japan developed into one of denuclearization, with a dramatically reduced population centered around an economy that promotes shared prosperity.[12]

What Is in a Name? *Nausicaä* and Allegory

Nausicaä was a turning point for Miyazaki because the success of the manga's adaptation into film directly led to the creation of Studio Ghibli in 1985. However, similar to Katsuhiro Otomo's multivolume *Akira* (1988), the corresponding animated feature film could not contain the full complexity of the multivolume manga and thus only scratched the surface of the manga's plots. The *Nausicaä* film roughly covers the first fifteen chapters of the manga, with several modifications to the plot to give it a more focused and conclusive narrative. This inconsistency created a complex response to the animation that was both beguiling and upsetting to many of its most ardent manga readers. Miyazaki continued to sporadically release chapters of *Nausicaä* the manga until its fifty-ninth and final chapter in March 1994.

Nausicaä draws from a myriad of cultural sources, including the Japanese twelfth-century tale, the "Princess who loved insects" (虫めづる姫君, Mushi-mezuru himegimi), and the Greek princess of the same name in Homer's *Odyssey*.[13] In this sense, *Nausicaä* is rooted in cross-literary intertextuality and is the animation's guiding metaphor combining Eastern and Western philosophy and literature. In the process, Miyazaki's graphic novel also draws from diverse ideological spectra that express notions of militaristic nihilism, war and peace, and overarching environmental concerns via a *shōjo* manga heroine who defies gender boundaries.

Postwar as Postapocalypse: Allegories of Childhood Trauma

Nausicaä seeded many of the environmental concerns that would be developed in later Studio Ghibli films. This pop cultural appeal, coupled with realistic environmental engagement, earned the film global accolades and fans in addition to a recommendation from the World Wildlife Fund. Even though Miyazaki's postapocalyptic narratives were released more than three decades after the end of the Asia-Pacific conflict, these animations are full of references to atomic bomb explosions and toxic natural environments, which not only evoke Japan's environmental movement but are also redolent of his childhood trauma. All of the plots play out their narratives under the threat of apocalyptic weapons of mass destruction. Thirty years after the end of the war, Miyazaki's psyche was still very much focused on the potential destruction of humanity and the world at large, as seen in the opening words of *Future Boy Conan*:

> July, 2008 AD
> Mankind was facing the fires of annihilation.
> Super electromagnetic weapons,
> far more destructive than atomic weapons,
> caused half the world to be wiped out in an instant.
> The Earth was seized by great tectonic upheavals.
> Its axis was tilted.
> The five continents were ripped completely apart and
> sank into the sea.[14]

The threat is similar in *Nausicaä*, where the most potent weapon is the *Kyoshinhei* (巨神兵, literally "giant God Warriors")—symbolic of not only the atomic bomb but also, more importantly, of the nascent danger of reawakening that destructive power despite its devastating legacy.[15] The message here is clear: Whenever environmental resources become scarce, new wars break out over territorial disputes, resources, or space for human settlement. This universal message remains relevant for future generations, as seen in the thinly veiled threats made by Putin during the invasion of Ukraine to potentially use his vast nuclear arsenal—just one example of the dormant power of the threat of nuclear weapons.

In *Nausicaä*, the *Kyoshinhei* are considered to have been the primary instruments of destruction during the so-called ancient "Seven Days of Fire," a reference to a devastating conflict that took place a long time ago. While the God warriors are believed to be extinct at the beginning of the story, their resurrection becomes the central focal point of the narrative development. Their ability to fly by "twisting space," and to use devastating energy beams that are fueled by nuclear energy, makes contact with them a potential cause for radiation poisoning. All of this suggests that the Seven Days of Fire may have been a nuclear holocaust reminiscent of the atomic bomb attacks on Japan.

Similarly, in *Laputa: Castle in the Sky*, the secret lies in the floating castles dormant weapon of mass destruction that can only be unleashed by a powerful crystal that unlocks its usage. The plot revolves around the attempt by Muska, the chief antagonist, to harness that power to conquer the world. Powerful weapons of mass destruction—reminiscent of Miyazaki's own childhood experience—form the *deus ex machina* of all three narratives and mirror not only the subliminal trauma of Miyazaki's own experience of surviving the war but also the postwar history of the Japanese nation at large.

The postapocalyptic vision in *Nausicaä* conjures images of war (the Asia-Pacific conflict, the Korean War, and the Vietnam War) or environmental catastrophes that released a large number of pathogens into the local community (Minamata) or globally (Chernobyl). For Miyazaki, who was born in 1941, the vision is that of the "generation of the burnt-out ruins" (焼け跡世代, *yakeato sedai*), or those who experienced the burnt-out city vistas of urban Japan as a result of vast firebombing campaigns during the early, preadolescent stages of their lives. Miyazaki commented, "if I was born a little earlier, I would have been a child-soldier."[16] He belonged to a generation who grew up amid total war, a generation of children whose psyches were not yet fully formed and who would later be exempt from any kind of culpability in the war. For the young Miyazaki, war was the natural status quo, and he has noted that some of his earliest memories are of "bombed-out cities."[17] In 1944, when he was only three years old, Miyazaki's family evacuated to Utsunomiya—the prefectural capital city of Tochigi Prefecture in the northern Kantō region of Japan. At the time, the common practice of "evacuating schoolchildren from major city centers" (学童疎開, *gakudō sokai*) was institutionalized. To protect the youngest generations, children left for the countryside, often without their families. Following the bombing of Utsunomiya in July 1945, he and his family evacuated further to Kanuma—a neighboring regional city. For Miyazaki and many artists of this generation, it took several decades before the post-traumatic stress of their childhood would be allowed back to the realm of consciousness, where it would be reimagined and laid bare via artistic expression.[18]

With a plethora of cleverly disguised allegorical allusions sprinkled throughout the narratives of *Nausicaä*—and, by extension, all three postapocalyptic works—Miyazaki's own childhood experience of war and the postwar home front is the final overarching allegory hidden deep within the penumbra of these works. All three works feature childlike, youthful protagonists who fight against the establishment and try to prevent a war and the implementation of powerful superweapons. Like all members of the *yakeato* generation who lived through the final devastation of the Asia-Pacific War, Miyazaki became disillusioned with the swift postwar ideological conversion, or *tenkō* mentality, whereby former enemies suddenly became friends and war was renounced forever by the pacifist peace constitution. Yet soon thereafter, with the outbreak of the Korean War in 1950 and the sudden implementation of the reverse course followed by the Vietnam War in 1955, the specter of war was suddenly looming once again over a generation that was just beginning to heal from the trauma of the Asia-Pacific War. It is for these reasons that war and destruction have remained a central theme throughout Miyazaki's oeuvre.

Why Read *Nausicaä* Now? Environmental Issues as Sociopolitical Allegories

"I don't need the nothingness to tell me that we are a cursed people. We're the ugliest of all creatures. We do nothing but harm to the earth—plundering it and polluting and burning it."[19]

Nausicaä, a story about two superpowers that vie for supremacy—the kingdom of Torumekia (王国) and the empire of Dorok (土鬼), with the small "valley of wind" caught in between— has many uncanny similarities to our present status quo.[20] What is more, the war between the kingdoms in *Nausicaä* takes place during an environmental disaster that threatens humankind; the catastrophe known as the "Sea of Corruption" (腐海, *fukai*) invokes the current global warming doomsday scenario. The work was also inspired by a major incident of industrial pollution in Japan and anticipates other environmental crises that followed, including the ozone hole discovery above the Antarctic in 1985 and the world's worst nuclear accident at Chernobyl in 1986. Miyazaki took as inspiration for his eco-fable the devastation wreaked by the Japanese industrial Chisso Corporation's protracted dumping of methylmercury into Minamata Bay. It was arguably the devastation wrought by Minamata that resurfaced Miyazaki's own traumatic childhood memories, where he observed helplessly as political bureaucracy led the people astray. It is this theme that he set out to explore in *Nausicaä*, where natural ecology becomes intertwined with human politics. Miyazaki revised the theme of toxic waste and focused his gaze on a post-pollution era, depicting a world where the environment has adapted to human pollution.

But this is only the beginning of *Nausicaä*'s tropes of intertextuality. The story's gigantic insect-like Ohmu (王蟲, オーム) are a continuation of the Godzilla trope that symbolically reflected the nuclear contamination of the Japanese archipelago.[21] *Nausicaä* follows the trend of Japanese *kaijū* films of the post-World War II era, where giant monsters created by the apocalyptical horrors of nuclear weaponry roamed the earth and fought back against humanity. Yet rather than following in the footsteps of Godzilla, Gatera, and many others— whereby nature is in continuous conflict with our Anthropocene—Miyazaki looked more closely at the post-disaster landscape toward a vision of what would happen if humanity persisted in a continuous fashion on its current path of environmental degradation. Minamata provided a unique prototype for *Nausicaä*; given the lingering effects of

Figure 6.3. Nausicaä in the Sea of Corruption.
Miyazaki Hayao, 1984, Studio Ghibli.

the mercury, Minamata Bay was off-limits to fishing, and consequentially, sea life anecdotally recovered, and the bay began to teem with life. In the image above, the female protagonist, Nausicaä, enters the surprisingly beautiful Sea of Corruption to investigate its true function in the natural world (figure 6.3). Miyazaki became interested in the way nature was adapting to the poisons that had been dumped into the bay, and rather than retelling the story of the human horror, he focused on the way nature synthesized the poison and bounced back.[22]

The fact that the interaction between the Japanese people and their environment was of major concern in the creation of *Nausicaä* is also exemplified in the preproduction memo for his crew during the making of the film in 1983:

> For the past few years I've put forth ideas for film projects with the following ethos. To offer a sense of liberation to present-day young people who in this suffocating, overprotective, and managed society find their path to self-reliant independence blocked and therefore have become neurotic; a major theme of this work is the manner in which people engage with nature, the nature surrounding them upon which they are dependent; can hope, exist even during this twilight era?[23]

It is for this reason that Miyazaki creates a young protagonist who is close to, and who actively engages with, nature. Nausicaä loves insects and plants and has a secret botanical laboratory in the basement of her castle. It is through her proactive interaction with nature that she is able to solve one of the central mysteries of the film. While most of the characters in *Nausicaä* believe nature is the villain intent on eradicating the human race, it is only the protagonist princess who realizes the giant forests in fact clean the Earth by absorbing poison from the soil and releasing it into the air, creating an environment where giant insects and arthropods can flourish, though it is harmful to humans.[24] Nausicaä discovers the secret of these forests during one of her frequent excursions there, when she accidentally falls into a huge vacant space underneath the forest floor that contains clean waters purified by layers of sand produced from the fossils of the forest wood. These forests, whose pollen are believed to be harmful to humans, are in fact purifying the lands and water originally contaminated by human warfare. Nature essentially restores the biosphere.[25] While the movie intuitively stops here and reconciles the nature versus human conflict via the self-sacrifice of the protagonist, Nausicaä is subsequently resurrected for the inevitable necessity of the happy ending. However, the manga significantly complicates the narrative.

While we never learn about the origin of the Sea of Corruption in the movie, the manga reveals that the Sea of Corruption was not a naturally evolved environment but rather an artificial "contamination purification system" (汚染浄化システム, *osen jōka shisutemu*) developed by humanity a thousand years ago with the purpose of purifying the earth over several thousand years after humans had lost control over environmental pollution. Once the poison had been removed, the Sea of Corruption would have outlived its purpose and faded away after having revitalized the earth. At the time of the tale, some revitalized land already existed, but some tribes who have learned to live with the Sea of Corruption, called the "forest people" (*Mori no hito*), are keeping this a secret.

In fact, it was the Doroks, one of the two warring nations described in the animation, who developed a genetically modified version of the mold from the Sea of Corruption. This biological weapon is introduced into battle against the Torumekians, but its uncontrollable rapid growth and mutation result in events referred to as a "great tidal wave" (大海嘯, *daikaisho*), which floods across the land uncontrollably and draws the insects into the battle. The unforeseeable outcome leads to the mass killing of both Doroks and Torumekians. Furthermore, the Sea of Corruption spreads across most of the Dorok nation, uprooting or killing vast numbers of civilians and rendering most of the land uninhabitable.

In a crucial revelation, Nausicaä discovers that the malevolent Ohmu—the giant monsters roaming the earth and believed to be hostile to humanity—are in fact another mechanism whereby nature cleanses the toxic biological spores developed by humanity as a weapon. Closer descriptions in the manga reveal that a profusion of fungi is sprouting from the Ohmu's body, growing rapidly within the miasma. The heroine realizes that the dying Ohmu is serving as a seedbed for the mold and that the giant species intend to merge with the mutant mold to create a new Sea of Corruption, meaning that it is the insects who fight human pollution and cleanse the environment after humanity has lost control over it. In this sense, the reader's perception of the Sea of Corruption gradually transforms from seeing it as a harmful entity to seeing it as a benevolent one. The narrative reveals nature's hidden potential as a force that actually purifies the world of toxins, and Miyazaki alludes to the fact that there are no absolute truths in our lives. As social beings, we are often misguided by our own self-interest, and the message of *Nausicaä* ultimately depends on our interpretations as readers.[26]

As such, the human interventions displayed in *Nausicaä* illustrate that despite our supposedly good intentions, we fail to tackle complex interrelated environmental issues like climate change and global warming. Just as the warring tribes depicted in *Nausicaä* misinterpret the encroaching toxic jungle, Miyazaki insinuates that our own comprehension of the complex natural environment is clouded by political and economic imperatives.[27] Remarkably, it is via its enduring relevance that *Nausicaä* continues to be applicable to contemporary environmental catastrophes. COVID-19 and the global coronavirus pandemic appear to be uncannily reminiscent of the deadly spores depicted in the film.

Conclusion

"History is in front of us; the future lies behind."[28]

「歴史は前にある。未来は背中にある」

Miyazaki adopted this phrase from the Japanese writer Hotta Yoshie (掘田善衛) to inspire political engagement and environmental consciousness in his viewers. Implicitly, Miyazaki's animations inextricably intertwine these two elements of our wasteful, modern-day consumer societies and the importance of the political choices we make. Both have deep ramifications that we need to be fully conscious of, and therein lies the *raison d'être* of his films. Stripped down to its bare essentials, the entire story of *Nausicaä* depicts an elaborate conflict for scarce environmental resources. Facing declines in population and productivity on a marginal planet, the territorial disputes of two major powers spill over and engulf the entire planet. In the end, humanity is decimated, and the scarce unspoiled lands are rendered uninhabitable. This is most certainly a narrative that we have heard about many times before, and at the time of writing, the Ukraine-Russia as well as Israeli–Palestinian conflicts weigh heavily on the global community.

The legacy of *Nausicaä* is that soon after this animation's success, Studio Ghibli was established in June 1985 by longtime cocreators Hayao Miyazaki and Isao Takahata, who teamed up with producer Toshio Suzuki and publisher Yasuyoshi Tokuma to create an animation studio that reflected a new environmentally focused ethos, which promoted the newly established ecological zeitgeist of the era. Like

Nausicaä, several of Miyazaki's films contextualize a powerful environmentally centered narrative that can subliminally transform our thinking and reconnect us with nature in unconscious ways. Studio Ghibli developed complex visual schema involving human-nature relationships that are cross-culturally and cross-generationally comprehensible. A key message of Miyazaki's work is that we must respect nature—or face our own destruction.[29]

The 1984 film version of *Nausicaä of the Valley of the Wind* ends abruptly on a happy note of coexistence between the kingdom and the toxic jungle. But the graphic novel reflects a much more complicated and nuanced philosophical treatise on our interaction with a limited environment that we all rely upon for sustenance. After a thousand-plus pages, Miyazaki ends his eco-saga with the final encouraging words that no matter how many mistakes we have made in the past, "Let us begin, no matter how challenging it is, we must live."[30]

Miyazaki's films stand as a pop cultural antidote to the legacy of environmental disasters that have besieged the Japanese archipelago from the early postwar period until the very present. The human pollution and environmental degradation climaxed most recently on March 11, 2011, when the Tohoku earthquake and ensuing tsunami destroyed the Fukushima Daiichi nuclear power plant, resulting in one of the worst nuclear accidents in history. Over a decade later, with concerns about childhood thyroid cancer on the rise, and massive amounts of contaminated coolant to be released in the ocean, a full accounting of the accident and its impact on human life is still a long way off. How much has Japan really learned in the past four decades after the animation was released?[31] Miyazaki's narratives subliminally convey important environmental concerns and keep them at the conscious level of his viewers by allegorically showing our relationship with nature.

Notes

[1] All translations throughout this paper are mine unless otherwise stated.

[2] See The Cambridge Language Collective, "Hayao Miyazaki, Studio Ghibli, and the 'Environmental Message.'"

[3] For eco-sagas, see Yuen, "The Ecological Imagination of Hayao Miyazaki"; and for a discussion of his ecophilosophy, see Gossin, "Animate Nature."

[4] Mason, "Whither Japan's Environmental Movement?" 190.

[5] Simon Avenell suggests that "Japan's ascent as a polluters' paradise and the struggle of its pollution victims propelled the country to the forefront of historic global environmental awakening in the 1960s." See Avenell, *Transnational Japan in the Global Environmental Movement*, 2. The high number of serious pollution incidents saw the Japanese environmental movement peak in the early 1970s. See Mason, "Whither Japan's Environmental Movement?" 187. Eventually, the focus shifted from purely localized pollution to the global environment in the late 1980s.

[6] Chapman, "56 Workers Contaminated in Japan's Nuclear Mishap."

[7] Mumcu and Yilmaz, "Anime Landscapes as a Tool for Analyzing the Human-Environment Relationship: Hayao Miyazaki Films," 16.

[8] Wake, "On the Ideological Manipulation of Nature Inherent in Japanese Popular Culture," 224.

[9] Yonemura, "Kaigai bunken shōkai."

[10] Hiatt, "Soviet Sub Bumps into US Carrier."

[11] Yonemura, "Kaigai bunken shōkai."

[12] Miyazaki, "Tokushu: Kenpo Kaisei," 7. See also McKirdy and Wakatsuki, "Animator Hayao Miyazaki Slams Japan's Abe Ahead of Controversial Security Vote."

[13] See Miyazaki, *Starting Point: 1979–1996*, 293.

[14] See Ghibli Wiki online at https://ghibli.fandom.com/wiki/Future_Boy_Conan. Accessed September 15, 2022.

[15] See, for example, Morgan, "Creature in Crisis," 180.

[16] See Miyazaki, "Tokushu: Kenpo Kaisei," 4.

[17] Miyazaki, *Starting Point, 1979–1996*, 239.

[18] See, for example, author Nosaka Akiyuki's semiautobiographical story *Hotaru no Haka* (Grave of the Fireflies, 1967), which was turned into an animation by Studio Ghibli in 1988 and directed by Isao Takahata, also a member of this traumatized generation.

[19] Miyazaki, *Nausicaä*, hardcover edition, vol. 2, 139.

[20] In addition to the current war in Ukraine, many other examples of using *Nausica*ä as a modern-day fable exist. See, for instance, Ethan Jeger's usage of the story in "Watching Nausicaä in the Age of Environmental Catastrophe" as a metaphor for the collapse of Australia's ecosystems and the Morrison government's refusal to combat climate change while failing to implement a policy for the transition to a 100 percent renewable net-zero emissions target by 2050.

[21] These creatures also insinuate the mercurial nature of humanity via homonymous analogy to the religious doomsday cult by the name Aum (オウム). Inaga, "Miyazaki Hayao's Epic Comic Series," 114.

[22] Schnelbach, "Nausicaä of the Valley of the Wind: A New Kind of Action Hero."

[23] Miyazaki, *Nausicaä of the Valley of the Wind Pre-Production*, cited in Ethan Jegers, "Watching Nausicaä in the Age of Environmental Catastrophe."

[24] Greenberg, *Hayao Miyazaki: Exploring the Early Works of Japan's Greatest Animator*, 122.

[25] Wake, "On the Ideological Manipulation of Nature Inherent in Japanese Popular Culture," 225.

[26] Yuen, "Nausicaä Vol. 1: The Valley of the Wind."

[27] Morgan, "Creatures in Crisis," 179.

[28] Miyazaki, "Tokushu: Kenpo Kaisei," 8. This quotation is by Yoshie Hotta, and it is used by Miyazaki in his essay in the Ghibli magazine, *Neppu*, July 2013.

[29] Yuan, "How Studio Ghibli Films Can Help Us Rediscover the Childlike Wonder of Our Connection with Nature."

[30] Miyazaki, *Kaze no tani no naushika*, 223.

[31] Masano, "Has Japan Learned the Lessons of Past Pollution Crises?"

Bibliography

Avenell, Simon. *Transnational Japan in the Global Environmental Movement*. Honolulu: University of Hawai'i Press, 2017.

Bryant, Nathaniel Heggins. "Neutering the Monster, Pruning the Green: The Ecological Evolutions of Nausicaä of the Valley of the Wind." *Resilience: A Journal of the Environmental Humanities* 2, no.3 (2015): 120–126.

Cambridge Language Collective. "Hayao Miyazaki, Studio Ghibli, and the 'Environmental Message,'" *Cambridge Language Collective*, 2022. Accessed September 15, 2022. https://www.thecambridgelanguagecollective.com/arts-and-culture/hayao-miyazaki-studio-ghibli-and-the-environmental-message.

Chapman, William. "56 Workers Contaminated in Japan's Nuclear Mishap," *Washington Post*, April 22, 1981. Accessed September 17, 2022. https://www.washingtonpost.com/archive/politics/1981/04/22/56-workers-contaminated-in-japans-nuclear-mishap.

Gossin, Pamela. "Animated Nature: Aesthetics, Ethics, and Empathy in Miyazaki Hayao's Ecophilosophy," in *Mechademia: Second Arc*, vol. 10 (2015), 209–234.

Greenberg, Raz. *Hayao Miyazaki: Exploring the Early Works of Japan's Greatest Animator*. New York: Bloomsbury, 2018.

Hairston, Marc, King Tyler, and Stacy Brian (eds.). "Now, after Nausicaa Has Finished" (Yom special story), *GhibliWiki*, June 1994. Accessed September 16, 2022. http://www.nausicaa.net/miyazaki/interviews/afternausicaa.html.

Hiatt, Fred. "Soviet Sub Bumps into US Carrier," *Washington Post*, March 22, 1984. Accessed September 17, 2022. https://www.washingtonpost.com/archive/politics/1984/03/22/soviet-sub-bumps-into-us-carrier/3c75515e-d492-4f6a-8f01-a023b6bc4c9c/.

Hisaaki, Wake. "On the Ideological Manipulation of Nature Inherent in Japanese Popular Culture: Miyazaki, Hyakuta, and Ishimure," in *Ecocentrism in Japan*, edited by Hisaaki Wake, Keijiro Suga, and Yuki Masami, 223–238. New York: Lexington Books, 2018.

Inaga, Shigemi. "Miyazaki Hayao's Epic Comic Series: 'Nausicaä in the Valley of the Wind:' An Attempt at Interpretation," *Japan Review* 11 (1999): 113–127.

Jegers, Ethan. "Watching Nausicaä in the Age of Environmental Catastrophe," *Tertangala*, June 21, 2021. Accessed September 12, 2022. https://tertangala.net/?p=67.

Lichten, Jack. "The Sun Also Rises: Miyazaki, Oshima, and the Politics of History," *MidnightEye: Visions of Japanese Cinema*. May 8, 2015. Accessed September 3, 2022.

http://www.midnighteye.com/features/the-sun-also-rises-miyazaki-oshima-and-the-politics-of-history/.

Lioi, Anthony. "The City Ascends: Laputa: Castle in the Sky as Critical Ecotopia." *Anime and Utopia* 2, no. 2. Accessed August 20, 2022. https://imagetextjournal.com/the-city-ascends-laputa-castle-in-the-sky-as-critical-ecotopia/.

Masano, Atsuko. "Has Japan Learned the Lessons of Past Pollution Crises?" *Nippon*, December 14, 2018. Accessed August 29, 2022. https://www.nippon.com/en/currents/d00383/.

Mason, J. Robert. "Whither Japan's Environmental Movement? An Assessment of Problems and Prospects at the National Level," *Pacific Affairs* 72, no.2 (1999): 187–207.

McKirdy, Euan and Wakatsuki Yoko. "Animator Hayao Miyazaki Slams Japan's Abe Ahead of Controversial Security Vote," CNN, July 14, 2015. Accessed September 13, 2020. https://edition.cnn.com/2015/07/14/asia/japan-miyazaki-slams-abe-security-bill/index.html.

Miyazaki, Hayao. *Kaze no tani no naushika* (風の谷のナウシカ), vol. 1–7. Tokyo: Animage Comics, 1982–1994.

Miyazaki, Hayao. *Starting Point, 1979–1996*. Translated by Beth Cary and Frederik L. Schodt. San Francisco: Viz Media, 2009.

Miyasaki, Hayao. "Tokushu: Kenpo Kaisei" (憲法改正) in Neppu『熱風』2013 年 7 月号 特集「憲法改正」. https://www.ghibli.jp/shuppan/np/009408/.

Morgan, Gwendolyn, "Creatures in Crisis: Apocalyptic Environmental Visions in Miyazaki's Nausicaä of the Valley of the Wind and Princess Mononoke," *Resilience: A Journal of the Environmental Humanities* 2, no.3 (2015): 172–183.

Mumcu, Sema and Yilmaz Serap, "Anime Landscapes as a Tool for Analyzing the Human-Environment Relationship: Hayao Miyazaki Films," *Arts* 7, no. 2 (2018): 16. https://doi.org/10.3390/arts7020016.

Pan, Yuan, "How Studio Ghibli Films Can Help Us Rediscover the Childlike Wonder of Our Connection with Nature," *The Conversation*, April 29, 2022. Accessed September 14, 2022. https://theconversation.com/how-studio-ghibli-films-can-help-us-rediscover-the-childlike-wonder-of-our-connection-with-nature-176612.

Penney, Matthew, "Miyazaki Hayao's Kaze Tachinu (The Wind Rises) 宮崎駿「風立ちぬ」," *Asia-Pacific Journal* 11, no. 30 (2013). Accessed September 10, 2022. https://apjjf.org/2013/11/30/Matthew-Penney/3976/article.html.

Schnelbach, Leah, "Nausicaä of the Valley of the Wind: A New Kind of Action Hero," *Tor.com*, March 29, 2017. Accessed July 25, 2022. https://www.tor.com/2017/03/29/nausicaa-of-the-valley-of-the-wind-a-new-kind-of-action-hero.

Yonemura, Miyuki (村みゆき) "Kaigai bunken shōkai: Takahato Isao or Miyazaki Hayao (Kim, Joon Yang) *Imēji no teikoku nihon rettō no animēshon*," [海外文献紹介：高畑勲あるいは宮崎駿 (キム・ジュニアン著『イメージの帝国日本列島上のアニメーション』; Introducing Overseas Literature: Takahato Isao or Miyazaki Hayao— The Animation of the Image of the Imperial Japanese Islands]. Tokyo: 専修国文』no. 94 (2014): 119–146.

Yuen, Isaac, "The Ecological Imagination of Hayao Miyazaki: A Retrospective on Four Fantastical Worlds," *Orion Magazine*, March 5, 2021. Accessed September 15, 2022. https://orionmagazine.org/article/the-worlds-of-hayao-miyazaki.

Yuen, Isaac, "Nausicaä Vol. 1: The Valley of the Wind" in *EkoStories: Essays and Stories by Isaac Yuen*, June 5, 2013. Accessed September 17, 2022. https://ekostories.com/2013/06/05/nausicaa-valley-wind/.

7

You Can (Not) Restore: Ecocritique and Intergenerational Ecological Conflict in *Evangelion*

Christopher Smith

The transmedia *Evangelion* series is undoubtedly one of the most important cultural phenomena in recent decades. Beginning with *Shin seiki evangerion,* the original 1995–96 television series, *Evangelion* expanded into two theatrical films in the nineties, multiple manga and video game adaptations, and, famously, untold multitudes of character goods. The most recent addition to *Evangelion* is a series of four *Rebuild of Evangelion* films (2007–2021) that retell and dramatically alter the original story. The story (in most iterations) focuses on a group of adolescents who must pilot giant robots to fight off giant monsters who attack their city, Tokyo-3. The series features nuanced psychological portrayals of the characters, a deep probing of protagonist Ikari Shinji's troubled psyche, an unfolding conspiracy that has dramatic implications for the future of humanity, and the frequent use of religious terminology and iconography. As such, the series has been fertile ground for analysis from a variety of disciplinary perspectives, including religious studies, psychology, media studies, genre studies, and women's studies.

Examining the original TV series, the two films from the 1990s, and the four twenty-first-century *Rebuild* films, this chapter argues that *Evangelion* can also be read as an eco-disaster story with a pointed ecocritical stance. Specifically, *Evangelion* depicts an intergenerational ecological conflict. Children of a generation that devastated the environment are left to live in a broken world, and they are furthermore forced by adults into painful battles with the giant monsters that manifest as a result of those adults' ecological carelessness. I argue that *Evangelion* can therefore be read as an ecocritique that denounces older generations who exploited nature instrumentally for their own purposes and then left their children to deal with the consequences of ecological damage and climate change. However, unlike many other eco-disaster films, in which restoration can only occur if nature is given time to heal itself, *Evangelion* seems to propose that the ecologies of earth can only be repaired if younger generations appropriate their parents' apparatus of exploitation and turn them toward deliberate ecological restoration. Furthermore, this ecocritical stance has become more prominent over time as the *Evangelion* series has iterated and the climate crisis has deepened.

Kaijū and Generational Ecocriticism

Briefly, fourteen years before the narrative present, a shadowy organization called SEELE unearthed a giant humanoid called Adam in Antarctica. In an attempt to analyze Adam and harness its power, SEELE triggered Second Impact, a giant explosion that caused global physical and ecological damage, including climate change and sea level rise. After Second Impact, SEELE created NERV, an organization that builds giant Evangelion "robots," which are actually clones of Adam. In the narrative present, NERV's commander summons his fourteen-year-old son, Shinji, to NERV headquarters in Tokyo-3 to pilot an Evangelion robot and fight off mysterious giant monsters called *shito*, or Angels, that are attacking the city for unknown reasons.

Although ecocriticism is not, perhaps, the most foregrounded aspect of a series with such a sweeping scope, the story centers around battles with giant chthonic monsters. The first such monster emerges from the sea, as do several other Angels, swimming through the urban streets and buildings of a coastal Japan now covered with water due to the rise in sea level engendered by Second Impact (figure 7.1). This creates clear intertextual connections with the *kaijū* (giant special-effects monster) genre. Indeed, Zoltan Kacsuk has argued *Evangelion* brings the giant robot genre back to its *kaijū* origins.[1] The progenitor of the *kaijū* genre is *Godzilla* (1954), in which the titular monster emerges from the sea to attack Tokyo because of nuclear weapons testing in the Pacific, which has both angered it and given it enormous power. Godzilla is therefore a potent symbol of the consequences of human-caused environmental destruction given concrete form, or perhaps even nature's instrument of revenge. It therefore follows that the monsters that attack Tokyo-3 in *Evangelion* can also be read as *kaijū* emerging from the consequences of environmental destruction.

Figure 7.1. The first Angel approaches from the ocean.
Anno, Hideaki, 1995, Gainax.

Others have remarked on the ecological commentary in *Evangelion,* mostly noting its critique of a Cartesian dualism between the self and other that walls off the subject from ecological systems and engenders an instrumental view of nature (i.e., that it can be exploited freely for human benefit). Giuseppe Gatti argues that the symbiotic relationship between the pilots and the Evangelion units (which are ultimately biological), and the contaminable bodies in the series are anti-Cartesian.[2] Stevie Suan, meanwhile, cites the "figurative acting" in the show, where characters are expressed through combinations of conventionalized codes. These codes are "all cited from prior instantiations of those codes by other characters," therefore emphasizing the interdependence between the subject and the world, a subject that can be formed only at the intersection of social and ecological systems.[3]

However, I argue there is also ecocritique to be found in the surface narrative of the series, specifically a critique of the ecological practices of older generations. There are clearly drawn divides between generations in *Evangelion.* The members of SEELE usually only appear as "sound-only" black panels in a teleconferencing system, but the head of SEELE is a white-haired older man named Kiel who wears a sort of visor. SEELE members also seem to have access to enormous economic resources and political capital, which they use to support the Evangelion program.

SEELE is therefore an organization of shadowy, well-connected old male power brokers whose machinations created the various problems facing the world in the present, including Second Impact. Next is the middle-aged generation that executed SEELE's plans. This generation includes Ikari Gendō, the head of NERV; a man known only as Dr. Katsuragi, who led the expedition to unearth Adam in Antarctica, which caused Second Impact; and Akagi Naoko, the scientist who built the supercomputers that run NERV and the Evangelion (Eva) project. Finally, the last generation is the children of the execution generation, who must fight battles they did not choose and barely understand: Gendō's son, Shinji, and the other teenaged Eva pilots; Dr. Katsuragi's daughter, Katsuragi Misato, who directs the military operations at NERV and commands battles against the Angels; and Akagi Ritsuko, the daughter of Naoko and the head research and development scientist at NERV. Although Ritsuko seems to know more about the true nature of the Evas and the larger conspiracy, Misato is kept in the dark about NERV's true purpose, as is Shinji, who is expected merely to pilot the robot.

Evangelion therefore very clearly assigns different roles to each generation in its narrative of battle against chthonic forces and transcendence: an older generation that pulls strings and makes plans; a middle-aged generation that is complicit with those plans, builds the infrastructure to execute them, and sets events in motion; and a younger generation that is forced to deal with the fallout of the older generations' machinations. Framed this way, *Evangelion* tells a striking story of one generation being victimized by their elders and left to deal with the fallout of their elders' choices. Certainly, this generational conflict has more than one dimension. As Patrick Galbraith has written, "the angst and anger oozing from Neon Genesis Evangelion, and its depiction of betrayed and vulnerable youth inheriting a world that is already destroyed, almost demand a reading of it as a product of the anxiety sweeping Japan in the 1990s."[4] Chief among the anxieties of the 1990s was the era's status as the "lost decade" after the collapse of the bubble economy, and here as well, we can see the relevance of a generational critique. The postwar generations built an economic system that benefited them enormously, then indifferently left young people to face a lifetime of dismal job prospects and zero growth when that system collapsed.

Yet, as stated above, *Evangelion* revolves around battles with *kaijū*, those giant monsters that, in genre tradition, emerge because of environmental destruction. Read in light of this intertextual ecological connection, the generational conflict in the series takes on new significance. SEELE desired the immense transformative power of Adam and sent an expedition, run by Dr. Katsuragi, to unearth and study it. Put another way, they excavated a fossilized source of energy, confident they could tame and harness it. Because of their hubristic and ill-considered attempt to harness this energy source, the world suffered the explosive disaster of Second

Impact, along with ecological consequences similar to global anthropogenic climate change: the climate warmed, ecosystems were disrupted, and sea levels rose. In the narrative present, Japan seems trapped in an eternal summer; we learn that cicada populations only recently recovered after being nearly wiped out (episode 4) and that Tokyo is now underwater (episode 7). Nonetheless, capitalism continues unabated. As Igarashi Tarō writes, despite Tokyo-3 being a post-catastrophe city, the shelves of convenience stores are buried in consumer goods.[5] Misato's apartment is also awash in the disposable detritus of consumerism. This world suffering from ecological disaster, yet where the wheels of capitalism and consumerism grind on unaffected, is a pointed metaphor for our own world. Furthermore, SEELE and the complicit middle-aged generation have not learned from their disastrous mistakes and have spent the last fourteen years continuing to build resources to attempt to harness the power of Adam and other mysterious life-forms.

It is the younger generation that is forced to live in this broken world of flooded cities, destroyed ecosystems, and attacking Angels. Misato, Ritsuko, Shinji, and the others of the younger generation must exert heroic efforts, drawing on all their intellectual and physical abilities to defeat the Angels, who manifest as a result of their parents' and grandparents' instrumental use of nature and ecological destruction. And the Eva pilots in particular suffer greatly because they are neurologically linked to the Evas and experience their pain. Shinji, for example, suffers the sensation of having his arm broken (episode 2), being stabbed and having his hands burned (episode 3), being shot and immersed in boiling liquid (episode 6), claustrophobic entrapment (episode 16), being strangled (episode 18), and having his arm severed (episode 19), among other things. Fellow pilot Sōryū Asuka Langley suffers the sensation of being burned by acid (episode 11), having both arms severed and being beheaded (episode 19), and more. Another pilot, Ayanami Rei, suffers bodily invasion and having her arm severed (episode 18), taking the brunt of an explosion (episode 19), being stabbed, and even dying (episode 23). All this suffering is inflicted on them because they are forced by older generations to fight the manifestations of those older generations' ecological exploitation and carelessness, exploitation they themselves did not participate in, having been born after Second Impact.

This generational conflict, where the young are forced to not only live with the consequences of their parents' and grandparents' ecological exploitation but also to do the hard work of cleaning up after them, can be read as a straightforward allegory for several pressing environmental issues, especially anthropogenic climate change. While older generations were able to enjoy the benefits of exploiting energy resources (fossil fuels) and carelessly dumping their waste products (carbon) into the ecosystem, younger generations face the prospect of living in a world of warming climates, rising sea levels, polluted ecosystems, and, as more resources are devoted to the monumental task of mitigating and repairing the ecological damage caused by older generations, decreased prosperity. And just as SEELE and NERV are still set on their plan to use Adam, those older generations are continuing their ecological exploitation with seemingly little inclination to change ecologically destructive habits. As David Ingram writes, an apocalyptic ecotext "displaces and contains the apocalyptic anxieties it raises."[6] By displacing the consequences of ecological destruction into Angels—essentially *kaijū* that take revenge for ecological exploitation—and by showing the young engaging in physical battles against these ecological avatars and enduring real physical and psychological pain as a result, *Evangelion* heightens both the suffering of younger generations and their cruel exploitation by older generations in this intergenerational ecological conflict.

Resistance and Restoration

Evangelion, therefore, offers a pointed critique of intergenerational conflict over ecological destruction and exploitation. But does it offer any possibilities of resistance to destructive regimes or a path to ecological restoration? Here, I turn to a comparison with a genre of ecocinema we might call the environmental postapocalypse film. In these films, some ecological disaster has occurred in the past that has destroyed or transformed human society and rendered the planet inhospitable to human life. In the narrative present, humans eke out a constrained existence in limited spaces. *Evangelion* fits into this general mold with the disaster of Second Impact in the past and rising sea levels that have forced humans to rebuild inland, although the living space available is less constrained than in some of the other examples of the genre discussed below. Almost invariably, in these environmental postapocalyptic films, "nature" is an independent force that exists as an exteriority to human society. Consequently, nature is capable of regenerating the environmental damage wrought by humans and repairing the ecosystem. Phillip Hammond and Hugh Breton note:

> Nature intervenes to rebalance and reorder the human world at the same time as reordering the ecosystem. . . . There is also an implied view of nature as in some sense intelligent or wise—the planet repairs itself by purging the pollution; the birds and zoo animals are the first to sense the impending catastrophe.[7]

In ecofiction, and especially apocalyptic ecofiction, nature often operates to repair itself independently of human agency, and humans usually have little to do with the ecological regeneration. At best, they can serve as stewards of the environmental repair nature is performing on its own; at worst, they hinder it.

This pattern can be seen, for example, in *Waterworld* (1995), *WALL-E* (2008), and *Snowpiercer* (2013). The most significant entry in the genre, however, is probably Miyazaki Hayao's *Nausicaä of the Valley of the Wind* (*Kaze no tani no Naushika* 1984), which *Evangelion* director Anno Hideaki worked on. A thousand years after the ecosystem was destroyed by an apocalyptic war, the planet is covered in a "Sea of Decay" (*fukai*), a jungle of massive plants and animals that has evolved to purify the ecosystem from the toxins humans created during their war in the distant past. Nature has acted independently of humans to heal itself and regenerate the environment. The protagonist, Nausicaä, is an agent of environmental regrowth only to the extent that she protects the Sea of Decay from being destroyed by other humans.

Mizobe Kōji traces exact parallels between *Nausicaä* and *Evangelion*, equating, among other elements, *Nausicaä*'s ancient humans with SEELE, and Second Impact with the purification of the jungles.[8] However, rather than faithfully follow the mold of *Nausicaä* and other entries in the genre, I argue *Evangelion* mixes postapocalyptic ecocinema with the *kaijū* genre. It is set after a (partial) apocalypse, but nature manifests as a destructive force in the *kaijū* tradition, a force that seeks to destroy humanity and that therefore must be confronted. "Nature," as a force external to humanity, is consequently not available to repair the damage wrought by apocalypse. *Evangelion,* therefore, proposes that other tools must be used, and these tools are the apparatus of ecological exploitation created by older generations, which the younger generation must appropriate and repurpose. However, this possibility of appropriative resistance and restoration has evolved gradually as *Evangelion* has iterated across more than two decades. In the remainder of the chapter, I will trace these changing approaches to ecological restoration across the various reworkings and retellings of the text.

Evangelion culminates in something called the human completion project, a shadowy plan created by SEELE and executed by NERV. The human completion project (although this is initially unclear) is a plan to use the power of Adam and its counterpart Lilith to merge all of humanity into a single organism, bringing down the physical and psychological barriers between individuals to create a single hive mind and body. The original ending to the television series, controversially, does not depict any of the events leading to the activation of the human completion project that viewers expected but instead moves directly into Shinji's internal psychological struggles as he is integrated into the collective mind of humanity that has been united into one being by the completion project. Ultimately, Shinji learns to accept himself as he is and that his existence is valuable. In the final scene, his closed-off world of misery opens up to a world with blue skies where all his friends are present, applauding him and telling him "congratulations" for overcoming his doubts and angst. Departing from Suan, who argues that the abstract meta-animation in this ending draws attention to the construction of the self from other codes and makes it the most ecologically conscious, I argue that this ending has the weakest ecological message of the three main endings.[9] I take this stance because in this ending, SEELE's human completion project seems to have worked and seems to have been recuperative for Shinji. In the end, Shinji seems to remove the barriers in his heart and join the hive mind of unified humanity, healed of his crippling psychological fears and anxieties. Human completion, in other words, was worth it. The pain and ecological destruction required to activate the human completion project seem to have been vindicated and commensurate here, an unfortunate but necessary sacrifice that seems to have paid off by achieving a better future for both Shinji personally and humanity in general. Allegorically, this ending seems to say that the ecological exploitation of older generations (through resource extraction, pollution, carbon, etc.) was justified because it secured the advancement of human prosperity.

These events are depicted more concretely in the follow-up 1997 film, *Shin seiki evangerion gekijōban Air / magokoro o / kimi ni* (English title: *The End of Evangelion*), which contained a completely new depiction of the human completion project, including the narrative events of its execution. In this version, due to ideological conflicts between SEELE and NERV, each of these organizations (representing, again, the two older generations in power) picks a teenager to use as a tool to execute human completion in their desired manner. SEELE picks Shinji, and Gendō of NERV picks fellow Eva pilot Ayanami Rei. Both, however, rebel against the plans of their elders. They do not refuse to participate in human completion but rather seize control of it and appropriate it for their own ends. Ayanami excludes Gendō from the final merging of humanity, where he hopes to meet his dead wife once again. She takes from Gendō an embryo of Adam that he had grafted on his hand—the key to initiating human completion— and with it merges with Lilith to begin human completion with her own agency, saying to him in parting, "I am not your puppet."[10] Shinji pilots his Eva unit, which is incorporated into Lilith as it begins converting all humans into an amniotic-fluid-like liquid and absorbing all human souls. He is thus in a position to guide the reshaping of the world. At first, he goes along with SEELE's plan but ultimately decides he wants to meet others again, even though they might hurt him. He therefore sabotages SEELE's human completion project; Lilith dies and falls apart limb from limb; and humans are reconstituted from the ocean of amniotic fluid to live independent existences again. In the final scene, Shinji and Asuka are shown to be living now as embodied, physical, individuated humans lying on a beach, capable of hurting and rejecting each other once again.

In this ending, two children of the younger generation are forced, once again, to be tools in the older two generations' ecologically destructive plans. However, they rebel and seize the mechanisms those older generations have put in place to instead create a world of their own choosing, exercising their own agency and ecological consciousness instead of being used as puppets. The younger generation's parents and grandparents destroyed the world (the final scene shows only a red ocean and a giant rotting head of Lilith in the distance), but the teenagers have subverted their plans and clawed back the possibility for ecological restoration, as at least humans now exist to restore the dead world. As human completion is in the process of being undone, Shinji's mother says humans can "find a chance at happiness as long as they are alive and have the sun, the moon, and planet earth," strongly indicating Shinji's new world will not be a cerebral (and Cartesian) paradise of joined minds but a world where humans find happiness in connection with ecosystems. This ending shows that, ultimately, the ecological destruction and exploitation older generations committed to achieve human completion was not justified or vindicated; their project was not desirable, and the younger generation seized the power of human completion to remake the world for themselves.

A decade after *The End of Evangelion,* Anno wrote a new set of four feature-length films known collectively as the *Rebuild of Evangelion,* or *Evangerion shin gekijōban,* although he codirected the films with his protégé, Tsurumaki Kazuya. These films completely retell the *Evangelion* story. The first two films follow the original TV series fairly closely but diverge sharply at the end of the second film when Shinji accidentally causes Third Impact. In the last two films, fourteen years have passed with Shinji in stasis, and his friends from NERV now run a resistance organization called WILLE that fights against NERV. In the *Rebuild* continuity, the ecological message of *Evangelion* becomes more strongly foregrounded. In this version, not only did Second Impact cause sea level rise and global warming, but it also sterilized the oceans and turned them red, which is the films' visual grammar for contamination. One member of the younger generation, Misato and Ritsuko's college friend Kaji Ryōji, has made it his mission to preserve and restore the marine life-forms and ecosystems destroyed by Second Impact. He operates a large oceanic facility that filters the red water into clean blue water and where marine animals can live in tanks and aquariums. Later, after Kaji's death, Misato carries on his desire for ecological restoration by launching seed vaults into orbit, ensuring the ecologies of earth will survive, even as humans wreak devastation on the planet, making ecological preservation a prominent part of the protagonists' mission.

While Second Impact turned the oceans red, Third Impact turns the land red as well, and it wipes out all life (humans are transformed into Evangelion cores and put in a kind of stasis). This dead, contaminated, red-filtered world is detailed for viewers in the fourth film, as Shinji, Asuka, and Rei trek past ordinary pastoral and urban scenes rendered alien and contaminated by red coloration until they are rescued by one of Shinji's former classmates (now an adult) wearing a protective suit. Igarashi notes that these images of contamination and ruin in the last two films (2012 and 2021) reflect the 3/11 triple disasters in 2011. He argues Anno and other directors:

> suddenly could witness scenes of ruin not in past records, or battlefields of far-off countries, or in scenes from anime or movies, but rather real ruins right here in Japan, over a huge area where convenience stores are everywhere. . . . The red sea that pushes in like a tsunami, the appearance of the protective suits that people wear when they enter contaminated areas and the devices like Geiger counters they use to measure L-Barrier density, all resemble the high-radiation areas damaged by the nuclear power accident.[11]

After 3/11, therefore, *Evangelion* shifts its ecological commentary to incorporate not only anthropogenic climate change and the destruction of ecosystems but also the environmental damage caused by nuclear contamination.

The pilots are rescued from the contaminated wasteland and taken to "Village 3." This area is protected from the red contamination by containment pillars supplied by WILLE, and within this confined area there is an explosion of colors—especially green—that contrast sharply with the monochrome red of the polluted world. In this village, survivors of Third Impact lead an agrarian lifestyle in harmony with nature, and this agricultural village becomes a place of respite and healing for Shinji after the trauma he suffered in a recent battle. Kondō Ginga writes that the portrayal of Village 3 is a betrayal of the feminist sensibilities of *Evangelion*, which, despite the sexualizing gaze it sometimes turns on its female characters, has always featured egalitarian gender roles and competent women in positions of authority. Life in Village 3 returns to traditional segregated gender roles, with women performing agricultural and child-rearing labor, while men assume roles as leaders and do technical work. She argues the theme of the first half of the fourth movie is the recovery of one's humanity, particularly for Shinji, and that the space of recovery is a gendered space.[12] While acknowledging this critique, I want to point out that the site of the recovery of humanity is also a green, growing space, filled not only with agriculture but with woods and wild animals, where humans live in careful harmony with ecosystems; we learn they only take deadfall from the forests, for example, and a small quota of fish from lakes. Village 3 represents an almost Tolkienesque intervention into the geometric, gray, concrete, and metal worlds of both WILLE and NERV. That this green space becomes the site of recovering humanity strongly suggests that "humanity" is a quality inextricably intertwined with natural ecosystems and cannot be found in the grand projects and mechanized worlds of either NERV or its resistance. But

Figure 7.2. Containment pillars protect nature within Village 3 from red ecological contamination. Anno Hideaki, 2021, Khara.

this natural space is only possible because Misato, the leader of WILLE, stole from NERV the containment pillars mentioned above that keep the red corruption from inundating Village 3 (figure 7.2). She also stole from NERV a giant flying warship built with Eva technology that allows her to wage resistance warfare against them. Here, a member of the younger generation appropriates the tools of older generations and uses them for ecological restoration.

This theme continues in the film's conclusion. Having healed from his psychological wounds and recovered his humanity in Village 3, Shinji goes on to participate in the final battle against his father. Gendō is once again trying to trigger human completion, and he has maneuvered all the pieces into place, including WILLE and the ship they stole. Shinji, however, manages to subvert his father, take over human completion, and turn it to his own ends. This is possible because Misato creates a "lance" from her ship, a mysterious device (one is given the biblical name "Lance of Longinus") that has the power to remake the world. Gendō had secured all the lances in order to remake the world in his image, but Misato—an older member of the young generation—makes an additional lance from appropriated NERV technology and gives it to Shinji. Shinji, in turn, uses the lance to destroy all Evangelions, which are precisely the devices the older generations built to harness the power of Adam (fossilized energy) and fulfill their environmentally destructive ambitions. Shinji then uses the power he has appropriated from NERV and SEELE to restore the environment in a miraculous reforming of the earth with the power of the lances. Humans are precipitated from Evangelion cores back into human form, but along with humans come various animals as well; humans are restored along with the ecosystems they rely on. The oceans are cleansed, and one shot shows a view from space of the planet turned blue once again.

Figure 7.3. The final shot, a photographic portrayal of the ocean restored
to its proper level and color. Anno Hideaki, 2021, Khara.

Shinji, therefore, uses the older generations' environmentally destructive
apparatus of power to create a world without any Evangelions, which might be
used for their grandiose ambitions, and where the natural environment is restored.
Nature cannot heal itself, as the destruction wrought by humans is too extensive.
But a teenager (and significantly, Shinji and the other pilots remain teenagers
despite the fourteen-year time gap) can use the older generations' devices and
turn them toward ecological restoration. As Michael Svoboda notes, in most
"cli-fi" disaster films, the environmental catastrophe is so large that there is a
disconnect from any action the audience might take to mitigate climate change,
and the only solution is to passively let nature itself take action to either heal itself
or destroy humanity.[13] *Evangelion,* however, suggests a path forward for younger
generations—even fourteen-year-olds—to take positive action by repurposing
existing systems of environmental exploitation.

The final scene shifts, quite abruptly, from grand montages of global
restoration to a scene of ordinary daily life, with Shinji and other characters at
the Ubeshinkawa train station in Ube City, Yamaguchi Prefecture. Ubeshinkawa
station is right next to the ocean and would have been submerged in Second
Impact. Its existence here shows that Shinji restored the world to its state before
Second Impact. The final shot of the film (and the whole *Rebuild* series) is an aerial
photographic (not animated) shot of Ubeshinkawa station, looking down from a
high angle at animated characters running out of the photographic station, then
panning up and around to look at the ocean, blue and at its proper level, before
cutting to the credits (figure 7.3). Shinji has created a world of restored ecosystems
and repaired ecological damage, including the damage of climate change and rising
sea levels. But the switch to photographic footage strongly suggests a connection
between this world and our own extradiegetic world. Admittedly, this could be
taken to mean that our own world is already restored, that no ecological work

remains to be done. However, I would argue this ending instead implies that the possibilities for resistance, for the young to seize the older generations' apparatus of ecological destruction and turn them instead to restoration, exist in our own world as well.

Conclusion

The *Evangelion* series has, from its first iteration in the 1990s, shown an intergenerational struggle between two older generations—which are complicit with climate change and ecological destruction for their own benefit and ambitions—and a younger generation they force into painful fights against *kaijū*, manifestations of their ecological destruction. Ultimately, the series seems to suggest that, contrary to most ecocinema, the restoration of the environment cannot be achieved by letting nature heal itself but can only be accomplished by this younger generation rising up to appropriate and repurpose their parents' and grandparents' systems of ecological destruction and turn them toward restoration. Humans must intervene and repurpose technologies that have heretofore been destructive to actively participate in restoring the environment. It is notable that this theme seems to have become a stronger focus of *Evangelion* as the series has iterated in various forms from 1997 to 2021. Over this period, not only did the Fukushima nuclear crisis engender a new consciousness of human contamination of ecosystems, but the climate crisis has deepened as well. *Evangelion*, with its depiction of rising seas, flooded cities, and endless summers, always dealt with climate change, but as decades have passed with little action by the generations in power, *Evangelion* seems to have strengthened its message that the only answer to the crisis is for the young to appropriate the political and economic apparatus of older generations and turn them toward the task of restoration.

Notes

[1] Kacsuk, "The Making of an Epoch-Making Anime," 235.

[2] Gatti, "The Mecha That Therefore We Are (Not)," 69.

[3] Suan, "Objecthood at the End of the World," 138.

[4] Galbraith, "The Evangelion Boom," 237.

[5] Igarashi, "Posuto katasutorofu no shinkeikan," 25.

[6] Ingram, *Green Screen Environmentalism*, 9.

[7] Hammond Breton, "Bridging the Political Deficit," 314–315.

[8] Mizobe, "Tsumi to shokuzai no shinwa," 48.

[9] Suan, "Objecthood at the End of the World," 141.

[10] Anno and Tsurumaki, *Air/Magokoro Wo, Kimi Ni.*

[11] Igarashi, "Posuto katasutorofu no shinkeikan," 29.

[12] Kondō, "Shin Evangerion to posuto feminizumu," 155.

[13] Svoboda, "Cli-Fi on the Screen(s)," 57.

Bibliography

Galbraith, Patrick W. "The Evangelion Boom: On the Explosion of Fan Markets and Lifestyles in Heisei Japan." In *Japan in the Heisei Era (1989–2019): Multidisciplinary Perspectives*, edited by Noriko Murai, Jeff Kingston, and Tina Burrett, 234–244. New York: Routledge, 2022.

Gatti, Giuseppe. "The Mecha That Therefore We Are (Not): An Eco-Phenomenological Reading of Neon Genesis Evangelion." *Series—International Journal of TV Serial Narratives* 7, no. 1 (July 29, 2021). https://series.unibo.it/article/view/12465.

Hammond, Philip, and Hugh Ortega Breton. "Bridging the Political Deficit: Loss, Morality, and Agency in Films Addressing Climate Change." *Communication, Culture & Critique* 7, no. 3 (September 9, 2014): 303–319.

Igarashi, Tarō. "Posuto katasutorofu no shinkeikan." In *Shin evangerion o yomitoku*, edited by Kawade shobō shinsha henshūbu, 22–35. Kawade shobō shinsha, 2021.

Ingram, David. *Green Screen Environmentalism and Hollywood Cinema*. Exeter: University of Exeter Press, 2008.

Kacsuk, Zoltan. "The Making of an Epoch-Making Anime: Understanding the Landmark Status of Neon Genesis Evangelion in Otaku Culture." In *Anime Studies: Media-Specific Approaches to Neon Genesis Evangelion*, edited by José Andrés Santiago Iglesias and Ana Soler Baena, 215–246. Stockholm: Stockholm University Press, 2021.

Kondō, Ginga. "Shin Evangerion to posuto feminizumu." In *Shin evangerion o yomitoku*, edited by Kawade shobō shinsha henshūbu, 147–160. Kawade shobō shinsha, 2021.

Mizobe Kōji. "Tsumi to shokuzai no shinwa: 'shin gojira' 'Kaze no Tani no Naushika' kara kangaeru 'Shin evangerion gekijōban ‖.'" *Ōtemon Gakuin Daigaku chiiki shien shinri kenkū sentā kiyō* 14 (March 2018): 35–56.

Neon Genesis Evangelion. Houston: Gainax, ADV Films, 2002.

Santiago Iglesias, José Andrés, and Ana Soler Baena, eds. *Anime Studies: Media-Specific Approaches to Neon Genesis Evangelion*. Stockholm: Stockholm University Press, 2021.

Shin Seiki Evangelion Gekijō-Ban: Air/Magokoro Wo, Kimi Ni. Gainax, Kadokawa Shoten, 1997.

Sontag, Susan. *Against Interpretation: And Other Essays*. New York: Doubleday, 1990.

Suan, Stevie. "Objecthood at the End of the World: Anime's Acting and Its Ecological Stakes in Neon Genesis Evangelion." In *Anime Studies: Media-Specific Approaches to Neon Genesis Evangelion*, edited by José Andrés Santiago Iglesias and Ana Soler Baena, 135–180. Stockholm: Stockholm University Press, 2021.

Svoboda, Michael. "Cli-Fi on the Screen(s): Patterns in the Representations of Climate Change in Fictional Films." *Wiley Interdisciplinary Reviews: Climate Change* 7, no. 1 (2016): 43–64. https://doi.org/10.1002/wcc.381.

8

Jellyfish Eyes (2013) and the Struggle for Reenchantment

Laura Lee

"In this vast universe, we encounter one another miraculously.
In the darkness a ray of light flashes and we gather there."

— opening text, *Jellyfish Eyes*

In this chapter, I analyze internationally renowned artist Murakami Takashi's *Jellyfish Eyes* (*Mememe no kurage*, 2013), a speculative film of imagined environmental annihilation that explores the coexistence of dread and a playful imagination. This paradox is a clear extension of Murakami's artistic universe, which combines childlike cuteness with trouble that lurks beneath the surface; at the same time, *Jellyfish Eyes*—Murakami's first foray into filmmaking—is far from a standard "art film." Indeed, Murakami's global cachet as a contemporary artist facilitated the film's limited international release in art and cultural institutions in the United States, but it was in Japan, where it targeted a youth demographic and was released widely, that audiences were best primed to recognize its anime and other pop cultural motifs.[1] A coming-of-age action-adventure for children, *Jellyfish Eyes* mobilizes tropes from well-known genres—in particular, the destructive spectacles of giant monster films—and it shares in a long legacy of harnessing science fiction to confront social anxieties and give visual form to disaster. Beneath this recognizable genre packaging, however, the film makes a unique contribution to Japan's disaster discourse through its treatment of children.

While it is common for children to be featured as props that represent the myth of untouched, pure space, and as symbols of futurity that focalize the long-term effects of disaster, often by serving as the prime objects of safety concern, *Jellyfish Eyes* positions children as complex individuals. By taking children's subjectivity seriously, the film eschews the idea that they are "pristine" objects that materialize adult fears, and instead refigures them as subjects with a rich inner life who have much to teach older generations. They emerge as multidimensional individuals whose emotions and problems mirror those of grown-ups: they are already marked by loss, and alienation, loneliness, anger, and fear are palpable dimensions of their lives. Yet they simultaneously possess different capabilities of perception and powers of imagination that build adaptive resilience. This unfolds primarily through an emphasis on alternative visual modalities and the duality of visibility and invisibility. The film adopts an ecocritical perspective, which aligns children with the more-than-human, and positions both as alternatives to the hegemonic, debilitating paradigm that structures modern society and threatens the social and environmental stability of the planet. By both "seeing" children and acknowledging the importance of how they see, the film staunchly adheres to their unique perspective, which puts pressure on easy distinctions between the real and the imaginary. Privileging the role of fantasy and play, the film suggests that, rather than the child needing to abandon idealism in order to properly grow up, adults would do better to see the world through a child's eyes; in so doing, the film points to the urgency of reenchantment as a corrective to our disenchanted world.

Although the main narrative of *Jellyfish Eyes* engages with impending apocalyptic destruction, it is also set against a post-Fukushima landscape. The main character, Masashi, a boy in middle school, is an environmental refugee who lost his father to a tsunami, which is clearly implied to be the March 11, 2011, tsunami that triggered a meltdown at the Fukushima Daiichi nuclear power plant and caused the surrounding area to be unsafe due to high radiation levels. As a result of forced evacuation, he and his mother have been living in an evacuation center and have just moved to the town where her younger brother lives. Masashi's displacement to the new town after the 3/11 triple disaster motivates the film's "new kid on the block" trope, which makes him susceptible to the local bullies and vulnerable to other tween social woes, just as it establishes him as a child of trauma. Not only is Masashi haunted by his father's recent death, but he also himself becomes a victim of contamination prejudice, which activates associations with those affected by the radiation from the atomic bombings of Hiroshima and Nagasaki at the end of World War II and underscores the cyclical nature of crisis. His personal trauma thus gives focus to the collective trauma of 3/11 and previous nuclear threats, and it draws attention to both the plausibility and the extreme cultural fear of imminent nuclear disaster. At the same time, it finds itself at home alongside the myriad social problems that impact the other children, suggestive of a scarred society in which environmental trauma is enmeshed in a matrix of political, social, and technological precarity. With anxiety and sadness permeating the fabric of life, the world of the film is figured in terms of a series of crises, in which pre- and post- cannot easily be disentangled. Fear of repetition is a source of panic, and the acute sense that the human causes of previous disaster persist unaddressed generates dread.

In this respect, the filmic milieu echoes a temporal feature E. Ann Kaplan has associated with her notion of "pretrauma" of environmental crisis. Although pretrauma scenarios center on the experience of severe anxiety associated with a catastrophic future, awareness of a traumatic past is frequently utilized because that past is recognized to have shaped this feared future.[2] While *Jellyfish Eyes* is set in the present moment—and thus does not directly maintain the futurist orientation of Kaplan's pretrauma film genre—past, present, and future nonetheless collapse in on one another in a similar fashion, with the symbolic figure of the child— and Masashi in particular—representing pretrauma's "trauma of the future" by embodying both the traumatic past and anxiety about the future.[3] 3/11 functions as a linchpin that maintains this structure as the implied driving force behind a shift that embeds the ecological within the social and political and redirects focus to the human cause of nuclear disaster. Produced just after the Fukushima nuclear facility meltdown, the film captures this period of widespread mistrust of government and industry through various mechanisms, including its depiction of a rise in new religions and apocalyptic thinking, which is a phenomenon frequently associated with disasters and their resultant social and political instability. Specifically, the Earth Salvation Society prays to cleanse the land after the corrupt government caused radioactive contamination and laid waste to the environment. Most notably, however, the plot turns on nuclear intrigue, as Masashi stumbles onto a terrible clandestine government project that both responds to and repeats the failures that led to the Fukushima nuclear disaster.

Government-contracted researchers at the town's secretive Disaster Prevention Laboratory—a structure that visually echoes a nuclear power plant, and which the Earth Salvation Society sees as the key source of cruel power that will devastate the planet—attempt to isolate and accumulate the fundamental energy of the universe, ostensibly to restore the myth of absolute safety that the government is committed to, and which has been shattered in the wake of the recent disaster (coded as 3/11). The government hopes that by harnessing this universal life force, they will be able to control the mechanism that causes earthquakes and thereby eliminate future natural disasters. Yet the scientists' tactics and goals are nefarious. Because the highest source of this special energy is in children's negative feelings, they make the kids of the town—all of whom are lonely and alienated, largely due to troubles at home—unsuspecting participants in their evil, destructive plot. Children's sadness, anger, and frustration are harnessed and transformed, materializing as CGI creatures that resonate with them and absorb their negative energy for use at the lab. These creatures, known as "F.R.I.E.N.D.s" ("life-Form Resonance Inner Energy Negative emotion and Disaster preventions"), are visible only to other children, and the children work out their frustrations by commanding their loyal F.R.I.E.N.D.s to battle with one another in an after-school fight club at a local shrine (figure 8.1). They control the creatures through smartphone-like devices given to them by the corrupt scientists, which, unbeknownst to the children, enable the scientists to harness their special energy.

These devices are obviously analogous to the personal devices children routinely use in daily life, most prominently through their escapist function that aims to obscure their self-alienating effects, and the paradox that although they appear to be controlled by the end user, they in fact operate in the service of big industry and are vehicles of surveillance. The film's depiction of these devices evokes overlapping concerns associated with digital culture and gaming, such as cyberbullying, addiction, and abusive monitoring, and brings to the fore the hidden nature of these threats, especially to children. These unseen forms of harm that unevenly affect those who are vulnerable are thus conceptualized in the film as analogous to the "slow violence" that Rob Nixon has described: the gradual processes of environmental contamination that impact the disempowered, and which are frequently invisible, indirect, and difficult to measure.[4] The susceptibility of the children serves as a reminder that the dangers of nuclear energy have been felt unevenly, with poorer towns that house power plants taking on terrible risks

Figure 8.1. Children using devices to control their F.R.I.E.N.D.s at an after-school fight club. Murakami Takashi, 2013, Takashi Murakami/Kaikai Kiki Co., Ltd.

for the benefit of much wealthier city dwellers and large companies; and the alignment of the slow, incremental violence of technological culture with the punctuated, spectacular disaster of nuclear annihilation gestures toward the diffuse and ongoing causes—the human-generated roots—of environmental collapse. At the same time, this parallel highlights technological innovation and interference as two sides of the same coin, implicating both in developing and deploying energy that cannot be controlled and underscoring the world's thoroughgoing sickness, particularly its weakness in the face of unchecked power.

These connections unfurl in the film through the duality of visibility and invisibility. The secretive, dangerous energy of the scientists wreaks its havoc unseen. Work done at the top-secret facility is inaccessible to the children, who cannot see inside the laboratory, just as they carry on with daily life, unaware of the danger that surrounds them. This functions as a direct analogy to nuclear radiation, which is a silent, invisible killer—and one that, after 3/11, was widely perceived to be a special threat to children, not only because of their tender age, which makes them especially susceptible to radiation, but also because radiation accumulates in soil, trees, and water, which are often found in concentration in parks and playgrounds where children play. This invisible threat of dangerous energy, a form of unrecognized and unmeasurable violence akin to those Nixon describes, appears to stand in sharp contrast to the visibility—in fact, the vibrant visuality—of the F.R.I.E.N.D.s, who apparently materialize at the joystick request of each aggrieved child. However, because the F.R.I.E.N.D.s are rooted in the same powerful energy and have been appropriated by the scientists for their wicked purposes, the children are unwittingly contributing to potential destruction, despite believing they are in control. In this way, the film utilizes analogies to gaming and generational conflict not only to highlight the acute vulnerability of those who are sidelined and weak but also to underscore the apparent impossibility of resolving the matrix of social, technological, and environmental problems that afflicts the world: the troubled children must play games to escape the woes of real life, yet this is a self-perpetuating system that, over time, produces adults who cannot manage the increasingly dire problems plaguing society. This endless spiral of disorder within the film gives material form to the cycles of trauma and ongoing dread that figure prominently in Kaplan's notion of pretrauma.

With the arrival of Masashi, however, this dystopian arrangement begins to break down, specifically as a result of his exceptional capacity for sight. Although Masashi, from the outset, epitomizes the average misunderstood or overlooked child, just as he enters the town, a F.R.I.E.N.D. is accidentally released from the laboratory, and Masashi's unique resonance with the energy enables him to see and interact with this F.R.I.E.N.D.—whom he names Kurage-bō (Little Jellyfish, or Jellyfish Boy)—without a government device. On one hand, this soon alerts the researchers to the fact that Masashi is the key to effecting the singularity that will catastrophically break down space-time, which both exposes their evil plot and places Masashi in grave danger. On the other hand, conceptually purified as a result of his independence from the government researchers and their technology, Kurage-bō exists by definition as an ideal F.R.I.E.N.D. He is an agentive entity who, by not being secretly controlled by the lab, is uniquely free and unsullied, as he is neither bound to the limiting rules found in real life nor implicated in the pernicious scheme of the researchers. The film exploits this conceptual freedom to explore a possible intervention in the unrecognized yet ongoing processes of environmental and social collapse. That is, if the other children and F.R.I.E.N.D.s call up the doomed repetition of environmental and technologically rooted devastation, Masashi and Kurage-bō act as a disruptive force that might end the cycle of trauma and halt the process of intensifying dread; that Masashi does not require a device to see Kurage-bō not only frees him from the evil scientists' grip in the narrative but also, in a broader sense, opens a space for make-believe that is dislodged from negative associations of video games and digital culture as avenues of empty (at best) or dangerous (at worst) escapism. *Jellyfish Eyes* thereby redirects focus to the purity of play and the importance of children's culture, treating earnestly the role that imagination and fantasy perform in people's lives.

This reclaiming of play and wonder as a potential antidote to the troubles of the real world comes through strongly in the film's cinematography and use of CGI, which draw attention to the complementarity of idealism and despair. The F.R.I.E.N.D.s, especially Kurage-bō, are photoluminescent, contrasting strongly with the drabness of the live-action cinematography (figure 8.2). Kurage-bō's jewel-toned brightness and positivity drive home the F.R.I.E.N.D.s' allure in light of the grayed-out, melancholic world of the preteen characters, whose lives are marked by parental negligence, illness, and other traumas. In this respect, government corruption and impending nuclear annihilation are not the only threats to a stable system: the children's parents are weak and troubled, passing their scars on to the next generation, and societal structures such as schools are cold and unresponsive. In a world that is rendered dark, ominous, and foreboding, it is no wonder children seek out colorful, phantasmal friends who seem to be incapable of betraying them. Significantly, this requires a mechanism of sight that is differentiated from the normative human visual system. Just as parents cannot see a child's imaginary friend, in *Jellyfish Eyes*, the F.R.I.E.N.D.s reside only within the purview and perception of children, evading detection by adults by becoming temporarily invisible when necessary. Their invisibility to adults (with the exception of the researchers at the lab) shores up their contrast with the mundane world, including its rules and restrictions, just as their visibility to children links them with creativity and imagination. Although for most of the children, this special sight has an ugly side, tainted as a result of the scientists'

Figure 8.2. Kurage-bō looking up at Masashi as they play together outside.
Murakami Takashi, 2013, Takashi Murakami/Kaikai Kiki Co., Ltd.

intervention in the same way that the F.R.I.E.N.D.s themselves have been co-opted for dark purposes, Masashi possesses an uncontaminated vision that connects him with the equally ideal Kurage-bō. Through the lens that Masashi provides, the bonds between children and F.R.I.E.N.D.s are conceptualized as supreme as a result of their shared life force that sets both of them apart from normative adult society. Particularly given that they materialize from devices and are controlled through them as if they are video game characters, the F.R.I.E.N.D.s epitomize childlike play: joyful amusement that is experienced only outside real-world rules. In short, the children possess a distinct mode of being, and of imaginative vision, that permits them to see the F.R.I.E.N.D.s, and this exceptional faculty of sight both underscores a special connection between them and represents resilience in the face of abounding troubles.

The film's title itself points to the significance of this unique perceptual bond. At one level, it must be seen in light of Murakami's *Jellyfish Eyes* print series from the early 2000s, which, for the most part, comprises works of a multitude of cutesy eyes against an undifferentiated background. The series highlights both a multiplicity of perspectives on the part of the viewer and a sensation of being surveilled, such that the cute style seems innocent and adorable at the same time that the masses of eyes generate anxiety. The fact that the film shares a title with this series plainly marks it as an extension of it. Most conspicuously, the film shares its focus on seeing and being seen, and the dichotomy of the whimsical and the disturbing translates clearly into the tone of the film, which is distinguished by cynicism and wonder and simultaneously generates hope and oppression. Additionally, some images in the series include a little boy with an adorable character friend, and a related lithograph, *Jellyfish* (2003), is of a multi-eyed character, Oval, who appears at the end of the film as a giant monster who happens to be the manifestation of all the F.R.I.E.N.D.s combined.[5] Although a detailed analysis of how the film integrates with Murakami's conceptual universe in general is warranted, most pertinent to the current discussion is how this sinister yet cutesy landscape acquires a range of associations via the original Japanese title, *Mememe no kurage*, which might more accurately be read as "Jellyfish's Three Eyes," therefore connoting a multiplicity of eyes. This use of "*mememe*" has significance across multiple fronts.

In the first place, it clearly references the work of legendary manga artist Mizuki Shigeru, whose most famous work is *Gegege no Kitarō*. Not only is Mizuki famed for his cute but creepy style, he is also responsible for introducing *yōkai* (spirit-like figures from Japanese mythology) into the Japanese popular imagination by giving them visual form, by making seen entities that typically reside outside visibility and, thus, outside rational, modern perception. One of Mizuki's recurring characters is the *yōkai* Hyakume ("One Hundred Eyes"), whose eyes maintain individual agency and can leave Hyakume's body to interact with the human world, notably in order to stop criminal activity. As a well-known mythological and manga character, Hyakume's disembodied, floating eyes epitomize the unease of being watched. Eyes have additional significance in *Gegege no Kitarō* via the main character, Kitarō, a *yōkai* boy who has only one eye, as well as Kitarō's deceased father, Medama-Oyaji ("Eyeball Father"), whose reincarnated remains have taken the form of his (anthropomorphized) disembodied eyeball. Medama-Oyaji's extensive knowledge of *yōkai* and other occult topics assist Kitarō as he seeks to create peace between humans and *yōkai*, and he usually resides in Kitarō's empty eye socket, covered by a lock of hair. With these connections in mind, the similarity between Murakami's title and Mizuki's work emphasizes feelings of strange discomfort, anxiety, and dread about the seen and unseen, which emerge clearly in the film in terms of constantly being watched, as well as of the government corruption that takes place behind closed doors. Oval makes perhaps the most overt visual connection to Mizuki's work, in that his many eyes obviously reference Hyakume. Most significantly, however, the "*gegege*" in Mizuki's title speaks both to liminality and the special perception of children, containing multiple associations that provide important context for Murakami's title. The term "*gegege*" is a sound-symbolic word—that is, a word that suggests a range of feelings or sensations based on its sonic qualities. At a basic level, "*ge*" is a sound of revulsion or shock, which is contextualized in relation to the ghoulish storyline. This general eeriness is highlighted in the opening song for the original animation of *Gegege no Kitarō*, in which frogs (whose Japanese onomatopoeia is "*gero-gero*") sing the "*gegege*" of the title; and a general spookiness is foregrounded due to a sonic likeness to the onomatopoeia for cackling: "*kera-kera*." Yet for all this croaky creepiness or witchiness, *gegege* is simultaneously well-known to have derived from Mizuki's mispronunciation of his own given name (Shigeru) when he was a child. As such, it is a representation of children's speech that hints at the perception and understanding of children; in this case, it is related to the boy Kitarō, who straddles the human-*yōkai* world, living in a liminal space between scientific rationality and the supernatural and having adventures with other-than-human creatures. It thus connotes a childlike behavioral or sensory modality, a penchant for delightful imagination and play, and an access to an in-between realm coded as magical and premodern that resides outside the normative sensory range of humans in the modern world.

By extension, "*mememe*" acquires a similarly ambiguous identity. If Kitarō exists in a weird, primeval world uniquely accessible to children, Kurage-bō likewise belongs to a primordial universe beyond ordinary sight that bears a special relation to children. In this way, cosmology in Murakami's film parallels the mythology in Mizuki's work; F.R.I.E.N.D.s and *yōkai* become aligned as preternatural entities that reside at a sensory threshold, transcending the distinction between extraterrestrial intelligent life-forms and folkloric phenomena. Through the character of Kurage-bō, the film's title names the liminality of the F.R.I.E.N.D.s in the film and suggests they are ubiquitous—despite residing outside standard visibility—while also underscoring their peculiar connection to children, with Kurage-bō and Masashi epitomizing a pure relationship between the other-than-human ally and the child. In this regard, while the film's title might initially appear to refer simply to the wide-eyed Kurage-bō and his single-focused, pure love for Masashi (and simultaneously, from an alternative perspective, the F.R.I.E.N.D.s' intended role as surveillants of the deep state), the *Gegege no Kitarō* intertext prompts a more nuanced understanding. It emphasizes the reciprocal nature of sight—the seeing and being seen—and contrasts this with invisibility or the inability to see or be seen; and it leads *mememe* to verge on the notion of a third eye, which denotes a special power and perception beyond ordinary sight. Although the film makes the strongest connection to Kitarō due to its title, this core thematic is shored up through references to other pop cultural texts in Japan as well, perhaps most clearly to the film *Spirited Away* (*Sen to Chihiro no Kamikakushi*, Miyazaki Hayao, 2001). Like *Spirited Away*, *Jellyfish Eyes* opens with a child in the backseat of a car on the way to a new home, overlooked by adults; in both films, this backdrop of being jettisoned or going unseen facilitates the protagonist child's entrance into a liminal realm in which they have access to a distinct mode of vision. These well-known intertexts spotlight the fact that Masashi and Kurage-bō (and in turn, the other children and their F.R.I.E.N.D.s) are connected through a heightened, substratal capacity for sight that permits entry into a zone of enchantment at the same time that the adult (modern) world—which is variously figured as passive and ineffective, distressed and incapacitated, or cold and apathetic—lacks this special modality of vision and is thus excluded from this zone of playful ambiguity.

In the second place, the title *Mememe no kurage* foregrounds the multiple eyes of jellyfish, positing an ecological context by showcasing alternative modalities of vision in the natural world. Although commonly thought to be simple creatures, box jellyfish in fact possess an extremely complex visual apparatus comprised of multiple visual photosystems: not only do they have multiple (twenty-four) eyes, but they also possess four different types of eyes, all of which perform special tasks necessary for survival and environmental adaptation. Scientists believe it is these unique powers of vision that enable the animals to manage complex behaviors in the absence of a highly developed nervous system or brain. Unlike the box jellyfish, many other jellyfish do not have conventional eyes, yet they still engage in multiple types of vision. They possess special sensory structures that act as a diffused light-sensing organ, a network of nerves and proteins that enables them to sense their environment; this is known in some cases to register shadows in order to avoid predation. They additionally possess extraocular vision that is critical for adaptive behavioral responses, such as avoiding excessive UV radiation. As a result of these multiple photosystems, jellyfish, and especially box jellyfish, are frequently studied to understand eye evolution.[6] This complexity and multiplicity of jellyfish vision acquires tremendous significance in the film in light of the title's homage to *Gegege no Kitarō*, with its evocation of the unique perception of children and their special relationship to the other-than-human world, as it seems to straightforwardly connect the jellyfish's physiological simplicity with the primitivism often applied to children but then overturn that assessment by foregrounding the significance of different types of intelligence. A reference to jellyfish points to the surprising sophistication of children's "primitive" ways of seeing. At the same time, calling up the tremendous variety of eye and sight-providing organs found in nature suggests a multiplicity within the mechanism of sight that extends far beyond the human model, which itself encompasses associations with the rational and objective. In this sense, the film takes an ecocritical approach that merges the concept of sight with sentience, highlighting the different perspectives from which our world might be perceived.[7] The child, as a category, thus blurs the boundaries between human and more-than-human, thereby emphasizing the human as but one entity in our universe and suggesting we might have something to learn from stepping outside our standard mode of perception. Additionally, this uniting of jellyfish and child links ecological resilience with psychological resilience. Although typically conceived of as rudimentary or undeveloped, the alternative modalities of sight associated with each pull the viewer's focus to resilience. This term, commonly used in disaster risk reduction, has been frequently utilized in ecology and children's psychology to conceptualize resistance to disaster shocks in human-environmental systems and social systems, respectively: the capacity to adapt, accommodate, and rebound after exposure to a hazard.[8] Particularly in light of the film's depiction of disasters as recurring events, this ecological framing in the film highlights the need to transform in response to shifting circumstances, and privileges the capacity to adapt and thrive, and to respond creatively and dynamically, amid disruptions. The children's unique ability to see the F.R.I.E.N.D.s comes into view as just such an adaptive perceptual behavior that facilitates their survival and flourishing. In this way, the future orientation provided by the figure of the child, which deepens anxiety about what is to come, transfigures here into a possible power to escape from the conditions of the slow, unseen deterioration Nixon has described. In *Jellyfish Eyes*, those who are vulnerable possess a mechanism to circumvent an endless descent into deprivation.

Combining these two dominant associations of *Mememe no kurage*, the film's title works to create slipperiness between the natural and the paranormal, with both bearing a unique connection to children through their distinct perceptual modalities. This unification takes shape overall in the film through a conflation of the ecological and the cosmological. The narrative unfolds in terms of a connectivity between the planet's environmental instability and the fundamental, originating energy of the universe that can be mobilized via rituals of ancient religious cosmology (and which is most concentrated in children). Most notably, though, this merging manifests in relation to Masashi's two dreams early in the film, just as Kurage-bō is entering his life. In his first dream, bioluminescent jellyfish gather in front of him as he tosses part of his Chee-Kama snack into the water to feed them. In his second dream, his father is with him. Masashi is enjoying his Chee-Kama—a snack food that his father manufactured before his death—and again sharing it with the fluorescent pink jellyfish. This time, a multicolored luminescent tsunami, which forms a graphic match with the jellyfish, appears behind the father in a visual reference to his death. The F.R.I.E.N.D., who appears to Masashi in a manner that expressly recalls *E.T.* (Steven Spielberg, 1982), boasts a pink, cap-shaped head and tentacles that graphically resemble these jellyfish, causing Masashi to announce that he looks like a jellyfish and to name him Kurage-bō. Kurage-bō's strong appetite for Chee-Kama completes the set of connections formed between "alien," animal, and child, as filtered through Masashi's perception and experience of loss. With this in mind, Kurage-bō and Masashi's powerful resonance as twin manifestations of the universe's core energy brings together multiple conceptions of the primordial—in developmental psychology, evolutionary biology, and cosmology—to conjoin children, jellyfish, and F.R.I.E.N.D.s.

This tethering of divergent entities effects a decentering of the human that activates a sense of awe, gesturing toward the marvelousness of the universe as it emphasizes the symbiosis among organisms that undergirds the sustainability of the planet. It draws attention to the planet as a shared, finite space that can be preserved only through an awareness that the human species is but one component of an integrated system, and through an appreciation of our shared existence as a precious, fleeting miracle. This is established in the opening of the film, which, replete with asteroids and the dark vastness of outer space, evokes the cosmic cataclysmic event that set the universe in motion. As such, the film's beginning sets the stage for the impending singularity and breakdown of space-time to parallel the profundity of the big bang. At the same time, through its opening text, which is reproduced in the epigraph for this chapter, the film points to the wondrousness of connections and chance encounters in the universe. In this respect, the film early on establishes the duality of wonder and dread via a planetary orientation: a perspective that steps outside modern history to conceptualize humans as deeply enmeshed within deep geological, evolutionary, and environmental processes, as it also symbolizes the rescaling of community—the planetary understanding—that actual nuclear contamination necessitates.[9] In a general sense, the film leans on a prevailing view that nature and humanity are inseparable, and that non-Western models—coded as primitive and long disparaged—which embed humans within a deep planetary context, offer a corrective to ways of thinking that have facilitated environmental destruction.[10] By aligning the primitiveness of the child with elemental life-forms and the primeval universe, the realm of play and wonder likewise becomes intertwined with the worldviews, peoples, and nonhuman entities that have been systematically marginalized in the modern world. That is, the film braids together childlike enchantment and the "nonmodern" or "nonadvanced," such that fantasy and play as an overlooked source of reenchantment for timeworn adults becomes inextricable from, and a conduit to, a more profound notion of reenchantment as a revitalized understanding of ecologies and the cosmos that embeds the human within larger systems—with both thereby serving a healing function in our disenchanted world.[11]

At a narrative level, this planetary orientation both reframes the children as authentic stewards of the world and raises the stakes, shoring up dread. Although the film centers on a specific group of children in one town, the government's ability to tap into the universe's core energy to effect a total apocalypse prompts an interweaving of the local, national, and planetary that renders Masashi and the other kids responsible for joining forces to save the totality. The evil scientists take advantage of an escalation of negative energy among the children and set their endgame in motion. They lure children to the lab for a battle royale among the F.R.I.E.N.D.s, with the promise that the winner will receive the ultimate power-up to make their F.R.I.E.N.D. the strongest of all. By accumulating the negative energy released in this 3D video game-esque battle (which significantly involves one of Murakami's most famous characters, Miss ko2), they are able to trap Masashi into acting as a medium to summon a giant creature named Oval, who is an unstoppable energy form that they hope will destroy the earth and enable its rebirth. Oval embodies all the F.R.I.E.N.D.s' energy and visually repeats the 3/11 tsunami and ensuing nuclear meltdown at the end of the film, thereby

Figure 8.3. Oval, the physical manifestation of all the F.R.I.E.N.D.s' energy, echoes the visual form of a tsunami when he appears at the end of the film. Murakami Takashi, 2013, Takashi Murakami/Kaikai Kiki Co., Ltd.

giving full visual form to ongoing cycles of disaster (figure 8.3). Emblematic of widespread anxiety, this climax clearly establishes the fantasy film as part of the *kaijū* (giant monster) genre, thereby contextualizing its nuclear dread within a well-understood cinematic framework.

In this case, the children must make the ultimate sacrifice to save the world: giving up their F.R.I.E.N.D.s. Through friendship and teamwork, they are able to hack the government technology and find Oval's weakness, but they are aware that defeating Oval will destroy the F.R.I.E.N.D.s as well. In a final surprise, one boy, a video game whiz, stuns everyone with his technological prowess; by hijacking the system, he finds a way to restore all of the F.R.I.E.N.D.s, who are now completely dissociated from the evil, secret lab and free as other-than-human agents, just as Kurage-bō has been from the start. This idealistic reversal represents a thorough overhaul that remakes the world through the children's eyes, with wonder and play interceding fully in the open-ended, attritional processes of environmental degradation and societal desperation. It at once recuperates technology—which initially functioned in the film as an insidious instrument of damage and impediment to true relationships but now is a positive tool of play and restorative imagination and a vehicle for genuine connections—and breaks down the wall separating the children's world from the adult realm. The children's will to save the planet meant that the F.R.I.E.N.D.s had to show themselves in public and step in to protect adults and save the community; now, their secrecy is irrelevant, and adults too both see and appreciate them. Though pitifully naive in one sense, this utopian ending is both instructive and inspiring. In the first place, the F.R.I.E.N.D.s' role in rescuing the planet and its human inhabitants underscores the reciprocal relationships that sustain our world, and it is therefore suggestive of the ways in which human actions affect, often in traumatic ways, the more-than-human world. Moreover, the ending confirms that childlike powers of imagination signify dynamism and adaptability and are ultimately liberatory. Because of their resiliency, they, in effect, triumph over the modern, such that the split between the visible and invisible is overcome. The film thus depicts childlikeness as a gateway to healthy development and urges a recapturing of its prized sensory modalities—its capacity for enchantment—in the quest for knowledge and sustainability.

While it is not new for ecocritical approaches to look to the premodern past or Indigenous worldviews in order to step outside the modern paradigm and transcend its problems, *Jellyfish Eyes* focalizes this process through the figure of the child. By granting the subjectivity of the child the importance it deserves, and by simultaneously aligning the child with the other-than-human, it overturns images associated with primitiveness, transmuting them into perspicacious saviors of the planet. Specifically, the film accomplishes this by contrasting the weariness and despair in the modern world that has resulted from processes of disenchantment with a possible reenchantment. In other words, it suggests that the mechanistic, human-centered worldview that we associate with modern, Western societies, and which has ravaged the environment and resulted in social, religious, and political crises, might find a solution in the magical wonder that appears to have been lost in the adoption of this "mature" worldview. Much as it is in Murakami's artistic work more generally, rather than trivializing play and disparaging children's culture, the film recognizes the appeal—and the fundamental power—of fantasy, thereby positing zones of wonder and childlike fancy as core components of life that serve an adaptive function, offering resilience in the context of a sick, unequal society. In other words, boasting the potential to intervene in processes of cyclical violence, trauma, and the ongoing accretive degradation denoted by slow violence, enchantment becomes a possible antidote to, rather than a dangerous escape hatch from, the problems of the real world. By focusing on the overlooked and vulnerable, the film thus invites us to see with new eyes and envision and believe in possible futures that halt ongoing and repeating processes of exploitation, disparity, and devastation across the globe. In this respect, the film's environmental commentary transcends its antinuclear premise to advance a sustainable imaginary, suggesting that we have it within us to construct a viable planet.

Notes

[1] The film additionally saw one screening in Milan (in Japanese with English subtitles), in a theater specializing in foreign films.

[2] Kaplan, *Climate Trauma*.

[3] Kaplan, *Climate Trauma*, 28.

[4] Nixon, *Slow Violence*.

[5] See *Jellyfish Eyes, Simon in the Strange Forest* (2004).

[6] Garm, et al., "Multiple Photosystems."

[7] This aligns with an approach in ecological discourse that is most closely associated with David Abram. See Abram, *Becoming Animal*; and Abram, *Spell of the Sensuous*.

[8] Initially linked to C. S. Holling in 1973, this term has since been used in various fields. See Alexander, "Resilience."

[9] The term "planetary" has been conceptualized as distinct from "global," particularly for its focus on deeper time and a consequent decentering of the human. See Chakrabarty, *Planetary Age*, chapter 3. For a discussion of the tension in environmentalist discourse between local and global, particularly in relation to the threat of environmental collapse and nuclear annihilation, see Heise, *Sense of Place*.

[10] See, for instance, Haila, "Beyond the Nature-Culture Dualism"; Gottlieb, *Oxford Handbook*; Imanishi, "A Japanese View of Nature"; and Morton, *Ecology without Nature*, 64.

[11] A seminal text on reenchantment is Taylor, *Secular Age*. See also Crawford, "Trouble with Reenchantment."

Bibliography

Abram, David. *Becoming Animal: An Earthly Cosmology*. New York: Vintage Books, 2010.

Abram, David. *The Spell of the Sensuous: Perception and Language in a More-Than-Human World*. New York: Vintage Books, 1997.

Alexander, D. E. "Resilience and Disaster Risk Reduction: An Etymological Journey." *Natural Hazards and Earth System Sciences* 13, no. 11 (November 2013).

Chakrabarty, Dipesh. *The Climate of History in a Planetary Age*. Chicago: University of Chicago Press, 2021.

Crawford, Jason. "The Trouble with Reenchantment." *Los Angeles Review of Books*, September 7, 2020. https://lareviewofbooks.org/article/the-trouble-with-re-enchantment/.

Garm, Anders and Peter Ekström. "Evidence for Multiple Photosystems in Jellyfish." *International Review of Cell and Molecular Biology*, vol. 280, edited by Kwang W. Jeon. Academic Press, April 2010.

Gottlieb, Richard, ed. *The Oxford Handbook of Religion and Ecology*. New York: Oxford University Press, 2006

Haila, Yrjo. "Beyond the Nature-Culture Dualism." *Biology and Philosophy* 15 (March 2000): 155–175.

Heise, Ursula K. *Sense of Place, Sense of the Planet: The Environmental Imagination of the Global.* New York: Oxford University Press, 2008.

Imanishi Kinji. *A Japanese View of Nature: The World of Living Things.* Edited by Pamela Asquith. Translated by Pamela Asquith, Heita Kawakatsu, Shusuke Yagi, and Hiroyuki Takasaki. London: Routledge Curzon, 2002.

Kaplan, E. Ann. *Climate Trauma: Foreseeing the Future in Dystopian Film and Fiction.* New Brunswick: Rutgers University Press, 2015.

Morton, Timothy. *Ecology without Nature: Rethinking Environmental Aesthetics.* Cambridge: Harvard University Press, 2007.

Nixon, Rob. *Slow Violence and the Environmentalism of the Poor.* Cambridge: Harvard University Press, 2011.

Taylor, Charles. *A Secular Age.* Cambridge: Harvard University Press, 2007.

Nuclear Anxiety
and Violence

9

The Reimagination of *Godzilla*: The Concealment of Nuclear Violence

Shan Ren

This chapter criticizes the political ignorance of nuclear and radiological violence on bodies and the anthropocentric attitude toward environmental damage by examining two recent films in the Godzilla franchise, the Japanese *Shin Godzilla* (Toho, 2016) and the American *Godzilla* (Legendary Picture, 2018). Unlike the original *Gojira* (Toho, 1954), the monster in these recent iterations loses its significance as ecological criticism. The films conceal, to the point of erasure, the existence of radiation victims and nuclear violence in Japan and the Pacific, despite the production of both movies in the wake of the 2011 Fukushima Daiichi nuclear power plant accident. Unlike the visual embodiment of radioactive harm to humans depicted in *Gojira*, in *Shin Godzilla*, there is a flattening and digitization of that harm from nuclear waste that erases bodies, while the American-produced *Godzilla* depicts radiation as both the final solution to save mankind and a natural force that can heal itself. These later films not only diminish the fatal environmental harm to humans caused by radiation, but they also whitewash history to represent nuclear violence as a natural phenomenon that can restore environmental balance. Victims are erased along with the radioactive harm and anthropogenic origins of this environmental damage.

My analysis employs a close reading of the different points of view, the characterization of the observer, the *mise-en-scene*, and the pace of editing in these films. I compare *Shin Godzilla* with the original 1954 version to show how the newer movie turns away from the direct depiction of the radiation victims in the earlier film. The absence of radiation victims in *Shin Godzilla* reveals the political discrimination toward this group of people, and its rewriting of the *Lucky Dragon No. 5* incident functions to downplay radiation's dangerous nature and to conceal the historical victims' suffering. By contrast, the 2014 American version is concerned with rewriting the negative wartime and postwar American nuclear image. In this film, the historical atrocity of the atomic bombing of Hiroshima and Nagasaki in 1945 is concealed, while the nuclear testing conducted on the Marshall Islands in the 1950s is reinterpreted as an American attempt to save the world. The actual nuclear victims become nearly invisible in this reimagining, as the US not only takes their place as victim but also plays the role of their savior.

As Kiu-Wai Chu suggests, we are living at a time when movies create "concealments of reality."[1] In these two contemporary Godzilla films, the reimagination of the nuclear disaster, the creation of Godzilla as a scapegoat, and the positive depiction of the government as the people's protector create a concealment of historical reality and environmental harm. Both *Shin Godzilla* and *Godzilla* are entertainment spectacles that provide the audience with easy solutions and avoid controversial and painful historical events, as the radiation victims who suffered from the nuclear bombs, nuclear testing, and nuclear power plant accidents are no longer visible and the government culpability in these disasters is concealed. As Yuki Miyamoto argues regarding female *hibakusha* (atomic bomb victims), sometimes the lack or absence of a group of people can further the discriminatory sentiment.[2] In this chapter, I argue that not only is this discrimination present in both governments' neglect of radiation victims, but their concealment of environmental harm also denies decades of nuclear violence and instead seeks to place both the blame and solution onto nature.

The Absence of the Direct Depiction of Nuclear Violence on Human Bodies in *Shin Godzilla*

When Godzilla rampages through Tokyo in *Shin Godzilla*, the audience is only shown the destruction of a series of empty buildings and streets. The lack of depiction of radiation victims and the nuclear harm upon their bodies, which is a direct result of the strong political gaze and the omnipresence of the government, seriously diminishes the effectiveness of the environmental message conveyed in the movie. Although the government is depicted as a bureaucratic nightmare plagued with poor efficiency, political hypocrisy, and dishonesty, the film positively points toward hope for reform in the future because both the older and younger generations of politicians share the same intention: to protect the people during major disasters. However, the "people" the government intends to protect do not include all citizens. An important group of people—radiation victims—is excluded from the "people" and becomes invisible in the government's view. With their existence erased, the interdependent relationship between human beings and nature is severed, and the long-term nuclear harm on human bodies is displaced by the immediate and visually arresting spectacles of the destroyed city. The only shot of exposed bodies appears in the final scene of the movie. The silhouette of several skeleton-like human bodies frozen in Godzilla's tail reminds the audience of the nuclear harm, but it downplays the long-term radiological impact on victims' bodies and deprives the actual victims of their identities and voices.

The political concealment of radiological harm is achieved in two ways in *Shin Godzilla*. The first method is the absence of the victims from the point of view of the government. Many scenes are intentionally narrated through the government's gaze, and radiation victims are hardly given any screen time. This erasure of the victims becomes more obvious when comparing scenes from *Shin Godzilla* with the original *Gojira*. Both movies open with an incident aboard a ship. In *Gojira*, the ominous nondiegetic soundtrack—"The March" and the monster's roars—plays behind the opening credits and into the establishing shot of ocean waves. Although the source of the waves is ambiguous, these waves and "The March" hint at the monster's awakening. The camera cuts to a ship called *Eikō-maru (Glory) No. 5* in the South Pacific, and the background music also shifts from the intense nondiegetic march to a peaceful diegetic melody of harmonica and guitar. The crew are playing music and chess when they suddenly hear a bang and see a flash of light. They run away, leaving the guitar and chessboard scattered on the deck. The camera cuts to a blast of light from an explosion that sets the ship on fire. The medium shots with the camera set close to the ground in this scene create a feeling of intimacy and immediacy, as if the audience is on the ship with the crew experiencing the mysterious attack, which, for viewers, is a clear reference to American nuclear testing in the Pacific.

Shin Godzilla also opens with a shot of a boat at sea, but it significantly shifts the camerawork, the location of the craft, the ship's occupants, and their purpose in a way that changes the audience's onboard experience. The first shot is of sea waves in Tokyo Bay, and a voice-over describes the discovery of an unidentified boat. The JCG (Japanese Coast Guard) sends three guards to check the boat, and the audience enters the ship *Glory-maru* by means of the JCG's handheld camera, point-of-view shots. The unstable camera moves from the entrance into the cabin and lingers briefly on several objects, including a document envelope, a book, a paper crane, and a pair of shoes. As the guard holding the camera reports to headquarters that there is no one on board and only some personal belongings are discovered, the ship suddenly starts to shake, and the scene cuts to an extreme long shot of Tokyo Bay as the ship explodes. There are three important differences between these opening scenes. First, unlike the original, no victims are included in *Shin Godzilla*. Second, this incident is filmed entirely through the JCG's handheld camera and narrated by JCG; or, in other words, the incident is observed through the governmental gaze. Last, as I discuss more in the next section, a critical geographical shift moves the incident from the distant South Pacific to Tokyo Bay.

All three changes of *mise-en-scene* serve to shift the focus from the victims and the environmental harm to the government. No civilians are injured in this incident in *Shin Godzilla*. Instead, the JCG sacrifice their lives for the nation's safety. The original location of the South Pacific in *Gojira*—which is far from Tokyo Bay, the center of Japan—is removed because it problematically draws attention to historical American nuclear testing in the Pacific, which undercuts the Japan-US alliance emphasized in *Shin Godzilla*. By relocating the explosion to Tokyo, *Shin Godzilla* emphasizes the significance of the JCG sacrifice—and, by extension, the disaster itself—as national rather than geopolitical.

The movie's second political concealment of the radiation victims is through the cinematic role of the observer, a character who serves as an affective register for the audience. In *Gojira*, Emiko—the daughter of the scientist Dr. Yamane— functions as an observer who witnesses Godzilla's rampage, while in *Shin Godzilla*, the observer is the stoic young politician Yaguchi, who embodies the governmental view.[3] Such a change clearly shows the shift of the narrative viewpoint from a female citizen who is sympathetic to the radiation victims to a male politician who ignores their existence.

Godzilla's radioactive harm to humans is clearly visualized through Emiko's perspective in *Gojira*. Emiko works as a nurse in a temporary hospital, where she sees firsthand the horrifying effects of radiation on the human body. The sequence, which is set the morning after Godzilla destroys Tokyo, starts with a full shot of a medical team carrying victims to the hospital, and the subsequent pan reveals a room full of wounded children. A doctor is diagnosing a child's radiation exposure with a Geiger counter while Emiko sits next to him. The camera slowly zooms in on the child's face, and the soundtrack amplifies the clicks emanating from the Geiger counter. In the following medium close-up shot, Emiko looks at the doctor, and the doctor shakes his head somberly. This scene visualizes the radiological violence in these children's bodies, and the doctor's and Emiko's affective responses are meant to show the viewers how to react to the scene. Similarly, in the following scene, a little girl starts to cry when her mother's corpse is about to be carried out. Emiko scoops the girl up in her arms. In the medium close-up, Emiko is gradually overcome with grief, and she cannot help but turn her head away from the crying girl (figure 9.1). Her sympathy and sadness set an emotional tone for the film and an affective gauge for the audience.

Figure 9.1. Emiko's sympathy. Honda Ishirō, 1954, Tōhō.

This sympathetic and benevolent female observer is replaced by the calm and rational young politician Yaguchi, and the radioactive harm to humans is blurred in *Shin Godzilla*. After Godzilla destroys Tokyo, the camera lingers on his face. Rather than sorrow, the close-up of Yaguchi's face reveals restrained anger and determination. The shallow focus draws the viewer's attention to Yaguchi's face, and the background bokeh prevents the viewer from seeing any victims. Instead, the cacophony of voice-overs of news reporters informs the viewer of the damage Godzilla caused and the government's response. Although the voices do report that a large number of people are missing, nothing about radiation levels or radiation victims is mentioned. In the next shot, a handheld camera follows Yaguchi, placing the viewer in the shot as a member of his team. The shot captures Yaguchi walking quickly past soldiers, police officers, and medical workers and finally arriving at the decontamination base. The silent young politician faces away from the camera, his emotional response concealed and his rational attitude emphasized.

The scenes of Yaguchi's reaction after Godzilla's rampage are completely different from Emiko's. The most obvious difference is the invisibility of the radiological violence. In the original, the audience witnesses the suffering of the radiation victims with Emiko and is expected to sympathize with them as she does. However, this group of victims is not present in the frame of Yaguchi's scenes. Even if we assume Yaguchi does see some radiation victims, his facial expression of anger does not telegraph any type of sympathy. His primary concern is not the victims but the elimination of Godzilla. Another important difference is the identity of the observer character. Emiko is a caring citizen/nurse and an emotional woman, while Yaguchi is a serious and dispassionate politician. On the one hand, Emiko's social status, job, and gender enhance the function of this character as an affective register. The camerawork leads the viewer to react to the scenes as Emiko does. On the other hand, Yaguchi embodies the government's attitude. His emotional reaction is either extremely restrained or concealed. From his point of view, the victims are more of an abstract concept than an actual group of people. The victims are either blurred in the background or reduced to numbers in the news.

The Digitalized Victim Experience and Historical Revisionism in *Shin Godzilla*

Although radiation victims are not physically embodied in *Shin Godzilla*, their existence and experience are implied but flattened through "digitalization." In this section, I explore the invisible victims in *Shin Godzilla* from two perspectives—their digitalization and the rewriting of history. *Shin Godzilla*'s concern about radiation is mainly expressed indirectly through modern technology like forum posts and live streaming. The incorporation of social media and the internet creates an illusion of intimacy and realism, but the entertaining tone, polyvocal narratives, and flattened people reduce the severity of the radiation disaster.

In *Gojira*, there are many scenes of people attacked by Godzilla, including sailors, passersby, news reporters, building workers, soldiers, and even children. The physical presence of these victims on-screen symbolizes the violence caused by nuclear bombs and its harm to human life and livelihood. In one scene, the camera focuses on a woman with her children, sheltering in the corner of a building while Godzilla burns the city with his radioactive breath. The woman tells her child that they will soon join their father. This one line reveals she is a war widow and recalls the violence of the war and the atomic bombs.

By contrast, the indirect depiction of victims' experience in *Shin Godzilla* is flattened and turned into entertainment through digitalization, as seen in the scene of a government rescue team helping the people who are trapped in a tunnel damaged during the *Glory-maru*'s explosion. It starts with a handheld phone shot recording the situation in the tunnel. This first-person perspective invites the audience to imagine they are experiencing the escape with the recorder, but there is no fear, anxiety, or anger expressed. Instead, the recorder enjoys the escape as if the tunnel was a water slide. The whole situation is entertaining for the characters and audience alike. In other words, the victims are turned into adventure tourists.

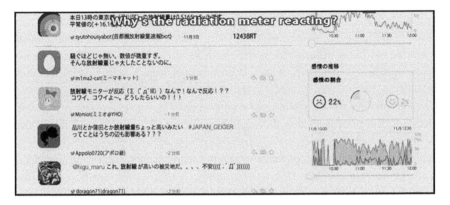

Figure 9.2. Netizens' comments on radiation.
Anno Hideaki and Higuchi Shinji, 2016, Tōhō.

The citizens' lack of concern about radiation in the abovementioned scene is somehow understandable because Godzilla has not yet made landfall. These adventure tourist/victims think they have only experienced an earthquake, but even after Godzilla's landing, the film's depiction of radiation is still problematic. After Godzilla emerges onto the land, many netizens reveal their concerns about radiation when they post on the internet about a news report: "the radiation in Tokyo is 16.1 times higher than normal" (figure 9.2). This scene incorporates contemporary social media technology into the film, but in the process, human victims are reduced to mere words, profile photos, and data without faces or bodies. Although this scene gives voice to various groups of people, the shot of fifteen posts is scrolled through in a mere five seconds of screen time, leaving the audience unable to read all of them without pausing the movie. Although the bulletin board contains the comments of victims, the disembodied emotional reaction stimulated by this scene, combined with the fast editing, makes it far less potent than the war widow's single line. Furthermore, the inconsistent opinions expressed by the netizens in this scene cast doubt on the significance of radioactive harm. For example, comments like "Please. The radiation level is insignificant . . ." express an indifferent attitude toward radiation while comments like "This is scary! What should I do?" display people's concern and fear. Such ambiguity significantly reduces these comments' affective power.

The second way *Shin Godzilla* conceals the existence of radiation victims is through historical revisionism. The ship's explosion at the beginning of the movie reminds the audience of the *Lucky Dragon No. 5* incident, but the movie downplays and rewrites the history of Japan's third nuclear exposure. On March 1, 1954, a Japanese fishing ship named *Lucky Dragon No. 5* was exposed to radiation generated by the Castle Bravo nuclear test conducted by the US on Bikini Atoll in the Pacific.⁴ The crew of *Lucky Dragon No. 5* were not the only victims. This nuclear test also contaminated twenty-nine populated atolls of the Marshall Islands (and many other ships in the South Pacific). Some of the islanders who were classified as "exposed" by the US government were resettled onto irradiated islands and became experimental subjects of research about the human absorption of radionuclides from an irradiated environment.⁵ Yu-Fang Cho argues that this incident "has been pushed to the edge of public history and memory" due to the overdetermination of both the dominant discourse of the bombings of Hiroshima and Nagasaki and the propaganda of the peaceful use of nuclear power as clean energy.⁶ As I argue below, *Shin Godzilla* not only eclipses the significance of this incident but also tries to downplay the two atomic bombings and the Fukushima Daiichi nuclear power plant accident.

In the original *Godzilla*, the ship incident occurred in the South Pacific, a reference to the *Lucky Dragon No. 5*, but *Shin Godzilla* relocates this to Tokyo Bay. This relocation severs the incident's connection with the Pacific and the exposed islanders. The *Glory-maru* incident in the 2016 film becomes a fully Japanese issue, with Tokyo functioning as a synecdoche for the nation. Furthermore, the relocation of the incident to Tokyo Bay also obscures the Japanese memory of the atomic bombs in Hiroshima and Nagasaki and downplays the nuclear contamination in Fukushima. In other words, the actual victims and the contaminated land in Hiroshima, Nagasaki, and Fukushima also become invisible in this rewriting of history.

Another change in *Shin Godzilla* is the source of Godzilla's awakening. In *Gojira*, the radioactive contamination is caused by the US nuclear test in the Pacific, but in *Shin Godzilla*, the monster is awakened by the unregulated dumping of radioactive material by various countries. This change has two implications. First, since this incident is not specifically caused by US nuclear testing in the Pacific, it allows the US to act as an ally aiding the Japanese. Second, the term "unregulated" transfers the responsibility to unspecified third parties, and such obfuscation further detaches the memory of nuclear violence from its historical context and obscures the responsible parties. In essence, no one is responsible for the historical victims' suffering.

In short, the rewriting and re-membering of the *Lucky Dragon* incident not only erases the historical radiation victims in the Marshall Islands, the atomic bomb victims in Hiroshima and Nagasaki, and the victims of the Fukushima disaster, but it also whitewashes US nuclear history and downplays Japan's responsibility in the Fukushima disaster. The absence of both physical radiation victims and specific responsible parties makes the disaster irrelevant and allows the audience to enjoy the spectacles without serious reflection or critical environmental concern.

Whitewashing American Nuclear History and Neutralizing the Ecocriticism Embodied in the Monster in *Godzilla*

If *Shin Godzilla* acknowledges the adverse role humankind plays in environmental deterioration, the American rendition of *Godzilla* goes a step further by completely disavowing the responsibility that human beings have to rehabilitate nature. This is accomplished through the whitewashing of American nuclear history in three ways: first, through the revisionist retelling of the history of nuclear weapons testing that favors the US government; second, by reimagining the US as a victim of the nuclear disasters, achieved by downplaying the suffering of local victims of the Castle Bravo test and the Fukushima tragedy; and third, through a remodeling of Godzilla as a potential ally of the US and a global protector rather than a representation of Japan's wartime memory and the devastating nature of nuclear violence. Radiation is interpreted as a natural phenomenon, and the film contends that nature possesses the ability to self-heal. Humankind is absolved of accountability for nuclear calamities, as these are now attributed to nature, with equilibrium being reinstated through natural means.

Godzilla opens with a series of events recording the history of Godzilla, which reconstructs the role the US played in the history of nuclear weapons testing and changes the meaning of the Cold War nuclear arms race. Although these opening scenes are a mixture of historical and fictional incidents, the movie's use of old monochrome documentary film clips and top-secret documents enhance the authenticity of this fictional history. The first historical incident mentioned is the *USS Maine*'s explosion in 1889, followed by newspaper clippings about two more submarine incidents. Next, a secret multination organization titled Project Monarch was established to investigate unknown creatures in the Pacific. Government men in white lab coats were secretly sent to Bikini Atoll to conduct research, and after discovering the existence of Godzilla, Monarch carried out an atomic bombing plan under the disguise of nuclear testing to eliminate the monster with the help of the US. Every event is accompanied by credits and comments related to nuclear threats and Godzilla, but these comments are immediately redacted on screen. The concealed comments create suspense and seed doubt about received history, implying the existence of an alternate, "true" version. This "true" version of history is explained to the audience later by two scientists working for Monarch. This history starts in 1954, when Godzilla was awakened by the launch of the *USS Nautilus*. The nuclear bomb tests in the 1950s, including those conducted at the Nevada Test Site and in the Marshall Islands, were attempts to kill Godzilla, an ancient alpha predator "from an age when the earth was ten times more radioactive than today."

The revised version of history effectively reshapes the perception of the US within the nuclear discourse from being a perpetrator to being a guardian. This transformation is accomplished through three key methods. First, historical elision deliberately omits references to World War II and the atomic bombings of Hiroshima and Nagasaki in 1945, thereby minimizing the destructive nature of nuclear violence and the environmental devastation inflicted by the US on Japan. For instance, in the film's opening scene, a map of Japan is shown before the mention of Bikini Atoll, yet neither Hiroshima nor Nagasaki is indicated on the map. In tandem with this deliberate suppression of wartime nuclear weapon use, the US's role in these events is also conveniently overlooked.

Second, *Godzilla* alters the catalyst for the monster's awakening. In the original narrative, Godzilla is roused by an American nuclear test, leading to his destructive rampage in Tokyo. Most scholarly discussions tie Godzilla to the themes of war memory, the fear of the destructive power of nuclear weapons, and American hegemony.[7] However, in *Godzilla*, the monster's Japanese origin is severed, and his anti-US sentiment is expunged. Instead, his awakening is attributed to the launch of the *USS Nautilus*, the inaugural voyage of a nuclear submarine to the ocean's depths. This revision significantly skews the environmental message inherent in the original. The atom's devastating might is supplanted by an ostensibly impartial scientific breakthrough, coupled with the human spirit's commendable pursuit of the unknown.

Furthermore, the film reimagines the history of the Cold War nuclear arms race between the US and the USSR as endeavors to annihilate this monster. The purpose behind the nuclear tests conducted at Bikini Atoll undergoes a transformation: they are no longer intended to scrutinize the design, effectiveness, and scale of nuclear weaponry before their real-world deployment but are now portrayed as efforts to safeguard the world from Godzilla's threat. The monster becomes living proof of the US's exertion in curtailing the nuclear peril.

Lastly, the experiences of the nuclear victims are completely concealed, as the US—whose actions caused their anguish—undergoes an abrupt transformation to emerge as their protector. This alternative history of Bikini Atoll is displayed through hyper-fast editing of a series of shots, including scenes, images, and text that interweave depictions of local people as victims, the US-led Monarch Project as the protector, and Godzilla as the ultimate nuclear threat. The sequence commences with a map pinpointing the location of Bikini Atoll, swiftly followed by a glimpse of a classified document, succeeded by the imposing phrase "Monarch Project." Subsequent shots imply that members of the Monarch Project intend to use nuclear bombs to exterminate the monster near Bikini Atoll, with some frames featuring local children. Notably, one frame, extracted from historical footage taken on Bikini Atoll, captures the moment when an American soldier joins a cluster of local children in a photograph (figure 9.3). The following frontal shot of a girl smiling at the camera displays her internal happiness directly to the

Figure 9.3. Local children on Bikini Atoll welcome the American soldiers.
Gareth Edwards, 2014, Warner Bros./Legendary Pictures.

audience. Within the film, this scene serves to illustrate the locals' welcoming of American soldiers as rescuers from the monster's threat.

While local children take a prominent role in these shots, their actual suffering remains conspicuously absent. The cause of their tragic fates undergoes an abrupt transformation, recasting the nuclear bombs that wrought enduring damage upon their bodies and lands as now safeguarding them. Ironically, such an implication aligns with the political propaganda of that era. Commodore Ben H. Wyatt, the US military governor of the Marshall Islands, communicated to the Bikinians that the nuclear tests were conducted "for the good of mankind and to end all world wars."[8] This adept utilization of historical footage thus effectively reconstructs history in favor of the US, at the expense of erasing the Bikinians' anguish.

In addition to the role of protector, the movie also constructs the US as the victim. The experience of a nuclear disaster of the American protagonist's family in the story reminds the audience of the 2011 Fukushima nuclear disaster, but it becomes a US-Japan shared trauma rather than a Japanese problem. The actual incident was caused when the Tōhoku earthquake and tsunami flooded the backup generators at the Fukushima Daiichi nuclear power plant on March 11, leading to multiple meltdowns. In the aftermath of the nuclear crisis, the Japanese government attempted to pacify the citizen's fears and downplay the damage through information manipulation.[9] In *Godzilla*, an earthquake caused by an awakening MUTO (massive unidentified terrestrial organism) damaged a nuclear power plant in the fictional Japanese city of Janjira and killed the mother of the American protagonist, Ford Brody. His father, Joe Brody, becomes a conspiracist and spends years debunking the Japanese government's false claim that the nuclear power plant's meltdown was a purely natural disaster and that the quarantine zone is contaminated.

The US's self-victimization and self-heroization embodied by the Brody family erases the existence of radiation victims. The only nuclear victim depicted in the movie is Ford's mother, who died in a nuclear power plant accident. Witnessing her death, Joe spends years researching the cause of the disaster and neglects Ford, who then tries his best as an adult to protect his wife and child from the monsters' attack. The focus on the American family appeals to US viewers, but it also erases the Japanese experience in the Fukushima incident. Unlike *Gojira*, in which the US is critically associated with the horrific monster, or *Shin Godzilla*, in which the US is willing to sacrifice Japan to save the world, the image of the US in *Godzilla* is redemptive. The US shares nuclear trauma with Japan, and Ford is a synecdoche for the American public. Both the US and Japan become pure victims, and the monsters—like Godzilla and MUTOs—become the scapegoats who take full responsibility for the nuclear disaster.

The final method through which the film conceals the radiation victims is its reimagining of the symbolic significance of the monster Godzilla. Despite some lingering ambiguity, Godzilla assumes the role of humanity's protector. In the scene in which he is approaching the Golden Gate Bridge in San Francisco, he protects a school bus on the bridge from the US army's gunfire. After he defeats the MUTOs, he is named the "King of the Monsters" and celebrated as the hero who saved the city. The clash between Godzilla and the MUTOs veils the part played by humanity in the history of nuclear violence. Past environmental catastrophes are no longer the result of human activities, and consequently, humanity is absolved of the responsibility to safeguard the environment. Instead, the movie proposes that Godzilla is an integral aspect of nature, and nature possesses the inherent capability to restore equilibrium. The genesis of Godzilla is traced back to an ancient era marked by heightened radiation. In other words, radiation is rationalized as a natural phenomenon, and hence, the power of the atom is also a natural power. As Dr. Serizawa in the movie suggests, "Nature has an order, a power to restore balance. I believe he [Godzilla] is the power."

However, this so-called natural order is inherently anthropocentric. The evil MUTOs who imperiled human society's stability are eliminated by the benevolent Godzilla, enabling humanity to persist in its enjoyment of life amid nuclear power and weaponry. Ultimately, nothing undergoes substantial alteration.[10] The antinuclear message and criticism embodied in Godzilla in the original movie are diluted, and the film's stance toward the perils of nuclear power shifts from one of anxiety and apprehension to a more neutral, if not celebratory, perspective.

Conclusion

This paper delves into the political erasure of radiological violence and the anthropocentric manipulation of environmental messages in both *Shin Godzilla* and *Godzilla*. The former presents the narrative from the perspective of the Japanese government, revealing its challenges as well as its determination to protect the nation and its people. However, in the government's view, "the people" excludes the actual radiation victims. The government's narrative effectively sidelines these victims by reconstructing history and dissociating unaffected individuals from those affected by radiation.

In *Godzilla*, the role of the US in the realm of nuclear weapons and power is reimagined. This reconfiguration portrays the US as a casualty of nuclear disasters, conveniently omitting the historical victims of American nuclear bombings. The film's portrayal of the US as a heroic figure in the battle against the nuclear monster glosses over the failure of the US to take responsibility for the consequences of their actions. The positive characterization of Godzilla further obscures the ecological criticism inherent in the original movie, transferring the accountability for nuclear disasters from humankind to nature.

This chapter highlights the overlooked and marginalized group of nuclear victims in the Godzilla movies, advocating for increased attention toward them and a greater awareness of humankind's active role in shaping the discourse surrounding nuclear issues.

Notes

[1] Chu, "The Imagination of Eco-Disaster," 270–271.

[2] Miyamoto, "Gendered Bodies in *Tokusatsu*," 1100.

[3] Rhoads and McCorkle, *Japan's Green Monsters*, 38.

[4] Cho, "Remembering Lucky Dragon, Re-Membering Bikini," 127.

[5] Cho, 132.

[6] Cho, 128.

[7] Rhoads and McCorkle, *Japan's Green Monsters*, 15–16.

[8] Niedenthal, *For the Good of Mankind*, 1.

[9] DiNitto, "The Fukushima Fiction Film," 1.

[10] Dew, "Godzilla. Film. Directed by Gareth Edwards. A Legendary Pictures Production, 2014," 217.

Bibliography

Cho, Yu-Fang. "Remembering Lucky Dragon, Re-Membering Bikini: Worlding the Anthropocene through Transpacific Nuclear Modernity." *Cultural Studies* 33, no. 1 (January 2, 2019): 122–146. https://doi.org/10.1080/09502386.2018.1428643.

Chu, Kiu-wai. "The Imagination of Eco-Disaster: Post-Disaster Rebuilding in Asian Cinema." *Asian Cinema* 30, no. 2 (October 1, 2019): 255–272. https://doi.org/10.1386/ac_00007_1.

Dew, Spencer. "Godzilla. Film. Directed by Gareth Edwards. A Legendary Pictures Production, 2014." *Religious Studies Review* 40, no. 4 (December 2014): 217. https://doi.org/10.1111/rsr.12174_3.

DiNitto, Rachel. "The Fukushima Fiction Film: Gender and the Discourse of Nuclear Containment." *Asia-Pacific Journal* 16, no. 1.1 (January 1, 2018).

Miyamoto, Yuki. "Gendered Bodies in *Tokusatsu* : Monsters and Aliens as the Atomic Bomb Victims." *Journal of Popular Culture* 49, no. 5 (October 2016): 1086–1106. https://doi.org/10.1111/jpcu.12467.

Niedenthal, Jack. *For the Good of Mankind: A History of the People of Bikini and Their Islands*. 2nd ed. Majuro, Marshall Islands: Bravo Publishers, 2001.

Rhoads, Sean, and Brooke McCorkle. *Japan's Green Monsters: Environmental Commentary in Kaiju Cinema*. Jefferson, NC: McFarland & Company, 2018.

10

The Walking Nuclear Disaster: Nuclear Terrorism and the Meaning of the Atom in *The Man Who Stole the Sun*

Eugenio De Angelis

Taiyō wo nusunda otoko (*The Man Who Stole the Sun*, 1979)[1] and its director, Hasegawa Kazuhiko, though generally neglected overseas, retain legendary status in Japan, as the movie ranked seventh in the Kinema Junpō's "Japanese All Time Best—Cinema Heritage 200," following worldwide renowned masterpieces like Ozu's *Tōkyō monogatari* (*Tokyo Story*, 1953) and Kurosawa's *Shichinin no samurai* (*Seven Samurai*, 1954).[2] Tremendously different from these works, *The Man Who Stole the Sun* is an uncompromising yet entertaining movie, dealing with issues regarding nuclear power, atomic bombs, and ecoterrorism (but also alienation and nihilism in society), embarking the audience on a 150-minute-long blockbuster filled with black humor and action.[3] In his seminal book *Slow Violence and the Environmentalism of the Poor*, Rob Nixon states, "The insidious workings of slow violence derive largely from the unequal attention given to spectacular and unspectacular time. In an age that venerates instant spectacle, slow violence is deficient in the recognizable special effects that fill movie theaters and boost ratings on TV."[4] In this chapter, I analyze *The Man Who Stole the Sun* as a film that wittingly exploits and subverts genre conventions, turning the "slow violence" linked to nuclear power precisely into a (comic and absurdist) spectacle.

Hasegawa is not what Nixon would call a "writer-activist," but as a *hibakusha* 被爆者 (survivor of the nuclear bomb), he has a clear antinuclear stance. Thus, he envisions a character who builds a nuclear weapon with his own hands yet soon starts to show the symptoms of radiation exposure. Turning him into what I call a "walking nuclear disaster" has a twofold effect: it makes this form of slow violence visible on the very body of the protagonist for the audience to acknowledge it, and it questions the alleged difference between "bad" atoms (used for military purpose) and "good" atoms (used for producing nuclear energy) and related containment policies. Here, Nixon's "poor"—those who unjustly suffer for the exploitation of resources by capitalist forces—are the Japanese citizens themselves, especially those living near the power plants who are deceived (and put in danger) by the myth of safety supported by the so-called nuclear village (原子力村), the complex web of politicians, businessmen, journalists, and scholars advocating for nuclear energy in Japan.[5]

The movie tellingly starts with a ticking clock and the images of a nuclear explosion, only to shift to a face squeezed against a metro window after the opening title. This is the lead character, Kido Makoto (played by superstar singer Sawada Kenji), a thirtysomething science teacher without friends and mocked by his middle school students for his detached attitude. In his private life, Kido nurses a wild idea: building a nuclear bomb with his own hands in his small five-*tatami*-mat-sized apartment. He steals plutonium from a nuclear power plant, and after many efforts, accidents, and one casualty (his cat), he achieves his goal. Kido starts threatening the authorities, his first demand being that they extend the broadcasting time of the nightly baseball games on television that were usually interrupted at 9:00 p.m. After his demand is granted, he teams up with the attractive radio disc jockey Zero (Ikegami Kimiko) and comes up with a second request—a Rolling Stones concert in Japan.[6] Meanwhile, the authorities and police, led by Inspector Yamashita (*The Yakuza Papers*'s legend, Sugawara Bunta), try to track him down, leading to a car chase, a helicopter shooting, and finally, a Western-like showdown that ends in favor of Kido, who walks away in the crowd with the bomb in his bag.

Director Hasegawa Kazuhiko and American screenwriter Leonard Schrader, the younger brother of Paul Schrader, devised this inventive plot after they met for the first time in 1977 in Hollywood, where Hasegawa went to write a travel journal for *Playboy* magazine Japan.[7] They became friends and started exchanging ideas for a new movie until Schrader came up with a plot line: "An ordinary guy develops an atomic bomb on his own and blackmails the government to 'keep airing the nightly baseball game on TV without disruption!' with this handmade atomic bomb."[8] It took them almost a year of exchanging drafts back and forth from the US to Japan (with the collaboration of Schrader's wife, Chieko) to come to the final version of the script. *The Man Who Stole the Sun* then became a four-hundred-million-yen-budget movie and had good critical success, being ranked second on Kinema Junpō's Best Ten, first on the readers' poll, and fourth in the PIA Top Ten (including Western movies). Nevertheless, the film struggled at the box office and exceeded its budget by one hundred million yen, leading Hasegawa to take an (ongoing) break from his directorial career after only two movies.

Laughing A-Bomb

There are countless Japanese films dealing with atomic bombs and nuclear power, especially after the March 2011 triple disaster, but it is hard to think of another movie as creative and provocative on the subject as *The Man Who Stole the Sun.* Hasegawa was born in Hiroshima in 1946, and therefore, he did not personally experience the atomic bombing, but his mother was pregnant with him at the time of the attack, and being a *hibakusha* clearly affected his childhood and later life. There are several interviews with Hasegawa in which he states that he was sure he was going to die young, a conviction that gave him the impetus to try to live life to its fullest.[9] It is exactly because Hasegawa is a *hibakusha* that Schrader decided to "give" him the original idea for the movie, in the belief that someone who had gone through such an experience could handle the subject better than someone who had not.[10]

In Japanese wartime memory, the two nuclear attacks came to symbolize the defeat of the country, the fall of the imperial system, and the start of the American occupation. Hiroshima and Nagasaki are also the reason why Japan went through a process of victimization in "a curious type of 'collective amnesia,'" which enabled the nation to "forget" the role of the offender that it itself played in World War II (and before).[11] During the 1950s, movies dealing with the war or, later on, with nuclear power often had a humanistic touch, carrying a universal anti-war or antinuclear stance, implicitly promoting the process of victimization. Only in the late 1960s, with New Wave directors like Ōshima Nagisa, were there attempts to shift this narrative. Nonetheless, later movies on the subject—one notable example being *Kuroi ame* (*Black Rain*, 1989) by Hasegawa's *maestro*, Imamura Shōhei— portray this tragedy and its aftermath through stories of individuals who have to make impossible efforts to survive and adjust to their life as *hibakusha*. Being one himself, Hasegawa claimed he did not feel uplifted by this kind of movie, even if they accomplished much from an artistic point of view. With *The Man Who Stole the Sun*, he is not making a movie to "cry about the A-bomb" because it would be but another example of Japan's victimization process.[12] In fact, the biggest change the director made to Schrader's final draft regards the fate of the lead character. Kido is a menace to his country, a terrorist of sorts, but he is also a victim, because soon after making the A-bomb, his hair starts to fall out—the main symptom of radiation exposure—his cat dies from eating plutonium remnants, and, later

Figure 10.1. Perpetrator and victim. Kido realizes he is the first casualty of his own plan. Hasegawa Kazuhiko, 1979, Tōhō.

on, his gums start bleeding (figure 10.1). To expose the protagonist to radiation was something Schrader strongly opposed, thinking that the resulting movie would have been too "heavy" to entertain the audience and so would lead to its failure. On the other hand, to shoot a "simple" action comedy was not enough for Hasegawa; he felt that a film dealing with the A-bomb should carry a certain degree of "weight."[13] Before Fukushima, Japanese cinema struggled to bring out the invisible dangers of nuclear violence (i.e., atomic violence not directly related to the A-bomb). Hasegawa's choice to make the threat of radioactive contamination visible on the very body of the lead character is one of the first examples of an effective way of putting this form of "slow violence" on display. It dramatically represents a strong antinuclear stance, matching the director's view of nuclear power as a burden for humankind: "I believe that the essence of nuclear weapons is that all mankind is both perpetrator and victim. That is why I made sure that the perpetrators are also exposed to radiation and become victims."[14] The bomb's deadly threat affects everybody, and when Kido realizes his condition, he briefly considers suicide. However, in the last scene, he finally accepts his mortality as he snatches up a lock of hair with his hand, quietly looks at it, and then simply blows it away. Hasegawa has always dealt with this threat in his life, and he wanted the audience to experience the same discomfort; he wanted to picture the nuke's toxicity because nuclear power is poison.[15]

"Good" Atom and "Bad" Atom

A Japanese citizen threatening his government with nuclear power in the only country that has ever been stricken by an atomic bombing during wartime inevitably raises questions regarding this source of power and artfully problematizes the illusory division between "bad" nuclear weapons and "good" nuclear energy. The use of nuclear power as clean energy in Japan was prompted by the US in 1955, when they launched a strong campaign, the "Atoms for Peace" program, to support it and defeat the obvious skepticism of the population.[16] The first reactor was then commissioned in 1966, and in the 1970s, several light water reactors were built. Despite the Three Mile Island incident (1979) and the Chernobyl incident (1986), the nuclear industry in Japan continued to grow throughout the 1980s and 1990s until 2011, producing around 30 percent of the country's electricity per year in this time span.[17] Nonetheless, the notion of "good" nuclear energy is itself problematic, because—as noted by Yoshimoto—"the mere existence of a nuclear power plant is already a form of violence. A nuclear power plant in peacetime signifies simultaneously a common fact of everyday life (in which the associated dangers are imperceptible) and the end of the world (due to the potentially irreparable effects of a radioactive contamination)."[18] While most of the nuclear-related movies focus exclusively on nuclear weapons or nuclear power, *The Man Who Stole the Sun* is one of the few films to feature both, linking them together through Kido stealing plutonium from a nuclear power plant and making a bomb out of it. Hence, it exposes the problematic aspect of this supposedly "good" use of nuclear energy and the obvious safety issues related to these plants.

In the movie, the nuclear plant looks like a technological station, even with some sci-fi elements, where the lighting (by veteran Suzuki Tatsuo) and the peculiar floor pattern play an important role (figure 10.2).[19] Hasegawa used this

Figure 10.2. The futuristic look of the nuclear power plant ironically hints at the myth of safety surrounding the nuclear discourse. Hasegawa Kazuhiko, 1979, Tōhō.

seemingly out-of-context setting (one that seems to ironically comment on the "futuristic" technology—both safe and sanitized—that nuclear power allegedly represents for the progress of mankind) to create one of the most inventive scenes of the movie, shooting the theft of the plutonium through a series of still frames with a fast-paced editing style that makes the sequence highly cinematic. Even if the style and development of the entire scene seem to draw inspiration more from *manga* than real-life actions, questions about the security of nuclear power plants remain, raising a red flag regarding the handling of nuclear energy in Japan.

American and, later, Japanese advertising campaigns on the civilian use of nuclear power sought to paint a positive image of the atom by detaching it from its military use. Nuclear energy was naturalized in the everyday life of Japanese citizens and incorporated into an economic discourse. It was marketed as a safe technology, minimizing its dangers. Nonetheless, the risks of nuclear disaster still loomed on the horizon, and the effects of nuclear incidents remained as devastating as ever. The "incident" at the plant portrayed in Hasegawa's movie predates several scandals that would strike Japan in the mid-1990s. In fact, accidents and cover-ups from authorities and electric companies at the Mihama, Monju, and Tōkai nuclear power plants between 1995 and 2000 raised questions about security and containment. The latter complex is also the one used in the movie, and in 1999, it was the site of the worst nuclear-related accident in Japan before Fukushima (two casualties). In these cases, the level of protest remained largely relegated to local associations, but the shift in the perception of nuclear power nationwide almost halted the construction of any new reactors. However, it was the tragedy of Fukushima in 2011 that sparked an antinuclear movement across the country, with demonstrations in Tokyo in September 2011 and July 2012 as big as those of the 1960s. Protesters sought to bring about the dismissal of nuclear power as a possible energy source, but at the same time, the movement requested more clarity from the government, which had allegedly omitted important information and acted in an obscure way to manage the disaster.

When Kido is finally able to complete the bomb and starts threatening the authorities, he has already obliterated the false distinction based on a radically different perception of good and bad nuclear power, which has been persistently reaffirmed in the public debate to the point that nuclear energy has been made virtually invisible to the eyes of citizens. Kido basically comes to embody a "walking nuclear disaster," initially as an unexpected element (i.e., a natural catastrophe) that exposes the containment policies and the myth of safety related to the "good" use of the atom, and then by embodying the bomb itself as a powerful criticism of the communicative strategies that the authorities deploy around the nuclear discourse.

Number Nine Teasing the Authorities

Hasegawa goes even further when he portrays the task force, which is composed of the politicians, police officers, scientists, and bureaucrats in charge of handling the threat. Mocking Japan's nuclear village, it is hardly depicted as reliable, as it fails to take any precautions on behalf of the population or come up with a clear strategy to stop the blackmail. After Kido—by placing a "sample" of his work in a toilet inside the Diet Building (the center of power *par excellence*)—is able to prove that he is the man who stole the plutonium and that he is capable of making a handmade nuclear bomb, the authorities start to take his demands more seriously. Nonetheless, they are always one step behind, spending half of the movie trying to track his phone down. As a director with anarchist tendencies and no love for those in power, Hasegawa often depicts the task force in farcical tones. Politicians give orders without knowing much about what they are dealing with, and they often speak through slogans while hiding their true colors (the minister has sent his family away from Tokyo while declaring that the terrorist is not really a menace). Once they are finally able to secure the bomb, they are embarrassed by Kido in an ironical action scene, where he breaks through a skyscraper window very much like Tarzan, surprises all the police officers in the room, and flees with the bomb in the same fashion. Later on, when the task force tries to use Zero as bait to catch him, they are tricked once again, as she starts a sort of romantic relationship with Kido and prevents him from being identified. Even Inspector Yamashita, the only one entitled to talk to him, cannot help but surrender to his demands, as he is obstructed by orders from his superiors.

Basically, the authorities seem unable to handle nuclear power, as they are often entangled by bureaucracy, divided by different opinions, or too worried by the possibility of media backlash. After Kido steals the plutonium and the news comes out, the authorities refrain from going public with the following developments, seeking to avoid panicking the citizens in the face of an atomic threat. At the same time, this cinematic treatment recalls how the government handled the Fukushima crisis in Tokyo decades later. As noted above, state-level discourses about nuclear power (and its related accidents) have always been characterized by missing information and cover-ups. While conveying the image of a "good" atom to the public, they refrain from disclosing the real risks entailed by nuclear technology; these would make the population realize how close they live to a potential nuclear disaster, with obvious consequences for the entire industry and the national economy. Therefore, the suppression or manipulation of vital information like radiation levels seems more designed to avoid responsibilities and preserve economic interests than to prevent mass hysteria. As a result, the unsuspecting population is exposed to the risk of contamination, as in Fukushima's case. Similarly, the authorities in *The Man Who Stole the Sun* act seemingly unaware of the consequences of a nuclear explosion, repeatedly risking thousands of lives in order to seize Kido. Their last attempt is even more potentially deadly, as they try to secure him during the Rolling Stones concert, when they plan to close up Budokan Hall, announce the concert cancellation—thus provoking mass hysteria—and arrest everyone in the building, hoping to find Kido among them. Yet the nuclear threat remains a challenge confined to the space between one individual and the authorities, removed from the everyday life of the population. Kido himself makes a phone call to a radio show hosted by Zero, announcing that he is the man who stole the plutonium and asking for advice as to what demands he should make to the government. This is the only time the nuclear threat is made public, but instead of hysteria, it is used by Zero to create a new feature for her program, *Mahō no genbaku kōnā* (Corner of the Magical A-Bomb), by asking the audience what they would demand if they had a nuclear weapon in their hands. The answers range from the personal to the universal, but they are generally shallow. It seems as though the communicative strategy of the authorities has worked, and the myth of safety has been accepted. The audience is no longer able to perceive the real danger that comes with nuclear energy, insofar as this is remote from their daily lives; hence, we can hear seemingly unrelated answers like, "I want to go to Morocco," or, "I want a new house" (*Morokko ikitai no*, 1:13:16, *Uchi ga hoshii wa ne*, 1:14:05).

One more notable element related to nuclear terrorism is the surprisingly long screen time devoted to the construction of the bomb—over thirty minutes in the first half of the movie. Through visually detailed images, Hasegawa shows all the passages that Kido has to go through to come to its realization. The process is actually handled with a scientific approach of sorts, and it is so realistic that Hasegawa had to cut some scenes to prevent the possibility of emulation.[20] However, the stoic nature of an anarchical director with a *hibakusha* background is especially visible when Hasegawa inserts scenes containing black humor and social commentary on the subject. For example, Kido explains to his middle school class the history of atomic energy and its subsequent use as a weapon against Hiroshima and Nagasaki. He does not show any particular empathy toward these events, and his students seem to be unaware of what it meant to postwar Japan, as they grew up in the high-growth era, when atomic power was synonymous with clean energy. When he starts to explain how to build the bomb in more scientific terms, only one student in the class seems to care about it, especially when the others find out it will not be part of their final exam. Several scenes even contain a grotesque kind of imaginary and highlight Hasegawa's satirical take on nuclear power, as when Kido's kitchen oven catches fire because he has misused it for "cooking" plutonium, or when he plays football with the bomb.

A private individual able to build a homemade nuclear bomb is obviously a concern for national security, but as Kido starts referring to himself as "Number

Nine" (eight was the number of official and unofficial countries equipped with the atomic bomb at the time), it may also symbolize a nation that "plays" with nuclear power on its home ground—one not fully prepared to handle the risk that comes with it.

The Walking Nuclear Disaster

The nuclear mushroom cloud is the most recognizable image of a nuclear catastrophe, but *The Man Who Stole the Sun* features it only once. It is placed extra-diegetically in the opening sequence, only to discard it for the rest of the movie, constantly teasing the audience with the promise of it without ever fulfilling this desire for destruction. Kido several times challenges the authorities to find the bomb before it goes off, but he never seems truly interested in killing. He feels frustrated by the society he lives in, but he is also reluctant to wipe Tokyo off the face of the Earth (a recurrent fantasy in Japanese cinema). These mixed feelings are exemplified by the recurring ticking of the bomb and the dreamy/nightmarish sequence of people playing in a pool where he fantasizes throwing scraps of plutonium metal at them, killing everybody (including himself), only to scream shortly after at everyone to get out of the water. On the other hand, he finds pleasure in exercising power over the authorities; he even starts calling himself "Number Nine," elevating himself to the state's level. Besides this feeling of power, he is an alienated individual in an entertainment-oriented society; what he is truly looking for is attention. His phone calls with Inspector Yamashita sound more like chats between old friends than offender-policeman conversations. Maybe Yamashita is right when he says that Kido only needs company (*yatsu wa tanin ni furetagatteru*, 1:38:05) and that the person he would like to kill the most is himself (*omae no ichiban koroshitagatteru ningen wa omae jishin da*, 2:17:50). Nevertheless, toward the end of the movie, he progressively seems to lose his human feelings in order to fully embrace his role as a "walking nuclear disaster," creating chaos and violence as the movie turns into a sort of escapist fantasy, becoming more and more unrealistic and spectacular. Kido and Zero flee from the police as though in a "Bonnie and Clyde" movie, but this getaway soon becomes a television show, as a TV helicopter following their car is in communication with Zero, who in turn provides live commentary. Kido and Yamashita start acting like superheroes, surviving what would normally be life-ending accidents, like jumping from a helicopter flying dozens of meters above the ground without sustaining any serious injury. After Kido survives an incredible leap with Yamashita from a rooftop using an electric wire as a liana (figure 10.3), the film ends on a freeze-frame of his face while a bomb goes off on the soundtrack. Hasegawa stated that Kido is not dead at the end of the movie; therefore, the audience is left wondering what that explosion means.[21]

Figure 10.3. Going off without a bang. Yamashita and Kido
jump from a rooftop with the A-bomb (that will gently land
on a tree). Hasegawa Kazuhiko, 1979, Tōhō.

As noted earlier, the only time a nuclear explosion appears on screen is at its beginning, in an extra-diegetic way, but it is telling that the subsequent images link it to a rising sun (Japan) and then to the face of the lead character. Indeed, by the end of the movie, Kido can be identified with the bomb itself, and the director does not need to show the iconic mushroom cloud to epitomize nuclear violence. He has become a "walking nuclear disaster," a bomb about to explode, as he brings death upon himself (he is already doomed by nuclear radiation) and upon others—a constant reminder to Japan of the risks of nuclear energy.

Epilogue

Yoshimoto wrote about a "systemic deprivation of imagination" concerning the way in which the nuclear village in Japan has dealt with nuclear power. By focusing on the division between "bad" nuclear weapons and "good" nuclear energy, it has confined the violence of nuclear power to its military use and sponsored a security system that is considered flawless, thus making radiation and related matters "doubly invisible" and removing them from the eyes of citizens.[22] As a *hibakusha* director—someone who knows what it means to deal with nuclear contamination every day, even if its effects are slow and invisible—Hasegawa fought hard against this systemic deprivation to bring nuclear violence to the fore in a multiplicity of forms. By refusing to exploit the spectacle of a nuclear explosion while making Kido's own body a nuclear battlefield, the movie highlights the "slow violence" inherent to invisible radiation. The director materializes it quite literally, making nuclear contamination and its deadly consequences visible on the body of the main character through hair loss and bleeding gums. He disguises it through the hyperbolic and unrealistic violence that characterize the last part of the movie (and the assault at the power plant), enabling the audience to imagine a form of this "unrepresentable" violence. The stealing of the plutonium exposes the lack of security measures surrounding nuclear energy, while the farcical representation of the authorities trying to catch Kido further symbolizes the fundamental inability to control a dangerous technology.

The nuclear discourse is no longer confined to sci-fi or *tokusatsu* movies, nor to individual stories of suffering human beings; it is brought right to the center of the consumerist society of the late seventies, making it part of Japanese citizens' daily life. Kido is its mediator, a "walking nuclear disaster" awakening the audience to nuclear-related issues, his body being the essential sacrifice to create a performative space capable of providing a usually neglected perspective. *The Man Who Stole the Sun* is a unique movie that exploits Hollywood-esque tropes and narrative devices while drawing from New Hollywood's "pop" in order to create a satire of nuclear power and the nuclear bomb in the form of an ironic action movie.[23] Well before Fukushima, when the government "sought to grant a sense of security that turned out to be as false as the myth of safety surrounding Japan's nuclear program itself," Hasegawa problematized the use of nuclear power as a source of energy, using nuclear terrorism to question safety issues that would become centerpieces of the antinuclear movement.[24] Thus, *The Man Who Stole the Sun* exposes the complex relationship between Japan and its nuclear program, while its anarchical undertone satirizes the authorities' inability to protect its citizens—even while they rely on this very false sense of security.

Notes

[1] The movie had several working titles: initially, Schrader proposed *The Kid Who Robbed Japan*, but Hasegawa was skeptical about it, as he was for *Plutonium Love*. Later, he came up with *Laughing A-Bomb*, but the distribution company—Tōhō—did not want any explicit reference to the atomic bomb. Finally, inspired by some promotional materials where the bomb resembled the sun, Hasegawa came up with the *The Man Who Stole the Sun*, which also calls to mind the Greek myths of Prometheus and Icarus, which in Hasegawa's opinion are somehow related to the story arc of the main character. Furthermore, nuclear power has often been linked—especially in American Cold War propaganda—to the image of the sun, as something beyond human control. Eigagogo, "Interview with Kazuhiko Hasegawa."

[2] *Ōru taimu besuto*, 1–20.

[3] Kimoto, *Kodoku to deai no eiga ron*, 12–20.

[4] Nixon, *Slow Violence*, 6.

[5] Kingston, "Japan's Nuclear Village," 1.

[6] At the time, the Rolling Stones were banned from Japan on drug-related allegations.

[7] He spent five years in Japan, married a Japanese woman, and had several Japan-related collaborations throughout his career. He wrote the script for the 1979 entry of the legendary *Otoko wa tsurai yo* (*It's Tough to Be a Man*) series by Yamada Yōji; Sōmai Shinji's *Shonben raidā* (1983); Sydney Pollack's *The Yakuza* (1974), starring Takakura Ken; and *Mishima: A Life in Four Chapters* (1985), directed by his brother, Paul.

[8] Eigagogo, "Interview with Kazuhiko Hasegawa."

[9] See, for example, Nishimura, "Hasegawa Kazuhiko intabyū"; Matsui, "Hasegawa Kazuhiko renzoku intabyū"; and "Wakuwaku suru koto."

[10] Miyahata, "Mō ippon totte shinu."

[11] Taylor-Jones, *Divine Work*, 160.

[12] Miyahata, "Mō ippon totte shinu," 2.

[13] Eigagogo, "Interview with Kazuhiko Hasegawa."

[14] Miyahata, "Mō ippon totte shinu," 2.

[15] Kobayashi, "Sakkashugi."

[16] After the speech delivered by US President Dwight D. Eisenhower to the UN General Assembly on December 1953, the US implemented a nuclear policy known as "Atoms for Peace" in order to promote peaceful uses of nuclear power. As part of this effort, they focused on lending nuclear materials and engineering help to underdeveloped regions in Asia and Africa. In May 1955, the "Hopkins Mission" arrived in Japan as an informal emissary of the program. Starting in Tokyo in November 1955, a series of "Atoms for Peace" exhibitions were subsequently organized in eight cities (including Hiroshima), with the support of prominent Japanese politicians and most of the national press. The success of the campaign marked a quick turnaround with regard to the public perception of nuclear energy; only a year before, one-third of Japan's population had signed petitions against hydrogen bombs. Nelson, *Nuclear Society*, 177–188.

[17] FEPC, "Results and Prospects."

[18] Yoshimoto, "Nuclear Disasters," 172.

[19] The reference in the movie is to the Tōkai nuclear plant in Tōkaimura, Ibaraki Prefecture. Built in 1960, it went active in 1966, becoming the first Japanese nuclear power station. Even if the reference is to an actual complex, for the outside shooting, Hasegawa used a thermal power station because there were no nuclear plants with a similar setting that would enable full-scale takes from the same angle used in the movie.

[20] Mes and Sharp, *The Midnight Eye Guide*, 275–277.

[21] Kobayashi, "Sakkashugi."

[22] Yoshimoto, "Nuclear Disasters," 173.

[23] Higuchi, *70nen dai Nihon no chōtaisaku eiga*, 240.

[24] DiNitto, "The Fukushima Fiction Film," 1.

Bibliography

DiNitto, Rachel. "The Fukushima Fiction Film: Gender and the Discourse of Nuclear Containment." *Asian-Pacific Journal* 16, no. 1 (2018): 1–13.

Eigagogo. "Interview with Kazuhiko Hasegawa." July 2011. Accessed August 12, 2022. http://eigagogo.free.fr/en/interview-kazuhiko-hasegawa.php.

FEPC (The Federation of Electric Power Companies of Japan). "Results and Prospects of Power Generation Volume by Source (1980–2014)." Accessed August 12, 2022. https://www.fepc.or.jp/english/nuclear/necessary/sw_necessary_02/index.html.

Higuchi, Naofumi. *"Suna no utsuwa" to "Nihon chinbotsu:" 70nen dai Nihon no chōtaisaku eiga.* Tokyo: Chikuma shobō, 2004, 234–252.

Kimoto, Shin. *Kodoku to deai no eiga ron.* Tokyo: Shin'yōsha, 2021.

Kingston, Jeff. "Japan's Nuclear Village." *Asian-Pacific Journal* 10, no. 1 (2012): 1–23.

Kobayashi, Jun'ichi. "Sakkashugi. Sakka ga sakka X Jiko wo kataru. Hasegawa Kazuhiko." *A People Cinema*, June 10, 2022. Accessed August 12, 2022. https://apeople.world/ap_various/various007.html.

Matsui, Osamu. "Hasegawa Kazuhiko renzoku intabyū. Part 1." *Eiga hihyō*, September 2001, 62–63.

Mes, Tom, and Jasper Sharp. *The Midnight Eye Guide to New Japanese Cinema.* Berkeley: Stone Bridge Press, 2005.

Miyahata, Yuzuru. "'Mō ippon totte shinu' Yonjūnen mo chinmoku tsudukeru 'densetsu no eiga kantoku' Hasegawa Kazuhiko ga gekihaku." *Tokyo Shinbun*, January 9, 2021. Accessed August 12, 2022. https://www.tokyo-np.co.jp/article/152936.

Nelson, Craig. *Nuclear Society: Atoms for Peace and the Origins of Nuclear Power in Japan, 1952–1958.* PhD dissertation, The Ohio State University, 2014.

Nishimura, Ichirō. "Hasegawa Kazuhiko intabyū. 'Taiyō wo nusunda otoko' wa yōkyū no nai jidai ni ikiru ore jishin no messēji da." *Besuto obu Kinema junpō.* Tokyo: Kinema Junpōsha, 1994, 1083–1087.

Nixon, Rob. *Slow Violence and the Environmentalism of the Poor.* Cambridge: Harvard University Press, 2011.

Ōru taimu besuto. Eiga isan 200. Nihon eiga hen. Tokyo: Kinema junpōsha, 2009.

Taylor-Jones, Kate. *Divine Work: Japanese Colonial Cinema and its Legacy.* New York: Bloomsbury, 2017.

"Wakuwaku suru koto wo motome tsudukete. Hasegawa Kazuhiko intabyū." *Kaijin 21 mensō no jidai 1976–1988 (Mainichi makku shiriizu 20 seiki no kioku).* Tokyo: Mainichi shinbunsha, 2000, 26–27.

Yoshimoto, Mitsuhiro. "Nuclear Disasters and Invisible Spectacles." *Asian Cinema* 30, no. 2 (2019): 169–185.

11

Representing the Unrepresentable: *Hibakusha* Cinema, Historiography, and Memory in *Rhapsody in August*

Adam Bingham

The subject of eco-disasters and popular culture has surely given rise to few more pressing and lasting reflections and discursive iterations than the example offered by Japan. Such has been the prevalence of reference points pertaining to the atomic bombings of Hiroshima and Nagasaki at the end of the Pacific War that both art and popular—and international and national—cinemas have been colored by their immediate impact and historical lineage. This in addition to a specific genre—*hibakusha* cinema, films about survivors of the atom bombs—means that the atomic bombings of Hiroshima and Nagasaki have continued to inform the social, political, and cultural facets of Japanese life; or at least this is certainly true of Hiroshima. Of Nagasaki, much less has been forthcoming, either in popular culture or in discourse pertaining to historiography, memory, and commemoration. To this end, the subject of the second bombing—the once important port town on the western tip of the southernmost of Japan's three major islands (Kyushu), an island of which it remains the capital and largest city—had tended not to be addressed in detail commensurate to its significance. Recent studies have begun to redress this imbalance, and Kurosawa Akira's *Rhapsody in August* (1991)—the acclaimed auteur's penultimate film—makes an instructive case study. Eco-disasters in general, long visited upon Japan as an ecologically vulnerable island nation, becomes a key framework within which to adumbrate this approach to Nagasaki and man-made eco-disasters. This is true to the extent that it offers a point of departure for questions pertaining not only to the bombing of Nagasaki but also to representations thereof (cinematographic and historiographic) and their probing of the lineage of the same at a key juncture in recent Japanese history. The chapter will explore this film from the perspective of these questions, the film's probing of the interrelated processes of memory, historiography and representation, and the significance of these questions at the time of its production— a seismic era of change in Japan.

Ecocinema: Trauma, Memory, History, and Storytelling

The subject of cinema and eco-disasters is something that, in Japan, has been of particular significance. From the Toei monster movies to *hibakusha* (A-bomb survivor) narratives, and from the politicized series of works by Noriaki Tsuchimoto and Sato Makoto to the more recent searing documentaries of Kamana Hitomi, the ecological effects of disaster and pollution have had a marked effect on Japanese films and filmmakers. One of the reasons for this continued importance has been the foregrounding of cinema's role in disseminating salient concepts and ideas and, to this end, the fact that it can further afford a chance to underline and indeed reflect upon the sociopolitical import and imperatives of cinema. That is, it can provide a self-reflexive or meta-cinematic imperative. Significantly, this pertains not only to historical events but also, and arguably more importantly, to processes of historiography, to how these events have been conceptualized, commemorated, and even challenged. Culture and politics are herein enmeshed, and the history and legacy of eco-disasters remain encoded within any and every representation so that—as it were—an intertextual signage takes precedence. It is this lineage that *Rhapsody in August* then uses to adumbrate its key themes.

The prevalence of eco-disasters and of their representation on film provides a key focal point for this exploration. Writing about and contrasting responses to Hiroshima and Nagasaki—a task that few in the West have undertaken—Jason Nicholls has argued that there should be a specific consideration of the second atom bomb that was dropped on Japan.[1] It has tended to be downplayed in textbooks, both in the US and in the UK, a conclusion with which Rachelle Linner concurs, stating that Hiroshima and Nagasaki are "yoked together, even though there are significant differences between them."[2] This difference pertains to the necessity for the second bomb to be dropped, an allusion to the complexity of discourse on the bombs, the contested reasons, points of view, and indeed histories that have proliferated. It is from this point of view that Kurosawa's *Rhapsody in August* becomes a particularly important work. However, this importance has still generally gone unrecognized and undervalued. It is a film that has been much neglected, and where it has been considered, it has been underestimated (if not summarily dismissed), a significant part of which neglect has been a result of its catalog of different viewpoints pertaining to responsibility and guilt over World War II. In the abovementioned context, it is thus an important text. Its narrative reflects national remembrance, mourning, commemoration, and historiography but moreover includes international—specifically US—views and the divisive reactions surrounding not only the dropping of the A-bombs but their official responses thereto.

The subject of eco-disasters and their representation is thus addressed as a narrative intrinsic norm. *Rhapsody in August* is set in present-day Japan and revolves around adolescents spending a summer with their grandmother (an A-bomb survivor) in Nagasaki while their parents are away in Hawai'i visiting an elderly relative, apparently the grandmother's elder brother. Here, the siblings learn about the bomb, visit the city and its key sites, and meet the Hawaiian's American son when he pays a visit. One of the key features of Japanese cinema's response to the A-bombs has been a desire to orient questions of tragedy around themes of individual identity. In contradistinction, the philosophical rumination of international films centering on these events have been attendant on explorations of what the dissemination of information reflects about how human beings assimilate and represent said information, as well as how it facilitates a reflection on the role(s) of cinema therein. In other words, the subjectivities of those relaying information (historically, culturally)—whatever their specific agendas may be—is taken up as a narrative theme. This is perhaps a natural bifurcation given the dichotomy outlined above, but the ways in which Kurosawa's film in various ways collates these approaches, questions, and perspectives means that it is one of comparatively few that make the issues of both approaches as a frame of reference. Productions such as Alain Resnais's *Hiroshima Mon Amour* (1959) or Nicolas Roeg's *Insignificance* (1985) take Japan as a point of departure. That is, they probe the role of memory and culture on a wider scale. Indeed, Resnais creates a textual dichotomy between populist and philosophical approaches by citing passages from a popular film of the 1950s—Shindo Kaneto's *Children of Hiroshima* (1952)—alongside his own. This then provides a foundation for a romance between a French actress (appearing in a film about Hiroshima) and a Japanese architect. Embracing in bed at the beginning of the narrative, they offer a gnomic exchange that accompanies the aforementioned pop cultural imagery. It begins with the actress stating, "The hospital in Hiroshima exists. How could I not have seen it?" Her interlocutor responds, "You saw nothing at Hiroshima," and this conflict of points of view continues through the film's extended opening and pertains increasingly to the extent to which the tragedy of the bombings has been subject to an almost touristic sense of spectacle, of the extent to which people have begun to engage with the bombs as they would with culture (hence, the juxtaposition of hospitals and museums).

Culture, Historiography, Storytelling, and the A-Bomb on Film

This bifurcation of approaches to Hiroshima throws light on a comparable division in what the different bombings suggest—how they have been represented. According to Robert Rosenstone, "[in *Hiroshima Mon Amour*] . . . the atomic bomb has nothing to do with honouring the dead or learning collectively . . . and everything to do with how the individual must come to grips with the traumas history inevitably inflicts."[3] It is, as Roth elaborates, most often the case that this particular disaster stands in for wider questions, both historical and philosophical. In this case, it is the use value of recollecting and of envisioning the past— about whose agency is revealed in such processes and "what desires are satisfied by this recollection."[4] If it is true, as Rosenstone has further elaborated, that one of the issues where cinema and representation is concerned is that "the filmic image cannot abstract or generalize . . . [that it] deliver[s] the past in a highly developed, polished form that serves to suppress rather than raise questions . . . rarely . . . push[ing] beyond . . . what we already know," then Kurosawa's is a particularly resonant approach.[5] At a time when what we "already know," or presumed we knew, was beginning to change based on using the past to mark out then salient aspects of the present, the fact that cinema has to deal with such a development was a consideration that fed into the construction of *Rhapsody in August*. This is not to argue that this work is more valid than others, to venerate it at the expense of other comparable films, as more populist fare offer their own perhaps more cathartic visions. It is merely to suggest that it is more complex, nuanced, and certainly far more interesting than has generally been allowed.

In *Rhapsody in August*, the myth of history as an objective record rather than a narrative is undermined. To equate history and narrative, as Hayden White argues, is to recognize that objectivity is not viable, not possible, in historiography.[6] It is a form of storytelling, a means of constructing a narrative and presenting a point of view. History and storytelling should be regarded as correlatives, and they remain processes that are perennially intertwined in dialogue throughout Kurosawa's film. The grandmother's memories vie for narrative space with her (often fantastical) stories about water sprites and local legends. The children's time with her is comprised as much with exploring the environs of her home and the stories that have been taken therefrom, something encapsulated in particular in a scene that becomes both story and history, in which the elderly lady talks about one of her brothers becoming a shoemaker and eloping with his boss's wife. This man apparently worked from the house that is now the grandmother's and absconded into the woods to live beyond social constraints. His-story here involves the shoemaker's wife seeing two trees that had been struck by lightning and that appeared to have committed double suicide, following which the pair decide to build a hut on the spot in which to live and work. This image of incineration and petrifaction from above offers a correlative to the bombing, a site of which the siblings have already visited in the city. They are profoundly impacted by this visit but are similarly influenced by the story of the lovers. The two elder siblings, brother and sister, visit said tree and (half-jokingly) profess to be under the sway of these ghosts, with the boy chasing his sister in apparently incestuous desire. As happens elsewhere in the film—for instance, when the grandmother's relating of a story about a sibling's obsession with eyes causes consternation when the protagonists are disturbed by a snake with the same eyes—such scenes inevitably feed into recollections by their grandmother or lead to moments in which the grandmother holds court over ceremonial remembrances. Reactions to one set of stimuli (the stories) facilitates and colors reactions to the other, to the history of Nagasaki, about which the young characters learn from scratch through their grandmother and their trips around the city. They remain impressionable, prone to being influenced by what they see and hear without necessarily processing said information and experiences rationally. Their proclamations about the forgetting of Nagasaki (taken by some to be key to the film's moralizing) thus need to be viewed critically. These proclamations occur as the protagonists traverse the city, visiting both memorial sites and the everyday places of the urban center, with the latter's lack of visible sites of remembrance facilitating their lamentations about a contemporary ignorance of the bombing. This is not to say that these adolescents are wrong but rather that (as with their reactions to the fantastical stories) they are presented as still lacking in maturity, and thus that they cannot offer instruction, moral guidance. Indeed, the point is rather that questions of correct or incorrect behavior are immaterial here. What predominates is simply a point of view, one not to be vilified but neither to be lionized, rooted as it is in the specific context of their ages and life experiences and their comparative lack of knowledge. That one of the siblings talks of how stories of the bomb had been akin to fairy tales suggests the extent to which history has, or can, become story, and although these young characters think themselves beyond such facets of childhood as these stories, the very fact of their emotional engagement with their grandmother's tall tales propels their summertime activities around her home and perhaps hints that this is not true. Critic Donald Richie attributes at least a potential dimension to the narrative wherein the grandmother is suffering from dementia; yet curiously, he does not seem to think that this would at least qualify any of the statements that he earlier takes to be among the keys to the film's perceived facile message.[7] As such, the veracity of the grandmother's recollections needs to be at least problematized— not taken out of the context of the narrative regarded as particularly privileged— as a source of secure knowledge and history.

Film Style

The abovementioned scenes of the children traversing Nagasaki offer a representation of this city that incorporates an implicit allusion to the fact that experiences thereof cannot be distinct from the perspective from which the city is viewed. These scenes are shot with the director's customary telephoto lens, a technique developed as a means of visually compressing physical space and flattening out the dimensions of the image. The distance of the camera from the subjects here posits a thematic imperative that, in the context of the narrative, suggests a distance from their points of view. The lack of physical proximity with regard to the camera suggests how the characters' optical viewpoints are almost summarily eschewed throughout. In their stead, an objective view of their experiences predominates. What we see throughout corresponds to no specific perspective, and consequently, their arguments do not become didactically those of the film. In other words, *Rhapsody in August* is not about Nagasaki per se. Rather, it uses this single cinematographic perspective on events as a point of departure for a wider engagement with what history means, how this meaning can change (inherent in the presentation of three different generations and both Japanese and US views in the film), and how it is communicated. Unsurprisingly, for the director of *Rashomon* (1951)—a film that offers an allegory of postwar Japan in its inclusion of contradictory viewpoints on a crime and an investigation of personal and social memory—meaning here is only meaningful to the extent that it is perceived to be so. There is no objective view of history, no such thing as a history without a story and no single way of expressing any event and its aftermath. Controversies in Japan pertaining to history books and what is taught in schools have for decades been pressing issues not only in school curricula but also in political campaigns, and attendant social protests underline this imperative. According to Claudia Schneider, this controversy "is a prism of . . . the heightened significance of the past for the present . . . [that] also holds a particular place among the region's numerous history debates . . . [serving] as one of the important arenas where the past, as well as the country's image of itself and others, is contested."[8]

The import of this to the wider historical and historiographic thematic of eco-disasters is to demonstrate the extent to which humanity's relationship with the world around it (especially in Japan) is perennially fragile, tenuous. Such events and tragedies do not simply happen in a vacuum. There is cause and effect, human intervention, and, most importantly, narrativization; even natural disasters are subject to such practices, as well as to processes of dissemination, exploration, or analysis after the fact that seek to situate it within a specific context for a specific purpose. To this end, Kurosawa said, when discussing *Rhapsody in August*, that he felt that a disaster of the enormity of the destruction wrought by the atomic bombs was essentially unrepresentable.[9] How, he asked, could the trauma of this devastation be communicated, be depicted directly without cheapening it or echoing the populist cinema of the past? The simple answer was that it could not. One is perennially faced with a presentation of points of view (be they cinematic, historical, or novelistic) when encountering history, and Kurosawa extrapolates from this to encompass his narrative. Echoing *Hiroshima Mon Amour*, Nagasaki itself becomes a museum throughout *Rhapsody in August*. The children make several sojourns to and around the city, prompted in each case by their discussions and interactions with others, and the long shots of citizens stress looking from a distance. These interactions then shape how they experience this locale. For instance, on their trip, which sees them visit the site very close to where the bomb exploded over Nagasaki, and thereafter, as they walk around the center of town, they talk about how the events (and like tragedies) appear to have been erased from popular consciousness or memory, how lives are being lived with almost no heed to this past event that, as it were, would seem to haunt the present like a specter, felt as a presence by a few but unseen, all but unknown, by the majority. Kurosawa has talked regrettably about forgetting, yet this is not necessarily either specific to Japan or necessarily a regrettable situation.[10] The children can, as they do, extol what they see as a lamentable feature of modern life. They chastise their parents, as does their grandmother, for their perceived ignorance and greed; but people cannot remain weighed down by events like the A-bomb, messages the Japanese have long since had to adapt to given the aforementioned fragility of their island nation and the concomitant necessity of living with disaster. The Japanese, then, like their country, have arguably needed to move on, suppressing the weight of history at the same time as they digest the same.

The very specific tension here between forgetting yet remembering, suppressing history yet keeping it alive, is an important part of *Rhapsody in August*. The need is to live within history, to regard it not as a past—something that has been and gone—but rather to live within it as a part of the present, a facet of life but not one at the forefront of daily living. As such, it is not part of the past but something that—as it is with any aspect of life as it is lived—is subject to change and transformation, and this has been attendant on thinking about the impact of the A-bomb. It requires a negotiation with how both history and historiographic processes in general are conceived, and with the historical specificity of this particular disaster and its ramifications, which pertain to questions directly related to *nihonjinron* (the post-World War II specificity of Japanese sociocultural expression and attendant racial homogeneity). To this end, the trajectory of Japan in the wake of World War II, its Westernization and economic miracle, must be remembered; and for all that, the parents' embrace of the material prosperities of their US relations reflects poorly upon their generation, such has been the context of their lives. Theirs is not a view of the bomb to embrace, but neither does their children's rejection of this offer a viable alternative. The cross-sectional protagonists of Kurosawa's film thus represent contrasting visions, but it must be remembered that the parents of the young protagonist do know about Nagasaki and its history, whilst their US relative (embodied by Richard Gere's thoughtful, caring Clark) is even more desirous of learning about his extended family and their experiences. Indeed, it is the middle-aged parents who explain to Clark a public shrine to the victims of Nagasaki. Thus, narrative here in fact disturbs the points raised and the attitudes expressed. Rather than offering a single, simple message, this raises a point that is questioned throughout the film. It is true that this apparent selflessness is contrasted with the perceived selfishness of the children's parents, who more than once extol a need to pacify the Americans and to benefit financially from these wealthy relations. In this, they may be argued to represent the Japan of the economic miracle—the drive toward material gain— while the past (grandmother) and future (the children) represent different values. They bespeak a Japan that—in the wake of the recession that was just beginning at the time *Rhapsody in August* was being made—was at least attempting to negotiate change and sociopolitical transformation. Nagasaki here becomes a ground zero, a historical nodal point in which concepts of nationalism become bound up with a capitalistic identity, and the extent to which the perceived common past of the bomb is, or can be, an amorphous entity can be contingent upon markedly different interpretations, depending on the present.

What is arguably more important is the conflation of actual spaces with perceptions thereof, perceptions that color and shape the experiential dimensions of such locations as Nagasaki. In other words, it is the ways in which "real" locations are charged with meaning that is at stake here. Space becomes indistinguishable from the subjectivities of those within its environs, something inexorably connected to the theme of eco-disasters. Much of the myriad work on cities and cinema as interconnected sites of experiential modernity has underlined this point, and in a sense, eco-disaster, long visited upon Japan as an ecologically vulnerable island nation, becomes a key framework within which to adumbrate this approach to Nagasaki and man-made eco-disasters. The changes wrought both after 1945 and after 1990 (when Japan's economic downturn began) mean that history and the bomb become elusive, ambiguous. To this end, the persistence of memory, problematic remembrance, and the vagaries of perception further complicate any clear message or simple unequivocal meaning, an imperative that Kurosawa was at some pains to suggest in his late films. His previous film, *Akira Kurosawa's Dreams*, is constructed almost exclusively around privileged vision, around people and spaces that suggest themselves for the singular edification, redemption, or damnation of the protagonist. Whether said protagonist's fate remains positive or otherwise is typically a question of his response to what form the eco-disasters take, as well natural and, indeed, supernatural phenomena.

The Eye

In *Rhapsody in August*, the image of an eye is raised in discussions between the grandmother and her grandchildren, when the former talks about a brother of hers who became obsessed with eyes in the wake of the bombing. She herself talks of seeing a great eye over the mountains at the time of the bombing, and it is not so much the specific eye of the male character—indeed, he is never present in the narrative—as it is the grandmother's, given that it is explicitly visualized immediately after she talks of her own experiences with this vision and that it approximates her optical point of view. Given the absence of such visions throughout, and the concomitant anomalous position of this as a point-of-view shot, it should be taken as representative of a single perspective, with all the limitations that have been noted as attendant on this character and perspective. The point, surely, is thus that this is a highly personal response, almost indistinguishable from the dictates of storytelling, given the references elsewhere to eyes and vision and an allusion to the individual proclivities that become attendant on these images as part of stories, tall tales. The prevalence of communal responses in commemoration and remembrance (something depicted later in *Rhapsody in August*) is thus subtly questioned here as a further means of problematizing didacticism rather than encouraging or enacting the same. Group activities of the kind seen in the film—where elderly Japanese clean and observe worship at the site of the bombing in the school seen earlier in the film—of course, have their place, but individual practices are also important. How trauma and tragedy are processed in a personal way is also significant, a way that perhaps forgoes the official strictures of communal commemoration. With this in mind, learning is a leitmotif throughout *Rhapsody in August*. The eldest of the young siblings is learning to play an old harmonium that he spends his summer vacation repairing, and sporadically throughout the narrative, his performance of different pieces of music, songs, and practice pieces forms the spine of scenes that depict the adolescents at both work and play. The film opens with said character playing scales, and throughout the narrative, he rushes back to this instrument to provide musical accompaniment to certain actions, typically when his siblings are playing around the house, as though to narrativize such actions, to underscore what is typically a time of joy for the characters, and to make of it an occasion replete with a sense of spectacle, making the film more grandiloquent as a means of engaging with representation. In this, it balances and mirrors the weight of the spectacle of history elsewhere in the narrative and complements said histories and the ways in which they have been disseminated in public discourses of remembrance and commemoration.

Reinforcing this aspect of the film is the fact that a nondiegetic rendering of the song that this boy plays, Schubert's "Heidenröselein," which is about a boy obsessed with the sight of a rose and is itself a compact story, occurs when, during a communal commemoration, the youngest of the siblings catches sight of a long line of ants ascending a rose. Literalizing the subject of Schubert's song, they move in single file up and down the flower, an image at once arresting yet ultimately disturbing, mournful in its implications of natural beauty eaten away. This is, in fact, a reframing of the Japanese philosophical concept of *mono no aware*, of an elegiac sadness at the passing of the time, the attendant transience and mutability of life, and its (not common) application to the bomb. The curious gaze cast on this image by this boy— frightened yet, at the end, smiling as his gaze is matched by Clark's—reinforces this ambiguity. Indeed, with the American character as central, the scene here also echoes the moment when, at the schoolyard site of the bombing during his first visit, a series of mourners emerge, almost like ghosts materializing from a sacred space (as the war dead emerge from sites of battle in *Akira Kurosawa's Dreams*) and, in a similar fashion, colonize the shrine and begin cleaning the objects therein. These mourners frighten the young boy—because, his brother tells him, they have witnessed the worst of the tragedy pertaining to the city's past (and thus, it is implied, they offer a direct link to said tragedy)—as the ants appear to similarly disturb him. It is a connection that is visualized here as the smile arrives as the boy has faced and seen through what was troubling his mind. A series of point-of-view shots show the ants' progress along the floor and up the stem of the flower, with cutaways to the boy's increasingly fraught reaction leading to a rising tension that is then released at the end of the scene when what has bothered him is dissipated—when, in other words, he has not hidden from what was scaring him and thus appears to overcome any fear.

Schubert's song reappears during the final enigmatic scene that sees the grandmother leaving her house during a storm, one that appears to trigger in her a reaction comparable to the initial bombing on August 9, 1945. It is as though she is reliving the trauma of this event, walking as she does into and against the storm, all the while pursued at a distance by her children and grandchildren. The music here links the image of the boy and his obsession with the children and the grandmother, the terror of the past literalized in a scene of pathetic fallacy and of facing one's fears (as her youngest grandson had faced what was earlier troubling him) as a means of assuaging it. Thus, the elderly woman seems here to be facing her past through reliving it, with memory and physical experience conflated. At the same time, the music and its diegetic connotations—as well as underlining the connection across generations—stress that this character's progression entails a temporal regression. Her personal demons are hers alone to assuage, as the cutaways to her family, apparently unable to catch up to her, make plain. This tension between self and others, past and present, mind and body, and forgetting and remembering is left to ring out across and after the end of the film, and it crystalizes its concern with the myriad complexities of dealing with a disaster such as the A-bomb.

Eco-disasters of the various kinds that have beset and continue to beset Japan offer a potent image of this fractious relationship between individual and nation. This is because responses thereto need individual actions (from mourning to engaging in acts of remembrance, charity, and writing/historiography); yet these acts need at the same time to proliferate on a wider scale. They require individuals to become communities, communities to become collectives, collectives (citywide concerns, for example) to become nations; and though these centrifugal practices are indexed almost inexorably to shared experience and endeavors of memory and recollection, nonetheless, the proclivities of the individual should not be overlooked, encapsulating as they do a heterogeneity of at least potential approaches and interpretations. It is a tension that lends itself to mainstream cinematic narrativization, which tends to stories about individuals, and Kurosawa dramatizes this in a scene in which the grandmother and a friend sit in silence and face each other, saying nothing, each encased in their own memories yet working through said memories together.

The complex intertextual lineage alluded to above also reinforces this thematic import by inferring a matrix of texts. An opening image looking up at the sky—a beautiful, placid, blue expanse, the movement of clouds across which suggests smoke—not only suggests the central tension between a peaceful present and a problematic past but also recalls the opening images of stasis and repose that open *Ran* (1985). In the earlier film, a mournful, violent transposition of *King Lear* into a historical era of social turmoil, Kurosawa's aim was to present the drama as though it were being viewed from the perspective of a sorrowful deity, conferring a feeling of distance and melancholy. Thus, from a film that looks down from the heavens, *Rhapsody in August* immediately presents an obverse, mirror image. It presents, and by extension and implication, immediately narrativizes, a look toward the heavens, one in which simple pleasures (of a sunny summer's day) remain in tension with the historical enormity of the bombings and the shadow it casts over contemporary Japan: a placid, calm sky nonetheless replete with a sense of foreboding, of expectation. Indeed, at this point in the narrative, there is no sense that this is not the sky over Nagasaki on the morning of August 9, 1945—Kurosawa thus drawing our attention to the potentialities and implicit narrativizations of this event, narrativizations that are then frustrated throughout. It is a history with an emphasis on the story, especially as the intertextual imperatives suggest a world in crisis and chaos but one whose chaotic dimensions have been internalized. It is a way of reflecting on the primacy of perception in that expectations and attendant stories are implicitly raised, expectations that refer back to a type of conventional drama on the bombing/s only to frustrate them in the subsequent conflict as a way of reframing how we engage with them.

Conclusion

Rhapsody in August stands out among films dealing with Hiroshima and Nagasaki in being as much about the legacy of 1945 as it is about the immediate aftermath thereof. As with a young boy killed in the blast who returns as a ghost in a recent Nagasaki film—*Nagasaki: Memories of my Son* (2017)—the persistence of memory is a salient concern and animates Kurosawa's inquiry into how remembrance is a personal and political undertaking. The import of the issues raised in this essay for considering the representations of eco-disasters is precisely that the central drama is built around the absence of such a representation. The narrative of *Rhapsody in August* stresses unrepresentability at the same time as it emphasizes the need for teaching and learning about history; and it is the tension between these two poles that opens up a liminal space that the film exploits in order to engage not with the bombing of Nagasaki but rather the historiography surrounding its social, political, and cultural lineage. To this end, the personal memories that anchor the narrative remain just that—personal memories: individual and specific points of view. This applies to the Japanese and US perspectives, as to the three different generational attitudes represented through the extended characters. Yet to suggest that the film privileges any of these attitudes is to misread its specificity. At a time when Japanese cinema was beginning to look nostalgically back to earlier eras, as their bubble economy was collapsing and the country was on the cusp of a recession that would go on to exponentially destabilize its industry, this engagement with the bombing of Nagasaki asks questions both specific and universal. To view it as a *hibakusha* film is to recognize its concern with the effects of the bombings in Japan, with their immediate impact and legacy; but in point of fact, Kurosawa's interest (as distinct, in part, from the novel the film is adapted from) remains not merely on this subject matter but on the limits of this genre. It thus confuses the boundaries between disparate eras and the interest attendant on their respective engagements with the past in general, and with Nagasaki and the A-bomb in particular, which have been subject to reinterpretation in recent years. This has been true in particular on international perspectives, specifically a link made in 2020 between the ideological and sociological foundations of the atomic bombing of Japan and the death of George Floyd in the US. These connections, built on a perceived commonality of racist attitudes that deny self-defense, show the ways that history fits the past, its stories not so much retold as remodeled and reinterpreted to fit the present.[11] Although *Rhapsody in August* does not, cannot, explore these issues directly, nonetheless, its approach makes it plain that different points of view have been and perennially can be brought to bear on understanding even so specific and apparently historical an event as Nagasaki, and its controversial inclusion of an American character demonstrates not a pandering to the US as much as a recognition that the A-bomb was and is an international incident. This specifically challenges the aforementioned victimhood that has beset Japanese responses to this tragedy and stresses instead a universality, wherein room for point of view and perception is paramount. To this end, discourse surrounding eco-disasters is broadened by the lack of representation and the primacy of presentation. It is a theme important for cinema in general, and for Japan and Japanese cinema in particular.

Notes

[1] Nicholls, "The Portrayal of the Atomic Bombing of Nagasaki in US and English School History Textbooks," 63.

[2] Linner, *City of Silence: Listening to Hiroshima*, 100–102.

[3] Rosenstone, "Introduction," 10

[4] Roth, "*Hiroshima Mon Amour*: You Must Remember This," 102.

[5] Rosenstone, *Visions of the Past*, 13.

[6] White, *Meta-History*, 112–115.

[7] Richie, *The Films of Akira Kurosawa*, 225–226.

[8] Schneider, "The Japanese History Textbook Controversy in East Asian Perspective," 108.

[9] Vox Populi, "Akira Kurosawa and Gabriel García Márquez: The Conversation."

[10] Vox Populi, "Akira Kurosawa and Gabriel García Márquez: The Conversation."

[11] Bulletin of the Atomic Scientists, "Memorial Days: The Racial Underpinnings of the Hiroshima and Nagasaki Bombings."

Bibliography

Kurosawa, Akira. "Akira Kurosawa and Gabriel García Márquez: The Conversation," *Vox Populi*. Accessed July 31, 2022. https://voxpopulisphere.com/2018/09/08/25245/.

Linner, Rachelle. *City of Silence: Listening to Hiroshima*. New York: Orbis Books, 1995.

Nicholls, Jason. "The Portrayal of the Atomic Bombing of Nagasaki in US and English School History Textbooks," *Internationale Schulbuchforschung* 25, no.1/2 (2003): 63–84.

Richie, Donald. *The Films of Akira Kurosawa*. California: University of California Press, 1996.

Rosenstone, Robert. "Introduction," in *Revisioning History: Film and the Construction of a New Past*, edited by Robert Rosenstone, 3–14. New Jersey: Princeton University Press, 1995.

Rosenstone, Robert. *Visions of the Past: The Challenge of Film to Our Idea of the Past* Cambridge: Harvard University Press, 1998.

Roth, Michael S. "*Hiroshima Mon Amour*: You Must Remember This," in *Revisioning History: Film and the Construction of a New Past*, edited by Robert Rosenstone, 91–101. New Jersey: Princeton University Press, 1995.

Scarry, Elaine. "Memorial Days: The Racial Underpinnings of the Hiroshima and Nagasaki Bombings," *Bulletin of the Atomic Scientists*. Accessed August 12, 2022. https://www.uwe.ac.uk/study/study-support/study-skills/referencing/chicago#websites.

Schneider, Claudia, "The Japanese History Textbook Controversy in East Asian Perspective," *Annals of the American Academy of Political and Social Science* 617, no. 1 (2008), 107–122.

White, Hayden. *Meta-History: The Historical Imagination in Nineteenth-Century Europe.* Baltimore: Johns Hopkins University Press, 1973.

Yoshimoto Mitsuhiro, *Akira Kurosawa and Japanese Film Studies*. Durham: Duke University Press, 2000.

12

Hibakusha Film as Genre, and the Slow Violence Depicted in Morisaki Azuma's *Nuclear Gypsies*

Jeffrey DuBois

The horrors of the atomic bombs and nuclear testing have inspired a range of filmic productions in Japan dubbed "*hibakusha* cinema," a reference to the victims of the bombs.[1] These range widely, from the birth of the monster, or *kaijū*, series with *Gojira* in 1954, to Kurosawa's *Record of a Living Being* (*Ikimono no Kiroku*, 1955), in which a businessman attempts to compel his family to move to Latin American to avoid being caught up in the crosshairs of nuclear warfare, to Kaneto Shindō's *Lucky Dragon No. 5* (1959), a dramatization of the fishing vessel irradiated by the US's hydrogen-bomb testing near Bikini Atoll in the Pacific in 1954, an incident that would not only launch the antinuclear movement in Japan but would also be tied to the awakening of Godzilla in Honda Ichirō's classic film.

This chapter proposes to expand the definition of "*hibakusha* cinema" to include all victims of nuclear technologies—human and nonhuman victims of not only nuclear weapons but also nuclear power. While the term *hibakusha*, or "those exposed to the bomb," emerged as a term to describe victims of exposure to the radiation unleashed in the blast of a nuclear bomb, nuclear power plant incidents—including the meltdown at the Fukushima Daiichi power plant and those before it—have allowed us to consider the term more expansively. In this chapter, I analyze one film that fits within this larger *hibakusha* film genre, *Nuclear Gypsies* (1985). The film, a fictional depiction of a real nuclear power plant in the

1980s, allows us to consider how the use of landscape and the depiction of slow violence can serve as powerful tools for films within the *hibakusha* film genre. In *Nuclear Gypsies*, a nuclear power plant in Mihama, Fukui, pervades the landscape as a constant reminder of its unending presence in the lives of the inhabitants. Meanwhile, the plant laborers are slowly falling victim to radiation poisoning, a violence that impacts them gradually and invisibly.

Hibakusha Film

While internationally, films of the 1950s, such as *It Came from Beneath the Sea* (1955) featured—in the vein of *Gojira*—radioactive mutants and suggested fear and panic of the ecological and global damage of nuclear testing, they failed to directly criticize the testing itself. That changed in 1964, when Stanley Kubrick's *Dr. Strangelove* and Sidney Lumet's *Fail Safe* both addressed the possibility of a launch of a nuclear weapon due to an accident or a rogue general down the chain of command. Such films taught audiences about the problems of the delegation of launch codes, of questions of mutually assured destruction, and the apocalyptic scenarios of nuclear war at any scale—warning that there is no such thing as a limited nuclear war. A strike against an enemy is also a self-strike, suicidal and omnicidal.[2]

While the edited volume *Hibakusha Cinema: Hiroshima, Nagasaki, and the Nuclear Image in Japanese Film* (1996) focuses on the bombs, it provides a useful moniker that can be expanded in order to consider nuclear-related films under a single category that takes the focus off the weapon itself and rather centers on those affected by nuclear technologies, the *hibakusha*. Broderick notes that the nuclear-related films analyzed in his volume express anxieties beyond the bombs themselves:

> Other concerns such as the stockpiling of plutonium by Japan, ostensibly for fast-breeder reactors but which could quickly be reused for weapons, and the ongoing proliferation of nuclear reactors around the country (currently over 40) have been addressed in dramas such as *Revenge of the Mermaid (Ningyo densetsu,* 1985) and *Dreams (Yume,* 1990).[3]

Use of the word "*hibakusha*" both decenters the bomb and helps us think through a more expansive meaning of victimhood. The *hibakusha* film genre, therefore, could include movies that deal with victims impacted by nuclear bombs or directly exposed to radiation, and those in the social and environmental ecologies that are also impacted.

Documentarian Hitomi Kamanaka had already embraced this more expansive meaning of *hibakusha* in 2003, as seen in the title of her film *Hibakusha at the End of the World* (ヒバクシャ ―世界の終わりに).[4] This film not only linguistically connected victims of bombs and other forms of radiation exposure, but it actively compared them through her transnational profiles of young victims of depleted uranium in Iraq, victims of the bombings of Hiroshima and Nagasaki, and women in Washington State in the US who were impacted by radiation from the Hanford Nuclear Site.[5] Kamanaka's other films, especially *Rokkasho Rhapsody* (2006) and *Little Voices from Fukushima* (2015), are similarly concerned with *hibakusha* victims of radiation exposure. For Kamanaka, the violence of radiation is not reducible to stories of national victimhood, and her approach compares (and sometimes brings together in gatherings of international *hibakusha* solidarity and support) the stories of communities in England and far northern Honshu, Japan, as well as Chernobyl and Fukushima.[6]

Kamanaka's films provide that crucial comparative link between nuclear weapons and purported "peaceful" uses of nuclear technologies, and they constantly explore the related environmental and ecological dangers. Her concern is not merely the health impacts of exposure to radiation but the ways in which nuclear technologies can disrupt entire ecosystems, alienating people whose livelihood is fishing, farming, or seaweed harvesting from the fruits of their labors (see especially *Ashes to Honey*, 2010).

I propose that "*hibakusha* film" can be used to denote two expanded categories: first, those impacted by nuclear weapons and those impacted by radiation from nuclear power plants; and second, nonhuman animals, plants, and the ecologies that sustain life beyond the atomized and singular individual. In other words, the relationships between living beings—the ecologies—are victims to the extent that they are severed, interrupted, or destroyed. As systems that support life, ecologies too can be *hibakusha*. Just as "atomic bomb literature" contains nonfiction and fiction, poetry and testimony, "*hibakusha* film" includes the diversity of moving images, from documentaries to fiction to anime. Indeed, anime that touches on nuclear themes ranges from the semibiographical anime of *Nagasaki 1945—The Angelus Bells* (2004) and *Barefoot Gen* (1983) to the nuclear-apocalyptic imagery in *Akira* (1988) or the focus on daily life amid war on the outskirts of 1945 Hiroshima in *This Corner of the World* (2015).

Slow Violence

I now turn to one *hibakusha* film and consider the concept of "slow violence" as articulated by Christine Marran in *Ecology without Culture*. I argue that the film *Nuclear Gypsies* (Morisaki Azuma, 1985) is a narrative fiction capable of depicting slow violence through the portrayal of laborers at a nuclear plant and their surrounding community. However, the film also employs spectacular violence to frame the slow violence of the radiation poisoning done to bodies and the environment within cycles, systems, or—shall we say—ecologies of violence.

In the second chapter of *Ecology without Culture*, titled "Slow Violence in Film," Christine Marran employs the term "slow violence," which was coined by postcolonial ecocritic Rob Nixon, to analyze the films of documentary filmmaker Tsuchimoto Noriaki, who spent years covering the mercury poisoning in Minamata. "Slow violence" describes the "violence done to humans, animals, and the environment over time, a violence that is often invisible because it is difficult to represent pollution events like radioactivity, eutrophication, mercury poisoning, and so on."[7] Such poisoning and degradation is invisible and difficult to capture with the moving image, which tends toward the spectacular (the "money shot" of the mushroom cloud or the image of the 2011 tsunami in Japan breaching the wave barriers in Fukushima). While Nixon privileged forms of writing as best suited for representing slow violence, Marran demonstrates how the many documentary films of Tsuchimoto depicted slow violence cinematically. She does this, as Marran writes:

> to illustrate how the specter of slow violence was visualized in his moving images. The filmic elements discussed in this chapter include: Tsuchimoto's avoidance of landscape shots that make the land and sea ambient; his refusal of montage and spectacle; his analytical rather than presentational approach to the body as revealed through an optics of ambulation; the lively ontology of his mise-en-scène; and the reconceptualization of the body in motion within the context of cinema history.[8]

For the purposes of my analysis here, the most important components of the representation of slow violence are the issues of landscape and spectacle. Landscape in film can be used as a break or pause from the narrative action. Like Ozu's pillow shots, it can give viewers time to catch their breath as they observe nature's serenity or a still object. It can also suggest an outside to the triviality and capriciousness of human daily life. Yet as Marran argued, Tsuchimoto refuses to make landscape ambient or background; rather, landscape is intimately bound to the ecology of life that includes the humans who ravage it. How might we consider the function of landscape within Morisaki's *Nuclear Gypsies*, a dramatic film quite different from the Minamata-related documentaries of Noriaki Tsuchimoto? What lurks behind the beauty of Morisaki's ocean views?

Spectacle is a useful device for keeping an audience engaged and has served a valuable role for the *hibakusha* film from its inception, as seen when the monster *Gojira* trampled the high-rises of Tokyo, melted steel beams with his radioactive blast, and toppled a radio tower with a crew mid-broadcast. Scenes of spectacle capture both events as they happen and their ruinous immediate aftermath. They cannot as effectively depict the slow violence of the long-term impact of the accumulation of toxins, the slow breakdown of ecosystems, or the diseases associated with exposure to radioactivity over time. Unlike Tsuchimoto's documentaries, *Nuclear Gypsies* is not without spectacle. But what is the purpose of this spectacle and does it undermine a greater message regarding the violence that nuclear power plants bring to the inhabitants of the area?

Nuclear Gypsies

Nuclear Gypsies is about the many layers of hidden violence wrought on communities that live in the shadow of a nuclear power plant. The film takes place in Mihama City, Fukui Prefecture, which came to be known as the Nuclear Ginza—named after Tokyo's high-end shopping district—due to its high concentration of nuclear power plants. A motley crew of characters, all originally from Okinawa, live above a small bar. Barbara is a dancer who returns from work on the road, looking to find her friend Aiko. Miyazato, Barbara's lover from decades prior, works at the Mihama nuclear power plant and is involved with the yakuza, but he is in trouble for not appropriately disposing of Aiko, who has knowledge of an accident at the power plant. Barbara hopes to help Aiko escape. Meanwhile, two teenagers—Tadashi, who Barbara brought with her from Okinawa as a child, and Tamae—kidnap their homeroom teacher, Noro, to extort money as payback for their canceled school trip, a rather ill-conceived plot. The principal suspects that Noro is part of the scheme and has no interest in paying the ransom to free him. Consequently, Noro allies himself with the group and comes to Barbara's aid.

The film's Japanese title, *Ikiteru uchi ga hana na no yo, shindara sore made yo*, translates to "Party Declaration: Life Is All Flowers until We're Dead." The title suggests that life ought to be embraced because it is a fragile acknowledgment of the precarity of life touched by yakuza violence and power plants. It is unclear why the English title was changed to *Nuclear Gypsies,* but the film makes explicit reference to transient nuclear plant workers through use of this term. The protagonist, Miyazato, himself self-identifies as a "gypsy." "Nuclear gypsy," coined by Horie Kunio in his 1984 expose, *Genpatsu Jipushii (Gypsies),* refers to a laborer on temporary contract with nuclear power plants.[9] They typically work dirty and dangerous jobs associated with the plants and are vulnerable to exploitation as subcontracted labor. In the film, Barbara explains that the transience of their labor is due to periodic inspections, which implies that they would be out of work if it was discovered that they had exceeded their periodic allowable radiation dosages. Consequently, they are forced to move around to avoid being prohibited from working, surely at a cost to their long-term health. The laborers hop from plant to plant, and Miyazato explains to another character how he had worked in nuclear power plants across Japan's main island of Honshu, from Fukushima Daiichi in Tohoku to the Genkai plant in Kyushu, and now at the Mihama plant in Fukui. He had declared the decision to pursue such work to Barbara when they fled Okinawa after the Koza riot of 1970, in which Okinawans clashed with the US military. Finding themselves on the mainland, Miyazato became a transient worker, a "nuclear gypsy," and Barbara turned to work as a dancer. Yet, fleeing the violence and military presence of Okinawa, which was still under the official occupation of US forces (which would revert sovereignty back to Japan in 1972), Barbara and Miyazato were akin to political refugees.

Displaced from their homes and community, the Okinawans living together in Mihama function as critical labor, and yet they are also pariahs. A traditional guardian statue from Ryūkyū, the *shiisa*, sits on the awning roof tiles, ostensibly to advertise their Okinawan pub, but it also serves as a marker of their outsider status in an unwelcoming land. The risk of radiation exposure is but one of the forms of violence in their lives. More immediate is the violence of poverty, the danger of yakuza affiliation, and sexual violence. The teenager Tamae, who works as a prostitute in a brothel run by the yakuza, has been impregnated, and a young gang member pressures her to get an abortion, something she considers but ultimately resists at the cost of running afoul of the gang; and Barbara speaks of young women brought from the Philippines as dancers whose passports are confiscated, leaving them exposed to further exploitation that may push them into prostitution. She recognizes that their cheap labor has devalued her own work, but she does not blame them. Barbara's final mission is to help one such Filipino dancer, Maria, escape Mihama with Tadashi, because she too knows too much.

Yet the central factor driving the violence of *Nuclear Gypsies* is the need to protect the Mihama nuclear power plant from scandal. If nuclear gypsies are exposed to high doses of radiation or are witnesses to a leak or mishap, they must be silenced, something rumored to be accomplished by shoving their bodies into waste barrels that are then removed by helicopter for disposal. In the film, one such worker, Yasushi, manages to hide in the immediate aftermath of an incident in which radioactive chemicals directly entered wounds on his leg; he and his lover, Barbara's friend Aiko, hatch a plan to get away. They hold a mock funeral for him, where he is literally buried alive in a makeshift grave, only to emerge and quickly marry Aiko, with Barbara serving as the officiant, before they are to escape. This scene happens on what appears to be a secluded hill in the woods. However, beyond the trees looms the presence of the Mihama nuclear power plant.

In fact, nearly every shot that includes the wider surrounding landscape includes the nuclear power plant. It is visible from the bus stop as Barbara returns from work. It is there when Barbara is running up a hill looking for Aiko (figure 12.1). It sits on the opposing shore of the serene beach where Barbara, Aiko, and Tamae spend the night reminiscing about their past (figure 12.2). It is the landscape behind Barbara and the others as they harvest vegetables in a field. It is

Figure 12.1. Barbara runs uphill, looking for Aiko with the nuclear power plant in the background. Morisaki Azuma, 1985, Kinoshita.

the opening shot of the pan that shifts the camera to the image of the runaways. The nuclear plant is in view through the sun-shower (the "foxes' wedding" in Japanese) shortly after the escapees, Aiko and Yasushi, are gunned down while fleeing on the distant shore (figure 12.3). The beauty of the rainbow appearing through the rain is pierced by the violence of Aiko and Yasushi's assumed deaths and the presence of the nuclear plant in the frame.

Figure 12.2. Barbara, Aiko, and Tamae reminisce about their past across from the nuclear power plant. Morisaki Azuma, 1985, Kinoshita.

Figure 12.3. The nuclear power plant seen through a
sun-shower. Morisaki Azuma, 1985, Kinoshita.

Simply put, the Mihama nuclear power plant is omnipresent in the film, a
constant reminder of the way it has invaded the life of the inhabitants. There is no
place to take a momentary pause from the pressures of the plant and the yakuza
who operate it. In no way can the landscape serve as a respite from the action
for the viewer. The landscape cannot be ambient—that which sets a background
mood without interrupting the narrative—because, dominated by the nuclear
power plant, it has been utterly transformed by human exploitation. It is in
this way that a narrative fictional drama film such as *Nuclear Gypsies* can share
a commonality with Tsuchimoto Noriaki's documentaries. To quote Marran,
"Tsuchimoto, who dedicated most of his life to documenting fisher folk living in
and around the Shiranui Sea, did not interpret landscape as aesthetic object or
ambient background. The good shot was not the one committed to landscape; it
was the one committed to ecological systems."[10] For *Nuclear Gypsies*, the good shot
was the one committed to the social and ecological systems; the landscape is not
separate but deeply entwined in the lives of the Mihama workers.

Moreover, the landscape shots, nearly all taken from the point of view of the
characters within the film, are both banal, in that they reflect an everyday visage
of the laborers of Mihama, as well as filled with significance, as the source of their
earnings and pain—the power plant—is omnipresent and inescapable. Scholar
and critic Yuriko Furuhata analyzes how documentary filmmakers in Japan
during the 1960s and 1970s engaged in theories of landscape (*fūkeiron*).[11] Adachi
Masao's *A.K.A. Serial Killer* (1969), Furuhata notes, "endlessly and disjunctively
strings together actuality footage of urban and rural landscapes," and yet it stands
apart from militant documentary filmmaking at the time "precisely because of its

peculiar obsession with the eventless images of quotidian landscapes."[12] *Nuclear Gypsies,* a narrative film rather than a documentary and therefore not engaging directly with filmmakers such as Adachi, plays with such understandings of landscape. In the film, the landscape shots are eventless and quotidian, yet they always point to the potentiality of what is occurring and what is to come.

There is no explosion at the plant or spectacular scene that indicates a large leakage of radiation into the atmosphere or water that would force residents to evacuate. Rather, such violence is slow and hidden. At one point, a detective who works hand in hand with the yakuza opens a duffle bag holding the possessions of Yasushi, the man exposed to radiation during an accident. He opens a magazine with pictures of naked women, but as he flips through the pages, the audience can catch a glimpse of an exposé about the "Dark Secrets of Nuclear Energy." He pauses before tossing the magazine aside. In this film, the secrets, of course, are the incidents and accidents that must be concealed to keep the plant running properly. If plants cycle through transient workers like the so-called "nuclear gypsies," they can avoid failing inspections for exposing their workers to high doses of radiation accumulated over time. This is the slow violence inflicted on the workers, who would normally be nameless and faceless drifters, but here, they are made the protagonists of the film. Miyazato is deeply enmeshed in the cycle of violence through his involvement with the yakuza. However, even Tadashi, the teenager who Barbara had cared for as a child, sees no promise of a future and begins working at the Mihama plant, submitting to life as a "nuclear gypsy"—that is, until he schemes to escape the area with Maria.

Were an incident to occur, evidence, including the bodies of injured workers themselves, must be made to disappear. The film features only a few dark scenes that depict a nuclear spill incident at night through the foggy face masks of the workers, or the arrival by night of a helicopter to collect the remains of a laborer tossed into in a waste barrel to decompose. But even these scenes of exploitation and violence appear in the film hazy or muddled, their veracity in question. For example, one scene of exploitation turns out to be nothing more than the nightmare of Noro, the kidnapped teacher.

It is only later in the film that Miyazato reveals that he himself is a victim, a *hibakusha.* The film leaves ambiguous whether Miyazato's injury was related to the slow accumulation of internal radiation or the result of a single incident of direct exposure, but Miyazato explains to Noro in the dark of night on the balcony that the damage of his radiation exposure plagues him. The dim light of a match reveals that Miyazato is attempting to cauterize a leg wound—his flesh is rotting away "because of the cesium," he says. His long hair, sunglasses, and yakuza swagger conceal his true vulnerability: he is slowly dying from his exposure to radiation. It is with this scene that the audience makes sense of the bandage wrapped around

Miyazato's leg in earlier scenes. When Miyazato next stands up, it is with a pained limp.

Yakuza gang members swing by the Okinawan pub to confront Miyazato about his inability to successfully kill witnesses to the nuclear accident, and they demand he turn himself in as a scapegoat. Miyazato seals his fate by shooting the yakuza member who confronts him, and he threatens to leak the incident to the newspaper. What ensues is a shootout between Barbara and the corrupt detective and yakuza, replete with an exploding car and flames. But this spectacle of violence can be connected to the slow violence of the film and the nuclear power plant: this violence is tied to the ongoing effort to conceal the violence of radiation, and this shootout, too, will be minimized as a "gang skirmish" to hide its significance.

The film here leverages the tropes of the yakuza genre: Miyazato is caught between his duty to the yakuza gang and boss and his immediate relationships, including with Aiko, and yet he must break with the yakuza out of a sense of righteousness and morality.[13] The slow violence that radioactivity did to his body pushes him to his breaking point. He no longer fears death if it means helping other victims escape the imprisonment represented by the omnipresent nuclear power plant and the communities it destroyed. Yet his self-sacrifice will not bring an end to the cycles of violence wrought by the yakuza and the power plant that leans on them—it will merely enable the escape of a few loved ones. His death, as well as the death of other gypsies and yakuza, will be concealed so that the slow violence, to the bodies of the nuclear gypsies and the surrounding environment, can continue without interruption.

Conclusion

Tragically, but perhaps predictably, the same Mihama plant that dominated the landscape of the film *Nuclear Gypsies* experienced an accident fifteen years later, in 2004, that killed four workers and severely burned five more. To date, it was Japan's worst nuclear accident, exceeded in seven years only by the disaster at the TEPCO Fukushima Daiichi plant. At the time, Kansai Electric Power Company, which owned the plant, assured the community that no radiation would leak into the surrounding environment. In a *New York Times* article about the 2004 incident, two sentences suggest that the slow violence depicted in *Nuclear Gypsies* contained more than a kernel of truth:

> Wariness has been fueled by accidents and by a cover-up culture in which employees show far greater loyalty to their companies than to the public's right to know. Last summer, the Tokyo Electric Power Company, the nation's largest utility, was forced to close all 17 of its nuclear plants temporarily after admitting that it had faked safety reports for more than a decade.[14]

In the post-Fukushima world we live in now, nuclear power is less viable in Japan, and KEPCO has plans to decommission the Mihama nuclear power plant.

Nuclear Gypsies lacks the cathartic spectacle of the nuclear explosion, and while it is neither documentary nor heavy social commentary, it offers a path for the *hibakusha* film. It demonstrates how a landscape heavy with the presence of a nuclear power plant can serve as a constant reminder of the oppressiveness of the industry on the lives of those who must live with it. It also allows us to identify whose pain—the pain of radiation poisoning that slowly deteriorates the body from within—is largely invisible. Finally, it shows us how the *hibakusha* film can jump through different genres to achieve its core function, the centering of the victims of nuclear technologies—the people, their communities, and the environment.

Notes

[1] Broderick, *Hibakusha Cinema*.

[2] Ellsberg, *The Doomsday Machine*.

[3] Broderick, *Hibakusha Cinema*.

[4] Released in the US by Group Gendai Film in 2005 as "Radiation, a Slow Death: A New Generation of Hibakusha."

[5] Marran, *Ecology without Culture*, 61.

[6] Kamanaka is not the first person to use the term like this, either. See the stories of victims of radiation on the "exposure" page of the Hiroshima Peace Media Center, where you can toggle back and forth between Japanese and English. It features a 1989 series on Sekai no Hibakusha 世界のヒバクシャ: http://www.hiroshimapeacemedia.jp/?post_type=exposure.

[7] Marran, *Ecology without Culture*, 58.

[8] Marran, *Ecology without Culture*, 61–62.

[9] Horie, *Genpatsu jipushī*.

[10] Marran, *Ecology without Culture*, 56–57.

[11] Furuhata, "Returning to Actuality."

[12] Furuhata, "Returning to Actuality," 364.

[13] MacDonald, "The Yakuza Film: An Introduction."

[14] Brooke, "Four Workers Killed in Nuclear Plant Accident in Japan."

Bibliography

Broderick, Mick, ed. *Hibakusha Cinema: Hiroshima, Nagasaki, and the Nuclear Image in Japanese Film*. London: Routledge, 2015.

Brooke, James. "Four Workers Killed in Nuclear Plant Accident in Japan." *New York Times*, August 10, 2004. https://www.nytimes.com/2004/08/10/world/four-workers-killed-in-nuclear-plant-accident-in-japan.html.

Ellsberg, Daniel. *The Doomsday Machine: Confessions of a Nuclear War Planner*. New York: Bloomsbury, 2017.

Furuhata, Yuriko. "Returning to Actuality: *Fûkeiron* and the Landscape Film," *Screen* 48, no. 3 (Autumn 2007), https://doi.org/10.1093/screen/hjm034.

Horie, Kunio. *Genpatsu jipushī*. Tokyo: Kōdansha, 1984.

MacDonald, Keiko. "The Yakuza Film: An Introduction" in *Reframing Japanese Cinema: Authorship, Genre, History*, edited by Arthur Nolleti and David Desser, 165–192. Bloomington: Indiana University Press, 1992.

Marran, Christine. "Slow Violence in Film." *Ecology without Culture*. Minneapolis: University of Minnesota Press, 2017.

13

Nuclear Visuality and Popular Resistance in Kamanaka Hitomi's Eco-Disaster Documentaries

Andrea Gevurtz Arai

*"The problem for Kamanaka is visualizing (the disasters)
in a way that spurs anti-nuclear awareness."*[1]

*"Long form documentary involves discovery and immersion in a social
problem . . . to describe the dynamics of its unfolding present."*[2]

"I don't want this to happen again to anyone else."[3]

Hitomi Kamanaka has been making documentary films focused on nuclear energy production and environmental disaster for the last thirty years. Her goal, preceding and following the triple disasters of Fukushima on March 11, 2011 (hereafter 3/11), has been to create a deeply contextualized, multilayered visual representation of the forms of eco-disaster associated with nuclear energy production. Through up-close encounters with the everyday and popular resistance actions of her documentary subjects, Kamanaka employs a strategy of what I refer to as "nuclear visuality" to expose the complex forms of nuclear eco-disaster, including what Katsuya Hirano has called "a logic of sacrifice," and Sabu Kohso "a land without people and a people without land."[4] Hirano's notion of "sacrifice" points to rationales employed by elected officials and electrification companies to justify unequal hardships imposed on local populations. Kohso's formulation highlights the catastrophic dimension of the "unseeable" disaster that renders uninhabitable human and natural landscapes.

I use the notion of nuclear visuality (following Rachel DiNitto in the first epigraph) to point to the challenge of visualization that Kamanaka takes on in her efforts to render radiation visible, as well as the immersive visual techniques she uses to bring the viewer face-to-face with irrevocably altered lives and landscapes. In the first film discussed below, the context is the aftermath of radiation disaster; in the second, it is the fight to prevent the destruction of biodiversity. Both films create the conditions for visual discovery, out of which a new visuality of the unseeable of nuclear eco-disaster emerges. As Megan McLagan (in the second opening epigraph) additionally notes, immersion and discovery are critical tools for independent documentary filmmaking that opens a space for possibility and difference, or what she calls "the unfolding present."[5]

For Kamanaka, this unfolding present is a space of possibility for nuclear visuality, one that animates awareness and popular resistance and that leads to what she has called a "revolution of feelings."[6] In her production of a new visuality, Kamanaka is in line with earlier female literary activists in Japan—in particular, Michiko Ishimure. A prolific writer, Ishimure was best known for exposing the Chisso Chemical Company's reckless dumping of raw mercury into the Shiranui Sea off the coast of Minamata City (on the island of Kyushu) in the 1960s, resulting in the destruction of animal and sea life, and the debilitating neurological disease now known as "Minamata disease."

In this chapter, I focus on the relationship between content and technique in Kamanaka's films, revealing how central one is to the other, how she accentuates victim's stories, juxtaposes locations, within and beyond Japan, and works to create a visuality that amplifies awareness of impending eco-disasters and their aftermaths. The victimized and exploited are central figures and actors in their own right in her films, participating in the relaying, remembering, and circulating of the conditions of disaster and exploitation.[7] Tracking an unfolding present—or something happening or about to happen in real time—requires time, care, and an attentiveness to struggles and complex conditions. Bringing all these tools to her filmmaking makes it possible for Kamanaka to create a visual story that has room for revelations and emerging forms of resistance.

Kamanaka is a devoted social activist off camera as well. Her films participate in exposing what Sabu Kohso has called the "apparatus" of growth and energy politics that continues to render some areas of Japan and those who live there into what economists call "externalities," or damages and hardships incurred to environments and human life that are left out and unaccounted for (or made external) to financial calculations.[8] Kamanaka's activism began many years ago when she was in Iraq following the first Gulf War (1991–1992) and she witnessed how the depleted uranium from American bullets resulted in elevated rates of childhood cancers. (Though many years later, she is still involved in one of the only childhood cancer care hospitals in Iraq, raising money for the hospital, supporting the doctors, and more.)[9] After she returned to Japan in 1995 to help the survivors of the massive Kobe-Osaka earthquake, she discovered along with the rest of the Japanese public that the damage from the 7.5-magnitude earthquake was exacerbated by the 1980s "bubble-era" deregulation of the construction market's seismic building codes. Thus began her filmic efforts to hold corporations and government to task, telling the stories and making visual records of those who were most disadvantaged by energy economics and its priorities, and at the same time shining a light on underrepresented alternative energy and livelihoods. This has meant, among other things, working to render visible the invisible atom and its invisibilized politics of externalities, its placement of nuclear plants, and its negotiations with local leaders. As Noriko Sakamoto discusses, prior to the meltdown of three out of six reactors in the Fukushima Daiichi plant on the highly seismic northeastern coast on 3/11 (2011), most Japanese people did not know where their energy came from, or about the everyday costs to local places to produce this energy.[10]

I focus here on two Kamanaka films about different moments and experiences of eco-disaster, *Ashes to Honey* and *Little Voices from Fukushima*. These documentaries bookend what is one of the most colossal nuclear energy disasters in world history—second only to the Chernobyl disaster of 1986—where Kamanaka takes her documentary team and visual techniques to build a story that is both local and global. I have chosen these two films because they take us inside the specific power dynamics brought to bear on local communities in their attempts to preserve their livelihoods and the biodiversity of their environments.

Ashes to Honey is the story of the twenty-seven-year battle of the inhabitants of Iwaishima (in the Inland Sea off the coast of Yamaguchi Prefecture) to prevent the construction of nuclear plants across the bay from their fishing and farming island. *Little Voices from Fukushima*, which takes place in the aftermath of the triple disasters of 3/11 (earthquake, tsunami, and nuclear plant explosion), is the story of how unlikely actors, ordinary housewives in this case, create a mother's movement—the Mama Rangers—to render visual the perils of nuclear energy production and the radiation sickness affecting their children and families. Well aware of the power of representation to support or contest the political order, these films by Kamanaka render visible the forms of political coercion and disaster cover-up of energy production in peripheral places like Iwaishima and Fukushima, together with popular resistance and energy alternatives.

This chapter has also been inspired by collaborative work with Kamanaka for a future documentary we began work on in 2019, focused on the responses of the younger generation to 3/11, which included exiting full-time salaried jobs, especially those related to nuclear energy production; refusing to participate in the reproduction of a growth economy at all costs and moving to local places to engage in projects of creative resistance. Our collaborative film project was put on hold due to the pandemic, but Kamanaka used this opportunity to do her own *turn away* from Tokyo and a way of life based on the unequal costs of energy production. Her own refusal, and the community she has helped revitalize, demonstrate another part of her commitment to creating a system in which costs are more evenly distributed and eco-disasters minimized.

Kamanaka is keenly concerned with the unseen politics of nuclear plant placement, and the unseen (and underreported) long-term dangers of low-level radiation for young, developing bodies. This is a danger that pediatricians from Belarus to Japan who were interviewed in *Little Voices* emphasize, and it is one Kamanaka exemplifies in the constant scans of thyroid glands and blood tests that must be done following nuclear accidents. The damages to the young can be mitigated but will never disappear. Moreover, the film captures the impossible choices faced by families in the aftermath of nuclear eco-disaster, to remain together in hazardous locations or separate and endure the tolls of displacement and family separation. How to choose between safeguarding oneself and one's children by taking refuge elsewhere when it involves a family breakup? As one of those interviewed in *Little Voices* tearfully tells Kamanaka: we want others to try and understand the hardship and perils of family separation.

"*Radiation contamination doesn't go away.*" (*Hōsha osen wa nakunaranai.*)[11]

Little Voices from Fukushima opens with a short cameo, with Kamanaka (on-screen and speaking) with Geiger counter in hand, taking a millisieverts (radiation-dose) reading of the area around the home she is about to enter to interview members of one of many families in Fukushima. As the title of the film suggests, Kamanaka elevates the voices of the small, those most affected over time by radiation contamination, and the mothers and fathers who seek to protect them from this contamination and the diseases that accompany it. Without giving the story and storytelling methods away too quickly, what is clear is that for Kamanaka—through collective action and as a result of the enormity of the hardship—these little voices can turn into powerful vehicles of resistance to the very political and discursive forces that have worked to suppress them.

Following the opening scene with Kamanaka, we meet Yuri (figure 13.1), the mother of two small children and someone Kamanaka follows throughout, in a shrine praying for her children's safety. The camera cuts to Yuri's kitchen in the early

Figure 13.1. Yuri in *Little Voices from Fukushima*.
Kamanaka Hitomi, 2015, Bunbun Films.

evening, where she is busily preparing the evening meal and being interviewed by Kamanaka. Yuri talks about her dread (*kyoufu*) at staying put with her family in Fukushima given the level of radiation that remains four years following 3/11. The alternative—to become evacuees from Fukushima and refugees (*hinansha*) in a different part of Japan, which some have chosen to do, and Yuri's family is contemplating as the caption below announces, "stay strong and move forward together," is a particularly difficult decision for their family. What those seeking to protect their families encounter, as Kamanaka skillfully shows us by taking us inside the clinics, radiation disease mitigation facilities, mothers' meetings, and more, is a complex world of terms and knowledge of health preservation (*hoyō*); reduction or abatement (*keigen*); the amount of exposure to radiation (*hibaku*); and refuge (*hinan suru*) that is challenging to navigate.

Several of my students were deeply affected by Yuri and her story. As one of them wrote in a discussion commentary on *Little Voices,* the opportunity to learn up close about one mother and her impossible choices, to be immersed in her everyday life and discover with her and her family what nuclear eco-disaster is and does, is to gain a new visuality. It is, this student wrote, "like Yuri is speaking to us. She's like us, one of us. This could happen to anyone." Kamanaka has helped this group of students and many others visualize and identify with ("she's like us; it could happen to anyone") the realities of different ways of life irrevocably changed by nuclear eco-disaster, closing gaps of time, space, geographic division, gender, and social class in the northeast region of Japan around Fukushima.

The Japanese government, according to museum anthropologist Fuyubi Nakamura, has employed design firms to construct a memorial museum structure. But as Nakamura relates, this is not what local people need or what they have requested of the government. Instead, as we learn along with Yuri and others in the film, what they are asking for is that others learn to visualize the "land without people and people without land"-type eco-disaster conditions of their lives, to provide ongoing mitigation efforts, and to shift away from what Natsuki Ikezawa has called "the bulldozer of postwar growth."

Kamanaka's film tracks how these mothers, fathers, and families learn to survive, support each other, and demand change, and how their present unfolds in surprising ways. Yuri's opening utterances of "zutto shinpai" ("[I'm] always worried") and her attempts to minimize the sources of radiation poisoning ingested by her children in their milk, vegetables, rice, and more are transformed from fear to collective action as part of the new group, the Mama Rangers, whose T-shirts announce their collective will and aesthetic. This group emerges out of the shared conversations between mothers (and perhaps also with Kamanaka).

Mama Rangers is an action-oriented group that takes the problem of health preservation, reduction, exposure, and prevention into their own hands. They garner support from outside of the prefecture and from post-Chernobyl Belarus, where this film goes next to learn from a well-known pediatrician on the front lines of child exposure care about the long-term effects (since 1986) of radiation sickness on exposed children.

This section of the film is heartening and disheartening all at once. Those exposed can get better, and many techniques have been created to try to mitigate the various vulnerabilities, pain, weakness, fatigue, nose bleeds, diarrhea, and of course, cancers, but those affected will never be free of radiation sickness. Some will live forever with long-term effects. Compensation money given by the government has often been spent not on care but on alcohol, as family units were devastated by the range of illnesses caused by the Chernobyl plant's radiation. As Dr. Anna (in Belarus) reminds the mothers—and all of us—it won't be the state that comes to your rescue; it will be the community (kokka de wa nakatta, minkan desu). The other reason for taking the film to Belarus is that the heavily exposed children of Chernobyl were sent to other countries that would take them. Japan was one of them. We meet young people who spent several years in Hokkaido and who have stayed in touch with their host families. Mothers in Belarus and Fukushima echo the sense of frustration (kuyashii) at having to send their children back to the exposed areas, knowing the ongoing danger to the younger ones but also the need to be with their families.

Kamanaka takes the viewer along with the Mama Rangers (figure 13.2) to Shinjuku Park in Tokyo to join in protests to protect the children, as Yuri, who

Figure 13.2. The Mama Rangers in *Little Voices from Fukushima*.
Kamakana Hitomi, 2015, Bunbun Films.

is front and center there with other moms in her group, says, we are here to remind everyone that radiation never goes away, neither do its effects. We want to make sure that this never happens again (*kurikaeshinai*). Back in Fukushima, we witness, as we did in Belarus, how ordinary lives have been forever transformed by radiation sickness. Children are regularly tested for thyroid tumors, and they undergo health preservation methods and retreats (one of these is on Hokkaido), as the young people wonder out loud what their lives would have been like without the need for these health interventions. What is a normal life like?

Kamanaka's *Little Voices* is the story of ordinary people subjected to the full force of eco-disaster, the so-called peaceful atom, as it was advertised by American and Japanese conservative (LDP) governments alike to convince the nuclear-opposed Japanese public that nuclear energy production was unrelated to the bombs dropped on Hiroshima and Nagasaki. This marketing campaign turned out to be highly successful within the conditions of the high-growth, energy-hungry 1960s–1980s, during which reactors were installed from one end of Japan to the other, replacing, in some cases, the hydropower dams that were dealing with varieties of after-effects (like sludge) and the need for expensive repair. Dam construction as well came with its own toll: displacing communities and shifting ecosystems dramatically. Enter the "efficient" and seemingly carbon pollution-less atom compared to these other energy sources. But as Jon Mitchell writes in *Poisoning the Pacific*, TEPCO chose to locate six reactors at the Daiichi plant in Fukushima on the coastline, ignoring the threat of a tsunami wave that would overwhelm its ten-meter seawall. On the afternoon of March 11, 2011, a 9.0-magnitude quake struck off the coastline of Tohoku. It was one of most powerful tremors ever recorded. It caused a fifteen-meter tsunami that flooded the complexes, knocking out the power supply to the reactors.[12]

In an interview with Katsuya Hirano following the 3/11 disasters, Kamanaka speaks of her sense of "powerlessness" following the nuclear disaster, as well as her ongoing commitment to produce "a thorough record" of what has gone on, from political decisions to the effects on everyday life. From the *little voices*, which can become large, to her ongoing recognition and commitment to the power of visual representation and documentary film, Kamanaka forces the politics of nuclear production out into the open, where their "undemocratic nature" can be seen, to create visibility around the issues of nuclear power production. This kind of visibility promotes, as Sara Pritchard and Jon Mitchell have argued in their books and articles on antinuclear protests, a larger discussion about what they call the "envirotechnical regime"—who benefits and who bears the uneven burden, like the seasonal and contingent workers at these plants who put their lives in peril to help with the cleanup, having lost their means of subsistence in the triple disasters.[13]

Some have laid the blame for the oversights and faulty decisions that facilitated the nuclear disaster at the Daiichi plant in Fukushima on the neoliberal policies and privatizations of the 1990s, which ultimately led to the bubble bursting in the financial and property markets and the ensuing recessionary climate. Allowing nuclear plants, particularly along the highly seismic northeast coastline, to be deregulated and turned over to the semigovernmental (and, therefore, partly private) Tokyo Electric Company is one part of this problem. However, the conditions of possibility for the location of the Daiichi plants along the Tohoku coastline, and the minimizing and cover-up of the Fukushima Daiichi nuclear plant disaster began much earlier with the production of a geographic and social unevenness or peripheralization in the late 1960s that prioritized the urban white-collar employment center of Tokyo, and its "credential and enterprise society," and turned local areas into industrial rust belts. Neoliberalization, or the shifting of risk from the government to the family and individual, and the state's concurrent retreat from the support and securitizing of education and labor—as I have argued at length elsewhere—did not create the unevenness between Tokyo and the rest of Japan, but it has exacerbated it.[14]

> "How can you afford oil in Japan? Why not use your natural energy sources like hot springs (geothermal) wind and sun? Deregulate your energy system so you can choose 'eco' energy rather than 'ugly' energy. You need to fix this. Start now!"[15]

> "We will never give up."[16]

Ashes to Honey: The Search for Energy Independence in Sweden and Japan opens with a quote about the buzzing of nature and human creative energy and then cuts to a pan of Miura Bay, Iwaishima (Japan), and a young man (Takashi Yamato) who has newly returned to the island and who is harvesting its prized seaweed, *hijiki*, with the older women who have shared their lifetime of know-how with him. He lends his youthful energy and internet savvy to this local enterprise, and in a matter of years, as he says, they have more orders than they can fill! The older women instruct Kamanaka, the director (and also interviewer and interlocutor), in how to tell *wakame* from *hijiki* and what to look for when harvesting and preparing. Theirs is the best because of the unpolluted water of the bay and the islanders' respect for the delicate ecosystem that provides them their livelihood. A montage of fishing and farming (rice and loquats, pollinating bees and honey included) and livestock follows. Little do we know at this point that their entire way of life, and the unique biodiversity of their bay, has been threatened from the outside, and the islanders have been belittled in the process by one of the large energy monopolies in Japan, Chugoku Electric. Our immersion in the landscapes of local life and environment, from seaweed cultivation to local agricultural products and a history of cultural events, leads to our discovery, along with the inhabitants of Iwaishima, of the unfolding present of their popular resistance and a new visuality around the possibility of alternatives, as those in Iwaishima and beyond announce: we will never give up on our way of life and its biodiversity.

Kamanaka pans to Tanoura Bay on the other side of Iwaishima that opens onto the Inland Sea. Chugoku Electric began over twenty-seven years ago to plan the construction of a nuclear plant across the bay from Iwaishima. It would raise the water temperature by seven degrees. These reactors rely upon a water source for constant cooling, which would destroy the biodiverse life in the bay. (Later in the film, a longtime fisherman tells Kamanaka that even a one-degree increase in the summer harms fishing). Older men and women, along with Takashi and his wife, protest every Monday at Tanoura Bay (over one thousand protests) and use their fishing boats to block the land reclamation. As they loudly proclaim, "We are totally against a nuclear power plant!" ("*Genpatsu zettai hantai*," figure 13.3).

Contrary to claims by the prefectural government, which stands to gain subsidies by allowing the plants to be built, and to the electric company representatives who promise there will be no adverse effects to the bay or the islanders' ways of life, and who promise free electricity and jobs at the nuclear plant, the inhabitants of Iwaishima are keenly aware of what is at stake environmentally and culturally.

Kamanaka, as observer and participant in her films, is as well. Her aim is to make visual the unseen dangers of nuclear energy production to natural and local life that the electrification company alternatively denies and justifies, and

Figure 13.3. Iwaishima citizen protest in *Ashes to Honey.*
Kamanaka Hitomi, 2010, Group Gendai.

to provide a deep sense of the island's unique ability to be a leader in sustainable energy and livelihoods. She does this through two additional sequences that are as visually revealing as they are moving and surprising.

The first scene is of a festival that the islanders have been celebrating since the ninth century. It commemorates the relationship with priests from Kyushu, who, having been shipwrecked over one thousand years ago on Iwaishima, were provided with food, shelter, and the repair of their boats so they could return home. What has followed is an annual festival of gratitude. The Kyushu priests arrive with gifts and ceremonies, and the villagers respond with local foods and longevity of relations between the two groups. For many years, this stunning festival of performance, prayer, and local specialties would attract visitors from across Japan. In recent years, however, as several inhabitants tell Kamanaka, the protests and the opposition to land reclamation and nuclear plant construction has taken its toll on the festival and its audience.

The second sequence takes the viewer outside of Japan to the small northern city of Overtornea, Sweden. This city was in trouble both economically (high unemployment and low income) and culturally until it embraced and became the forerunner of the "deregulation" of energy production and consumption in Sweden. Through interviews and visits to the sites of popular resistance and change, Kamanaka provides us with a visual and verbal close-up of what the

Iwaishima inhabitants have been persistently fighting for two decades. It is not a "pipe dream" or the whims of local people, but as a range of local people involved in new wind farm installation and waste processing plants demonstrate, healthy, vibrant, and viable livelihoods can go together with energy emancipation, local subsistence, and an example of what is possible environmentally. As one of the many participants in this project insists, this could happen in Japan. "How can you afford oil in Japan? Why not use your natural energy sources like hot springs (geothermal) wind and sun? Deregulate your energy system so you can choose 'eco' energy rather than 'ugly' energy. You need to fix this. Start now!"[17]

Back in Japan, we hear from sustainable energy experts, like Iida Tetsunari, who come to the support of the islanders of Iwaishima by speaking out about the benefits of energy deregulation, which in Japan directly threatens the monopolies on energy production and consumption that have made nuclear power seem inevitable. Shining the camera's bright light on a whole population's way of life and the natural environments that sustain them, the value of biodiversity to other forms of life—threatened by the very construction and normal operation of these nuclear plants—provides a staggering realization of the cascade of incalculable costs that range from their normal operation to the accidents that are inevitable in the "ring of fire" where Japan is situated.

We will never give up! We will save our way of life, shout the Iwaishima villagers at their protests on land and in the sea. Taking on the power and influence of a huge corporation backed up with political power is no small thing. Neither is this unique form of eco-disaster filmmaking, the purpose of which is to challenge the status quo story of nuclear energy production in Japan as a necessity with minimal costs.

By taking us to the two locations of Fukushima and Iwaishima—and from each to the locations of earlier nuclear catastrophe (Chernobyl) on the one hand and of sustainable energy production (Overtornea) on the other—we are witness to those who bear the burden and sacrifice for this energy, those who must choose to stay in a radioactive environment and live with these immanent health dangers and the realistic alternative of deregulated sustainable forms of energy production and its benefits to local communities and natural environments.

Conclusion

Writing about another form of political power and energy production—what he calls "the age of oil"—and the Middle East, Timothy Mitchell argues that the term "democracy" can have different meanings. "It can refer to ways of making effective claims for a more just and egalitarian common world. Or it can refer to a mode of governing populations that employs popular consent as a means of limiting claims for greater equality and justice." Or as he so aptly puts it, "what if democracy is not

202 : ECO-DISASTERS IN JAPANESE CINEMA

a carbon copy but carbon based?"[18] It seems to me that Kamanaka's eco-disaster documentary films, in particular the two discussed here, point us in a similar direction. They expose, through her method of nuclear visuality, the undemocratic nature ("democracy as mode of governing"). At the same time, this visuality also creates the openings to an unfolding present in which "making effective claims" can be an outcome of the eco-disasters as well. As Sara Pritchard writes about 3/11 and what we must finally learn about it and other disasters like it (at the time of this chapter's writing, the Zaporizhzhia nuclear plant in southeastern Ukraine is threatened by warfare rather than seismic activity), we need to understand the complex, dynamic, porous, and inextricable configuration of nature, technology, and politics that together helps us to understand all that the single word "Fukushima" now signifies.[19]

As Kamanaka's Swedish counterpart (in *Ashes to Honey*) argues virulently, "deregulate and choose eco (not ugly) energy . . . fix it now," to which the Iwaishima islanders echo, "we won't ever give up" trying to preserve our way of life and the biodiversity that makes it possible. Though chided for not being concerned with the future of the nation, in effect, their efforts to guard against ecological destruction over short-term gains respond precisely to the belabored message of the Belarus pediatrician, battling radiation sickness for thirty years, about the power of local communities (and individuals like Kamanaka) to make the difference.

Notes

[1] DiNitto, "Ecology. Toxic Interdependencies: 3/11 Cinema," 383.

[2] McLagan, "Imagining Impact: Documentary Film and the Production of Political Effects," 307.

[3] From the documentary film, *Little Voices from Fukushima*, directed and produced by Hitomi Kamanaka (Bunbun Films, 2015). A response by Yuri (to Kamanaka's question) about why she is taking part in an antinuclear protest in Tokyo. Yuri is one of the mothers featured in this documentary film. She helped form the Mama Rangers to protect her own children and others affected by the Fukushima nuclear disaster of March 11, 2011.

[4] Kamanaka and Hirano, "Fukushima, Media, Democracy: The Promise of Documentary Film," 5.

[5] McLagan, "Imagining Impact."

[6] Kamanaka and Hirano, "Fukushima, Media, Democracy."

[7] McLagan, "Imagining Impact."

[8] Kohso, *Radiation and Revolution*, 5.

[9] Kamanaka and Hirano, "Fukushima, Media, Democracy."

[10] Sakamoto, "Local Energy Initiatives in Japan," 5.

[11] Excerpt from Hitomi Kamanaka's film *Little Voices from Fukushima*.

[12] Mitchell, *Poisoning the Pacific*, 166.

[13] Brown, *Anti-Nuclear Protest in Post-Fukushima Tokyo*.

[14] Arai, *The Strange Child: Education and the Psychology of Patriotism in Recessionary Japan*. See also my "Notes to the Heart: Lessons in National Sentiment and Sacrifice in Recessionary Japan."

[15] Alternative energy spokesperson (Sweden) in Kamanaka's film, *Ashes to Honey: The Search for Energy Independence in Sweden and Japan* (Group Gendai, 2010).

[16] Iwaishima protestor in Kamanaka's film, *Ashes to Honey*.

[17] Alternative energy spokesperson (Sweden) in Hitomi Kamanaka's film, *Ashes to Honey*.

[18] Mitchell, *Carbon Democracy: Political Power in the Age of Oil*, 9.

[19] Pritchard, "An Envirotechnical Disaster: Negotiating Nature, Technology, and Politics at Fukushima," 269.

Bibliography

Arai, Andrea Gevurtz. "Notes to the Heart: Lessons in National Sentiment and Sacrifice in Recessionary Japan." In *Global Futures in East Asia*, edited by Ann Anagnost, Andrea Gevurtz Arai, and Hai Ren, 174–196. Stanford: Stanford University Press, 2013.

Arai, Andrea Gevurtz. *The Strange Child: Education and the Psychology of Patriotism in Recessionary Japan*. Stanford: Stanford University Press, 2016.

Brown, Alexander. *Anti-Nuclear Protest in Post-Fukushima Tokyo*. New York: Routledge Press, 2018.

DiNitto, Rachel. "Ecology: Toxic Interdependencies: 3/11 Cinema." In *The Japanese Cinema Book*, edited by Hideaki Fujiki and Alastair Phillips. London: British Film Institute/Bloomsbury, 2020.

Kamanaka, Hitomi, dir. *Ashes to Honey: The Search for Energy Independence in Sweden and Japan*. Japan: Group Gendai, 2010.

Kamanaka, Hitomi, dir. *Voices from Fukushima*. Japan: Bunbun Films, 2015.

Kamanaka, Hitomi, and Katsuya Hirano. "Fukushima, Media, Democracy: The Promise of Documentary Film." *Asia-Pacific Journal-Japan Focus* 16, issue 16, no. 3 (August 15, 2018): 1–28.

Kohso, Sabu. *Radiation and Revolution*. Durham: Duke University Press, 2020.

McLagan, Megan. "Imagining Impact: Documentary Film and the Production of Political Effects." In *Sensible Politics: The Visual Culture of Nongovernmental Activism*, edited by Meg McLagan and Yates McKee, 305–319. New York: Zone Books, 2012.

Mitchell, Jon. *Poisoning the Pacific*. New York: Rowman and Littlefield, 2020.

Mitchell, Timothy. *Carbon Democracy: Political Power in the Age of Oil*. London: Verso Books, 2001.

Pritchard, Sara. "An Envirotechnical Disaster: Negotiating Nature, Technology, and Politics at Fukushima." In *Japan at Nature's Edge*, edited by Ian Jared Miller, Julia Adeney Thomas, and Brett L. Walker, 255–279. Honolulu: University of Hawai'i Press, 2013.

Sakamoto, Noriko. "Local Energy Initiatives in Japan." In *Greening East Asia: The Rise of the Eco-Development State*, edited by Ashley Esarey, Mary Alice Haddad, Joanna L. Lewis, and Stevan Harrell. Seattle: University of Washington Press, 2020.

Ruined and Apocalyptic Landscapes

14

Diverging Imaginations of Planetary Change: The Media Franchise of *Japan Sinks*

Hideaki Fujiki

Originating from Komatsu Sakyō's 1973 science fiction novel, *Japan Sinks* (*Nihon chinbotsu*), a multimedia franchise has developed that has been adapted on a variety of media platforms encompassing print, film, television, animation, manga, radio, and the internet. Up to now (2022), this transmedial imagination of the fiction has enacted a dynamic process whereby some narrative elements, such as the title, setting, and characters' names, are shared across texts. The story and audiovisual configurations, on the other hand, have unfolded across them in divergent ways.

In this deployment of the franchise, one of the most crucial narrative components in the original novel that has been inherited by its subsequent adaptations and remakes with remarkable variation is diastrophism, the faulting and folding of the earth's crust, which could result in a mega-earthquake that endangers the whole Japanese archipelago. Komatsu's *Japan Sinks* articulated this ecological imagination of the geological force amid the historical context of the 1960s and early 1970s, during which a number of environmental issues came to the fore: a series of environmental pollution incidents in Japan (or *kōgai*, including Minamata disease), the publication of *The Limits of Growth* (a 1972 report by the Club of Rome predicting the inhabitability of the earth due to the continuing growth in population, industrialization, resource consumption, and pollution), and the rising global environmental movement.

How, then, has the ecological imagination unfolded through the subsequent media franchise? The three filmic variants—the 1973 film (dir. Moritani Shirō), the 2006 film (dir. Higuchi Shinji), and the 2020 animated film (dir. Yuasa Masaaki)—constitute vital parts of the diverging imagination of planetary change in the ever-growing *Japan Sinks* franchise. This chapter thus aims to disclose the imaginative vision of these three films regarding the diastrophism that endangers the entire Japanese archipelago, a fundamental narrative setting that originated in Komatsu's novel.

Like Komatsu's novel, all three works largely portray geological changes to the earth in a human and national framework. As their title succinctly indicates, they each, unsurprisingly, tell a national tale. Nevertheless, the three films are striking in their depiction of ecological change as a disaster to humans and the nation. After all, following Komatsu's original novel, they all represent the diastrophism as a more-than-human phenomenon or the other of humans. This depiction counters humanity's role in the history of modernity as having mastered many aspects of the planet by means of technology, from energy infrastructure to land development. At the same time, the three films depart from the original novel, and each offers a distinctive vision of planetary dynamics. I argue that through their narrative, audiovisual, and affective configurations, the three films respectively represent the planetary change as a tragic fate of the Japanese nation; as a crisis or even an enemy for it to overcome; and as a material condition for people and, by extension, the nation to survive. These ultimately lead to unique narrative conclusions to this national tale: a faint hope to revive Japan as a de-territorialized imagined community in the future, a dramatic preservation of existing Japan, and a flamboyant reconstruction of Japan as a techno-utopia. Made in different periods and constituting vital nodal points of the ever-growing *Japan Sinks* franchise, the three films provide a range of outstanding ecological imaginary visions in their representation of planetary change as a disaster to humans and the nation.

Planetary Change as a Fate: *Japan Sinks* (1973)

The 1973 version of *Japan Sinks* by and large represents the diastrophism and its resulting subduction of the nation as an act of fate. This is narrativized as a tale in which the nation loses its geological foundation—namely, the Japanese archipelago—thereby forcing the surviving population to immigrate to foreign countries. The loss of the land is depicted as a force that is absolutely impossible for humans or the nation to stop. And yet the film does not make the Japanese nation disappear completely. Rather, it intimates that while the nation is geographically de-territorialized, it can persist as a community shared in the imagination of the population and their offspring who will survive as a diaspora across various foreign countries all over the world.

A central charm of this overall narrative is sustained by what I call the "plot of a tragic chronicle." That is to say, the plot appears to show, chronologically and somewhat dramatically, a process in which the Japanese struggle not with the consequence of their prior actions but with their *fate*: the sinking of the Japanese archipelago. This process hinges on three key narrative tropes in particular: science, life, and politics. In the plot, science is not simply defined by intellect but tied up with mystery, suspense, and affect. It proceeds, in the main, in the following order: (1) the early scenes create mystery by showing characters wondering about the disquieting geological phenomenon and the behavior of animals (particularly that of swallows); (2) the government decides to take the extreme measure of forcing the population to migrate to other countries under scientific conditions that remain uncertain; (3) the scientist Tadokoro's hypothesis about the sinking of Japan is leaked by newspapers and television; (4) having performed a scientific simulation, scientists and government officials agree that the sinking of Japan is an inescapable fact. This shifts the narrative's main concern from mystery to suspense, centered around whether the population can successfully evacuate from Japanese land; (5) the information about the sinking is disseminated as definitive fact both inside and outside Japan via the media; and (6) the ending sequence unfolds around the point of whether the main characters will remain on Japanese land or migrate to foreign countries.

As this outline indicates, scientific doubt and certainty play a role in driving the mystery (number one above) and suspense (number four above). Yet, equally important, this science narrative is associated not only with objectivity and accuracy (which are represented by the information scientist, Nakada, and Professor Takeuchi, who was a real professor in geophysics at the University of Tokyo at that time) but also with the uncertainty and affect represented by Tadokoro. Indeed, Tadokoro repeatedly says, "I am not sure," and, "What is important for scientists is intuition (*kan*)." In a scene toward the end, he even explains that he loves Japan and will remain there so that his life will end with the sinking of the land, implying he is a nationalized affective body.

Technology, or the products of science, are also significant to the plot of the 1973 film, though they are portrayed as things that do not generally work. Technology is, fundamentally, part of the infrastructure of Japan that is destroyed. Though some narratively important technological devices, such as the state-of-the-art submarines, *Wadatsumi* and *Kermadic*, are effective in detecting unusual happenings on the deep-sea floor, they are powerless to solve the geological problem. Likewise, mass media technologies—specifically newspapers, radio, photography, and television—only function as one-way communication tools that convey information to the public. Nor do other means of communication, like the telephone, help characters resist geological forces. Almost as soon as Onodera—a submarine operator and one of the protagonists—has answered a call from his fiancée, Reiko, who is phoning from a public booth in a remote area, the call is disconnected by the earthquake. In this way, technology and media in the 1973 film have narrative significance insofar as they are largely dysfunctional, or at least less supportive of humans.

The narrative's nature, as that of a tragic chronicle, is reinforced first by human science and technology, which do not work, and second by human life itself, as it is epitomized by Onodera. To be sure, the film portrays him throughout, albeit loosely, as a character in a *bildungsroman*: despite his mental instability, he grows in maturity so that he eventually learns to value affection and connection. However, it does not provide him with a happy ending or any kind of reward: the last scene shows Onodera and Reiko on separate trains or separate cars of the same train—the narrative setting of which is ambiguous—running across vast plains beyond Japan, and their romantic love is never fulfilled. Moreover, the last sequence can also be viewed as implying that the younger characters, like Onodera and Reiko, embody *new Japan* as a de-territorialized imagined community. The elderly Watari and Tadokoro are, by contrast, older, and they embody *old Japan*. They will remain in Japan as it sinks. Yet it is uncertain whether young Japanese migrants like Onodera, Reiko, and their children will realize such an overseas community in a future; hence, the film comes to no clear conclusion. Since there is no clearly positive dramatic outcome, the protagonist's ambiguous narrative treatment may indeed be described as a tragic chronicle of his life course.

If Onodera and Reiko, as representatives of ordinary Japanese people's lives, heighten the sense of a lurking tragic fate, Prime Minister Yamamoto's representation of government politics has a similar effect. Yet as his voice-over suggests, his politics and personal perspective are not very far apart. Certainly, whereas Onodera's voice-over communicates his internal struggles over his abovementioned personal concerns, Yamamoto's tends to function as that of a disembodied narrator who communicates his thinking about "the fate of Japan" and "the protection of the nation." But the film uses voice-over only for these two characters, suggesting that they are equally privileged in being allowed to convey their interiority. In this regard, Yamamoto embodies the collective standpoint of the nation, which is at once objective and subjective, and thus his perspective facilitates the audience's sympathy with the nation.

As a political entity, Yamamoto creates significant drama in the chronicle of events. The plot often has him facing difficult situations in which he must make decisions for the nation-state. He tends to choose what will best serve the people rather than the interests of power. For example, he orders government officials to open the gate of the Imperial Palace to admit those who have flocked to it to escape the devastating earthquake. He is also the lead proponent of the measure compelling Japanese immigration to foreign countries, even though his advisor, the elderly Watari, tells him that "doing nothing" is an optional measure the government can take. Moreover, in contrast with the elderly Watari, who can be seen as the incarnation of an older type of Japanese government power, or *genrō*, who will die as the Japanese landmass collapses, Yamamoto will leave the territory together with Watari's niece, a young woman named Hanae, whom Watari urges to have a baby with a man from Japan or from anywhere else in the future. This suggests that Yamamoto has the potential to be of political service to a future Japan that persists in the personal lives of the Japanese.

Most importantly, Yamamoto's nationalist politics is a crucial characteristic of the tragic chronicle. The plot is not concerned with whether the Japanese government, represented by Yamamoto, attempts to stop the land from sinking. Rather, it highlights a process in which they accept the geological force as absolute fate and make efforts to negotiate with foreign countries so that a maximum number of Japanese—or the nation's— people survive, even if they do so in the form of a diaspora. Indeed, by the midpoint of the plot, which corresponds to a scene in which Special Envoy Nozaki asks the Australian prime minister to accept millions of Japanese immigrants to Australia in exchange for some Japanese national treasures of Buddhist statues, science and technology have turned out to be useless in preventing the destruction of the land. Moreover, the film doesn't portray the annihilation of the territory as the complete termination of the nation-state. Rather, it suggests both the end of old Japan and the possible survival of a newer Japan as a de-territorialized nation.

As such, the plot of the tragic chronicle traces the fate of the nation, particularly in terms of science, life, and politics. However, it should also be noted that the plot is, to an extent, accompanied by catastrophic spectacle, a chief attraction of this kind of science fiction disaster genre. As I mentioned above, the film contains moderate suspense around whether people can be safely evacuated from the sinking land. The spectacle, I would argue, is more integrated with the chronicle of the nation's fate than with this suspense. For one thing, the earthquake, which strikes the whole nation, represents the total destruction of old Japan, including the nation's attachment to the territory and to the illusion that high economic growth brings happiness. The film as a whole portrays the annihilation of the nation's entire geological foundation, from metropolitan areas to provincial and mountainous ones. It also shows the extensive demolition of anthropogenic civilization and cultural icons from its infrastructure (factories, roads, buildings, telephone booths, etc.) to symbolic national landmarks like Mt. Fuji and the Tokyo Tower, and even to everyday life itself. This destruction takes a variety of forms such as collapses, explosions, fires, magma eruptions, ruptures, tsunamis, landslides, and fault lines. The film positions humans as mere vulnerable beings in the face of a devastating geological force. In the overarching plot, as the earthquake occurs off the Pacific coast and then radiates from the central Kantō region and metropolitan areas toward the periphery of the archipelago (as far as Hokkaido, Kyushu, and Okinawa), more and more people have no other choice but to evacuate to lands overseas rather than stay and wrest with the force.

And yet, these spectacles also seem to create what could be described as an aesthetic of destruction or disaster, which allows the spectator pleasure in observing awesome destruction from a privileged safe position. Indeed, the spectacles of a series of demolitions, filmed from high angles, as well as the progress of destruction from off the Pacific coast to metropolitan areas in 1973's *Japan Sinks*, echo those in Honda Ishirō's films, including *Godzilla*. Yet whereas the spectacle in *Godzilla* relates to suspense around whether the characters can remove the source of danger, that of 1973's *Japan Sinks* has little direct connection with suspense. In short, while its series of disasters are foregrounded as sensorily stimulating attractions for the spectator, they are shown as part of the nation's fate rather than a driving factor for drama.

As such, 1973's *Japan Sinks* somewhat dramatically chronicles the nation's fate, its struggle with disaster in the face of uncontrollable planetary change, and its faint hope of constructing a future de-territorialized nation overseas imagined by Japanese diaspora and their offspring.

Planetary Change as Crisis: *Japan Sinks* (2006)

The 2006 *Japan Sinks,* on the other hand, represents the diastrophism less as fate than as a crisis that potentially endangers the Japanese nation. It does so by dramatizing the nation's confrontation with the geological force as if it were a crisis to be fought, or even a war against an enemy, with the eventual conquest resulting in the retention of a territory-based nation-state. Moreover, the nation's overcoming of the crisis not only strengthens its sense of national identity but also purifies the community, as utilitarian characters who see rescuing a maximum number of the population as a worthless effort are eventually excluded.

These overall characteristics are partly sustained by a problem-solution plot that drives suspense. Different sources of suspense are set up in both halves of the plot. Unlike the 1973 film, in which the first half centers around the mystery of something unusual happening to the earth, the 2006 film establishes the characters' consensus about the sinking of Japan in an early scene, in which a scientist from the American Geodetic Society presents a data visualization that makes him confident that the Japanese archipelago will sink within a few decades. Shortly after this scene, the scientist Tadokoro discovers through his own simulation that the nationwide disaster will occur much earlier—that is, within a year. This creates suspense concerning whether the Japanese can be successfully evacuated within the "true" time limit, that calculated by Tadokoro, which has not been announced publicly. In two subsequent scenes, however, the suspense shifts to another question: Will the nation successfully prevent Japan from sinking? In one such scene, Tadokoro proposes a challenging method of stemming the geological force to the minister of crisis management, Takamori (who is also Tadokoro's former wife); in another scene, Takamori realizes that Japanese migration to foreign countries is almost impossible following television news items on anti-Japanese movements overseas and official reports on the US government's decision to release Japanese government bonds.

Importantly, this shift of concern is morally rationalized in several ongoing subplots. In one subplot, Takamori expresses her preferred option to protect the whole nation and its territory rather than to prioritize the survival of certain groups of people. This leads, in turn, to her decision to try to overcome the geological force rather than to evacuate the people from the devastated land. This is in opposition to her rival politician's (Nozaki's) idea that the government should give some people's lives precedence over those of others. In an earlier scene, her idea is also articulated by Prime Minister Yamamoto, who tells Takamori that the option of "doing nothing [about the potential disaster] makes the most sense to me" vis-à-vis the moral debate about whose lives should be preserved first. This point is in sharp contrast with the one in the 1973 film, in which the elderly Watari says that this option ("doing nothing") is the least worth serious consideration.

In another subplot, the 2006 film characterizes the rivalry between Takamori and Nozaki (who becomes acting prime minister after the previous one is lost) as analogous to the binary opposition of spiritualism and utilitarianism. Nozaki cynically presents the data visualization so as to discourage the government from taking measures to limit Japanese deaths, and he works harder to protect the Buddhist statues considered national treasures than on rescuing people. Again, the motif of the Buddhist statue here is given a remarkably different meaning from that in the 1973 film, in which it is a tool used by the Japanese government to negotiate with their Australian counterparts to protect Japanese people's lives. Takamori's passionate actions are positioned as a counter to Nozaki's attitudes.

The rationale to try and stop the geological force is further reinforced by the portrayal of certain characters as moral and passionate, a narrative strategy that does not feature strongly in the 1973 film. An obvious example is the aforementioned rivalry between Takamori and Nozaki. The 2006 version also features Reiko, a member of the Fire Rescue Task Force (a.k.a. Hyper Rescue), and her dedication to rescuing children, which is also absent from the 1973 version. Equally important is the depiction of death caused by the disaster. The stricken characters are all good—in moral terms—which is conveyed both overtly and in subtler ways. Moreover, in a chain that links families, friends, and romantic couples to the nation and its territory, this affective connection between the dead and the living bolsters the rationale of those intent on taking on the geological force as an enemy.

And yet, the audience may wonder if it is wiser for the characters to evacuate from Japan rather than to dedicate themselves to rescuing the whole nation. Onodera plays a key role in solving this contradiction in the narrative in that he shows how three plots—love story, *bildungsroman*, and problem-solving— intersect. The romantic plot takes a much more central position in the 2006 film than it does in the 1973 version. This is reflected in its advertising, which foregrounded its two young stars: Kusanagi Tsuyoshi, a member of the Japanese idol group SMAP, and Shibazaki Kō, whose celebrated acting made her famous in the early 2000s. Though the 1973 film featured Fujioka Hiroshi, a popular actor of the superhero television drama *Kamen rider*, and Ishida Ayumi, a popular singer of a big hit song ("Blue Light Yokohama"), most of its advertising did not focus on their images; instead, the destruction takes center stage and the human characters are consigned to the edges of the poster.

Indeed, the opening scene of the 2006 version begins with an encounter between Kusanagi's character, Onodera, and Shibazaki's Reiko, a scene which strikingly differs from the opening scene of the 1973 version. The latter begins with the geological history of the earth. In the 2006 version, from the opening scene on, the romantic plot develops hand in hand with Onodera's mental growth from an "immature" individualistic personality to a "mature" patriotic one, a *bildungsroman* reminiscent of wartime Japanese propaganda films. The death of Onodera's close friend Yūki leads to the climatic sequence, which presents Onodera's transformation into a full-fledged "soldier" by showing his decision to go on a mission of self-sacrifice—like a *kamikaze*—to protect the Japanese land and nation instead of evacuating to a foreign country for his own sake. Importantly, Onodera's successful mission of self-sacrifice is completely opposed to the conclusion of the 1973 version, which rejects sacrificing youth in order to protect territory.

Furthermore, a reallocation of gender roles heightens the narrative's emphasis on the mission to salvage Japanese territory from the geological force. On the surface, the 2006 *Japan Sinks* appears highly conscious of gender balance: whereas the 1973 version is dominated by male characters and gives only secondary roles— such as the femme fatale-type and the housewife—to two female characters, Reiko and the prime minister's wife, who barely appear, the new version has many more female characters and gives Takamori and Reiko socially respected occupations previously held overwhelmingly by men. Yet from different standpoints, both Takamori and Reiko eventually take more conventional home-front roles in supporting the male-dominated mission to rescue the nation. Despite her status as a member of Hyper Rescue, Reiko ultimately sends her man off to the battlefield in the same way as the wives and mothers of wartime films. While Reiko embodies the standpoint of an ordinary person, Takamori performs the aforementioned spiritualism and nationalism from a government standpoint when expressing her passionate belief in rescuing the people and the nation and paying homage to the men who have dedicated themselves to the mission.

Science and technology further reinforce, in vital ways, the affective aspects of the mission to rescue the nation from the geological force. For instance, in contrast with the submarine as a state-of-the-art technology in the original novel and the 1973 film, the *old* type of submarine—named *Wadatsumi 2000*—that Onodera uses for the deadly mission strikingly epitomizes Japanese spiritualism, as it appears to be a technological yet lower-performance prosthesis that evokes the wartime Japanese "zero" fighter aircrafts (*zero sen*) used by the *kamikaze* suicide corps.

The spectacle of the geological force furthermore enhances the nation's confrontation with the planetary change. In the first place, utilizing far more advanced audiovisual technology, such as CGI, Dolby, and surround sound, the 2006 *Japan Sinks* highlights the earth's ferocity as the nation's formidable enemy by means of a more powerful and realistic spectacle than the 1973 version. It does so by producing from multiple angles the dynamic movements of diverse forms of water and land—such as tsunami, magma, and landslides—as well as the collapse of various human-made infrastructure and symbols—buildings, houses, towers, and Mt. Fuji (as a symbol of Japan)

It is furthermore interesting that, whereas in the 1973 version, the geological force attacks the Japanese archipelago in a centrifugal direction from the Kantō region (including Tokyo) to provincial and mountainous regions, in the 2006 version, it advances in a centripetal direction—that is, from relatively peripheral areas such as Kyushu and Hokkaido to urban areas such as Osaka, Kyoto, Nagoya, and Tokyo. This evokes a war metaphor—that is to say, a known traditional Japanese maneuver—to "bury the moat" (*sotobori o umeru*)—which means that a military force (the geological force in this case) tries to get rid of obstacles from the periphery first before moving toward the center in order to weaken the opposition's (in this case, Japanese) power. In effect, the geological force is depicted as the nation's wartime enemy.

In short, 2006's *Japan Sinks* dramatizes the Japanese nation's, and, by extension, humans' confrontation with planetary change and their eventual overcoming of it, so that the territory-based nation is maintained and strengthened. At the same time, it shows the nation sustained by the affective connection between "good" characters and nationalized land, and their purification through the exclusion of utilitarianism.

Planetary Change as a Condition for Survival: The Animated *Japan Sinks* (2020)

The theatrical anime film of *Japan Sinks* represents the diastrophism as a material condition for the people's—and by extension, the nation's—survival. In this anime, the geological force that sinks the national land is not taken to be the enemy of either humans or the nation. Rather, it is simply the uncontrollable condition for their survival. But in the end, the force is overcome (in the sense that Japan is recovered as a nation with only minimal land) by means of human technology and, more specifically, the digital archive of memories of the past nation. In this narrative, survival, I argue, is not simply there to produce thrills but also to raise questions about the contingent nature of collective identity and the signification of death. This process of survival leads to the film's conclusion, in which a recovered Japan is flamboyantly presented as a techno-utopia with a new Japanese identity based—in moral terms—on contingent human relationships and diversity.

One of the key characteristics of the 2020 anime is that its plot is motivated not by protecting Japanese territory from the geological force but by surviving it. Thus, neither particular places nor the nation's land are objects of characters' affection but conditions for their survival. The opening scene of the 2020 anime, for instance, begins by showing members of a family located in different places when the earthquake strikes: a teenage girl, Ayumu, is at an athletic field; her younger brother, Gō, is at home; their mother is on an airplane; and their father is on the construction site of the planned Olympic stadium. Although they all escape disaster and reunite at a historic temple site, once the father, who is a construction worker, colorfully illuminates this place, it appears to be more of an artificial meeting point than a firm physical foundation or a historically rooted piece of land. Indeed, they quickly leave the site and never subsequently find another stable place until the ending sequence.

While the geological force and land itself have little more meaning than that they form conditions for the characters' survival, the survival plot has several important functions and meanings. In the first place, it operates as a kind of game that solicits the spectator's excitement regarding how the protagonists might survive their journeys. As in a game, the plot presents characters with moments of choice throughout. A few examples, among many, include whether they should go west or east, and whether they should believe Onodera's message or not.

The survival plot also presents a series of opportunities for the family to encounter people with a variety of social positions and identities, and this foregrounds the contingent nature of human relationships. During their journey, the group acquires Nanami, Koga, Kite (a YouTuber), Hikida (the aged shopkeeper of a convenience store), Daniel (a Yugoslavian hitchhiker), Onodera, and a fisherman, although several die or leave the group as time goes on. Their relationships are mostly fortuitous and temporary rather than essential and permanent. Nor does the survival plot involve romantic love. It is the contingent encounter that constitutes the group's fluidity throughout the survival plot, regardless of whether their relationships are based on blood ties, official marriage, or any other recognized bond.

Vitally, the survival plot illuminates death as an issue. Death in the anime sometimes occurs by accident or suddenly (such as the father being killed by an unexploded bomb and Nanami being poisoned by natural gas), but it is sometimes motivated by characters' thoughts and actions (in the cases of the mother and Koga). The geological force is usually the direct or indirect cause of death, though not always. But characters do not view the disaster through hostile eyes or as an enemy. In the 2020 anime, what is important are the meanings of death per se, which are more greatly influenced by the game the characters play to survive than they are by the nation's sinking. For instance, Ayumu's losses—of family members and friends—function, at certain moments of the survival plot, to highlight her affection for them and, more vitally, to activate her memories of them, which are repeatedly presented in flashback until they culminate in the last sequence.

All these significant characteristics of the survival plot—contingent relationships, technology, and death—converge in the last sequence, which reveals the techno-utopia that enables Japan to be reconstructed as a virtual nation with no physical foundation (but ultimately with minimal land). In the first place, the recovery of the nation is realized by digital media technologies, which include photography, video, and digital data and archives, all of which function as tools for recovering and sharing memories. Media technologies, on the other hand, serve to revive community or the Japanese nation toward the last scene of the narrative by linking three levels of memory: individual, familial, and national. Hence, Onodera and Tadokoro are celebrated as the inventors of the digital technology that will preserve the nation's memory rather than heroes who have saved the nation's land. Accompanying the visual presentation of technology, Ayumu's voice-over is a vitally important mediator of the different levels of the nation's recovery. From the opening of the penultimate sequence, Ayumu relates, in voice-over, her memories of her past experiences with her family without any visual references to technology, but in the final sequence, the specific references in her voice-over and the visual images are synchronized. Both technology and the memories she voices contribute to the recovery of the nation, overcoming both the spatial and temporal gaps caused by the sinking of the land and the irreversible fact of the deaths of some of the characters.

And yet, while Ayumu's voice-over emphasizes the recovery of "Japan," the concept of what is assumed to be the nation in this anime significantly differs from the 2006 film. For one thing, the entire narrative has a highly reflexive consciousness of the issues of nation and ethnicity. As already noted, it shows people from a variety of ethnic and cultural backgrounds gravitating toward the traveling family. Disability is also highlighted in the last scene, when Ayumu, who loses a leg in the course of survival, appears on the athletic field with an artificial one. In addition, Japanese identity itself is questioned rather than taken for granted in certain episodes, such as those involving the mother from the Philippines, Gō, who often speaks English, or the debate in which Gō, Koga, and Ayumu each express their opinion of Japaneseness through rap music. Moreover, in keeping with the survival plot, Ayumu's voice-over in the last scene stresses that the family and the nation have been built on contingent encounters rather than being essentially rooted in the land. After all, the nation has been recovered as a techno-utopia, not only because spatial and temporal losses are magically overcome by means of technology but also because it is presented as a community free of conflict despite its significant diversity.

Finally, it should not be overlooked that this anime mobilizes spectacle more in the service of revealing the techno-utopia than in conveying disaster. The geological force is largely narrativized as an accidental condition in which the survival game is played, and it follows the main characters' journey as they move from Tokyo to mountainous areas. On the other hand, the ending sequence presents a dazzling montage combining fragmented images of the family's memories, the ruined old city under the sea and the newly constructed island city, and traditional and modern Japanese cultural icons (such as a temple, cherry blossoms, cosplay, Mt. Fuji, and so on), constantly accompanied by light, rhythmic electronic music.

The 1973, 2006, and 2020 versions of *Japan Sinks* are part and parcel of a media franchise that has developed from the original 1973 novel in diverging ways. On the one hand, following Komatsu's 1973 original novel, they all function as an ecological imagination of the planet in the sense that the diastrophism is represented as a more-than-human phenomenon, or the other of humans. On the other hand, the three films have provided astonishingly varied imaginative visions of planetary change: as a fate for the nation to accept, as a crisis for it to overcome, and as a condition for it to survive. In this genealogy, while preserving a national framework, the 2020 animated film, albeit in a utopian way, distinctively shows technology and media not as the means for mastering the planet but for harmoniously inhabiting it. In any case, the 1973, 2006, and 2020 *Japan Sinks* films, which themselves have constituted vital parts of the franchise's media ecology, have demonstrated fascinating variations of an imagined eco-disaster.

Filmography

Japan Sinks (a.k.a. *Tidal Wave, Submersion of Japan, Nihon chinbotsu, Nippon chinbotsu*), 1973, directed by Moritani Shirō, produced by Tohō eiga and Tohō eizō, and distributed by Tohō.

Japan Sinks (a.k.a. *Thinking of Japan, Nihon chinbotsu, Nippon chinbotsu*), 2006, directed by Higuchi Shinji, produced by Eiga "Nihon chinbotsu" seisaku iinkai, and distributed by Tohō.

Japan Sinks 2020: Cinema edition (*Nihon chinbotsu 2020 Gekijō henshūban: Shizumanu kibō*), 2020, directed by Yuasa Masayuki, produced by "JAPAN SINKS: 2020" Project Partners, and distributed by Avex Pictures Inc.

15

Technology, Urban Sprawl, and the Apocalyptic Imagination in Hiroyuki Seshita's *BLAME!* (2017)

Amrita S. Iyer

"All media contain messages about the environment."[1] These messages have the potential to "propagate beliefs about the relationship between humans and the living systems that sustain them."[2] What is debatable is whether these messages have more positive or negative consequences, specifically in their representation of eco-disasters. Positive results might include the development of a more eco-conscious society that is eager to build on sustainability to mitigate and manage disasters. Negative consequences might be the cultivation of "psychic numbing"[3]— that is, a feeling of indifference due to the constant bombardment of similar messages regarding eco-crises, or a misrepresentation of the state of things.[4] A related issue is that media representations are often part of commercialization, which in turn results in an increased ecological footprint, despite the messages they might present.[5] However, if media propagates beliefs, it also has the potential to shift those beliefs by influencing the popular imagination. This chapter arises from a very general question: What does the representation of eco-disasters in media, specifically animated films, contribute to alternative modes of thinking about them?

For one, cinematic representations of disasters use the audience's ability to stretch their imaginations and comprehend worlds where life as we know it is over.

For the purpose of this chapter, Hiroyuki Seshita's anime film *BLAME!* (2017), based on the manga series of the same name by Tsutomu Nihei, imagines a reality where humans have become nearly extinct as a result of urban sprawl caused by lively sentient machines.[6] Japanese cinema has a long history of representing lively nonhuman entities, with one of the most notable examples being Ishirō Honda's *Gojira* (1954), in which a "prehistoric creature reanimated and irradiated by American nuclear bomb testing . . . in turn irradiates and otherwise lays waste to Tokyo until 'destroyed.'"[7] Due to the multiple social, political, historical, and environmental implications of the creature, *Gojira* is not only a spectacular "monster-film," but it also arguably illustrates the eco-disastrous consequences of nuclear weapons.

In this chapter, I consider the eco-disaster caused by the machine-constructed city in *BLAME!* as an allegory of urban sprawl in real life, with the notable difference that the film's sprawl is machine-generated, while in real life, sprawl is an anthropocentric manifestation. My argument has two parts. First, I contend that the film's move to have sentient machines cause the sprawl exemplifies an inversion of anthropocentrism, as the humans become passive subjects adversely affected by the sprawl with little control over their dire circumstances while the technological forces thrive and modify the environment according to their designs. Outside of the allegory, the film's machine world potentially visually signifies the transformative power of technology that affects both human and nonhuman worlds in far-reaching ways. Second, I argue that despite the seemingly contentious relationship between humans and technology, the film also posits that humans and technology are closely interconnected at various levels, which might allow us to perceive them as complementary and collaborative forces in constructing possible futures. From this, we understand that the machine world in *BLAME!* not only signifies a physically transformed landscape but also human-technology interconnections on deeper and more intimate levels, which need to be critically interrogated.

At this juncture, it must be noted that for cinematic representations of eco-disasters to lead to serious discussions, they must not be treated as mere spectacles or narratives but as *representations* that can lead to reflections and critique. One of the ways Japanese cinema achieves this process of reflection through representation is through the apocalyptic mode. In what follows, I examine how the apocalyptic mode converges with the "anime" form to bring forth critical reflections.[8]

While the most common association with the term "apocalypse" is the "end of the world," the original meaning can actually be traced to "revelation" or "uncovering."[9] For noted anime critic Susan Napier, it is this uncovering of the secret and reason behind the apocalypse in films that fuels the narrative tension.[10] In *Anime: From Akira to Princess Mononoke*, Napier points out that

Japanese anime holds a lot of sway through displaying apocalyptic images. The apocalyptic mode is not just an aesthetic choice; instead, it is "deeply ingrained within the contemporary Japanese national identity."[11] Napier attributes this to the haunting memory of the atomic bombs as well as the recession that signified the end of Japan's economic boom. Furthermore, she cites "various geographical and climactic factors peculiar to the Japanese archipelago"—such as earthquakes, volcanic eruptions, and typhoons—that support the prevalence of the apocalyptic mode.[12] These have collectively contributed to the creation of a sensibility that indicates an awareness of the precarity of human life.

While the precarity of human existence is due to several factors, one of the major themes in apocalyptic anime is "human transgression, most often the misuse of technology."[13] The human misuse of technology can disrupt and destabilize natural cycles, which can have cascading effects and result in irrevocable changes. However, what if the situation were reversed and humans were at the mercy of lively and sentient technology? This alternative situation is explored in *BLAME!* By foregrounding a world that is dominated by sentient machines, the film refuses to let the environment be treated as a passive backdrop. This is because the observable landscape is animated by machines that are constantly rebuilding and expanding the city for *no apparent purpose*, as established early in the film when the humans come across "Builder" machines. The constantly changing city becomes unfamiliar to the humans, thereby increasing their difficulty of traversing it. Furthermore, the city also becomes an active threat to the humans as the "Exterminator" machines try to kill them. Due to the indirect threat of the changing city and the direct threat the Exterminators pose to humans, the setting becomes the site of critical reflection on the animateness of technologies. In this regard, sentient technology is presented as environmentally harmful in the film, as it has completely taken over the biosphere and destroyed most organic lifeforms (figure 15.1). More significantly, these shots of the city also show the absence of other naturally occurring forces like sunlight, water bodies, and land. Not only does this make the film's environment even more cognitively estranging, but it also highlights the near-complete dependence of the humans on machines in this world, as the possibility of sourcing food and water is through the machines alone.

Such animated technologies in *BLAME!* indicate the wider role of animation as an aesthetic form. Animation is a way "through which industrial societies have reflected on the animatedness of the nonhuman, the inanimate, and the object. In some cases, animation has given rise to vivid portrayals of a natural world shaped by perceptions, agencies, and intentions—of animals, plants, and even features of the landscape—some of which resemble those of humans, and some of which remain resolutely alien."[14]

Figure 15.1. A panoramic shot of the city that illustrates the expanse of the machine-landscape and shows the absence of any organic growth. Hiroyuki Seshita, 2017, Tsutomu Nihei, KODANSHA/BLAME! Production Committee.

To understand what the alien world of *BLAME!* conveys through the liveliness of sentient technology, it is important to first review the plot. The film opens with a postapocalyptic scenario in which a small community of humans are survivors of a past "contagion," which resulted in humans losing control over the technologies that made up their city.[15] Based on their roles, the systems are referred to by different names, such as the Builders, the Safeguard, the Exterminators, and the Authority.[16] At some point, due to an unknown cause, the systems began to perceive the humans as "illegal residents" and hunted them. The humans sought shelter in an enclave that is the only place the machines cannot access.

The plot moves into action when a character named Killy appears, claiming to be a human traveler. Killy states that his purpose is to find humans with something called the "Net Terminal Gene," which is a genetic component that would allow humans to reprogram the technologies. Killy's search leads him and others from the community to a scientist named Cibo, who has kept herself artificially alive using technologies for centuries. Cibo then brings up the idea of creating a machine that would synthetically simulate the function of the Net Terminal Gene. The attempt fails when the Safeguard infiltrates the enclave and attacks the community. Despite the losses, Cibo is able to get the location of another enclave that is not actively monitored by the Safeguard. The film ends with the human community thriving in this second enclave while Killy continues his search for humans with the Net Terminal Gene.

This summary shows that *BLAME!* depicts a technologized postapocalyptic scenario. I consider "postapocalyptic" to mean a spatial and temporal setting that not only estranges us from but also reveals something about our present reality. One of the most estranging aspects of the fictional world in the film is its absence of organic life apart from humans. Through several visual frames, the setting of the film is revealed to be a sprawling, machine-dominated, and apparently purposeless city. This nonfunctional city becomes a difficult terrain for humans to traverse. Furthermore, the absence of other organic life and the presence of hostile machines create specific ecological relations that are not conducive for humans. By "ecological relations," I mean "the totality or pattern of relations between organisms and their environment."[17]

In what follows, I uncover the conceptual implications of these new and unfamiliar ecological relations (apropos to the definition of apocalypse cited earlier) in *BLAME!* that have already led to the extinction of nonhuman organic life and brought humans to the brink of extinction. Notably, even though the fictional world is estranging for the audience of the film, in many ways, the technologized and growing city parallels the urban sprawl of the real world. In the manga, this fictional techno-controlled sprawl is the "consequence of a governmental urban development programme gone awry."[18] While the spatial and temporal ambiguity of the film's setting allows for its allegorical association with any culturally specific urban sprawl, it arguably has specific resonance with sprawl (*supurōru*) in Japan, mainly because the term has a slightly different connotation in the Japanese context. Historically, urban sprawl was a consequence of the Japanese *government's* effort to rapidly redevelop the country between 1955 and the early 1960s, which caused environmental destruction and adversely affected public health due to an increase in pollution.[19] This haphazard and unregulated nature of government-sponsored development is mirrored in *BLAME!*, albeit in an exaggerated way. This parallel creates a worrying reflection that the eco-disastrous situation in *BLAME!* is a possible future for humanity unless measures are taken. Moreover, the eco-disaster is relatively more of a threat in the Japanese context, since sprawl there might potentially spread to zones that are at increased risk of other prevalent disasters such as landslides and tsunamis, thereby creating a cascading effect.[20] While the situation at present is not as dire as the ones presented in *BLAME!*, the film does serve as a warning against unsustainable urban expansion.

In actual practice, urban sprawl is the result of human actions, which encroach on nonhuman habitats, often with devastating effects on the organic life that thrives in them. For instance, globally, nearly four hundred cities are expected to sprawl into the habitats of endangered species by 2030, further endangering their habitats and continuity.[21] What *BLAME!* offers is an inversion of the position of power that humans command in the real world. In the film, it is the humans who are fearful and isolated, who face the lack of food availability and the constant threat to their lives and habitat, finally culminating in a forced migration to find another habitat. The threat to humans is comparable to the threat to the lives and habitats of nonhuman organisms that are caused by rapid and unsustainable human-driven urban expansion in present times. While at first glance this may seem like a way to blame technology and to build sympathy for the nearly extinct humans, the situation has deeper critical implications. The film periodically reiterates the "legend" of how *humans* were once in control of the city and the machines, indicating that the destructive out-of-control technologies are possibly a consequence of past human actions. Furthermore, the transposition of humans into the position of animals works at an empathetic level, as the human characters express bewilderment at their situation. Their lack of understanding of the reason behind the machines' constant attacks on them and their habitat parallels the bewilderment animals face when their lives and habitats are threatened and destroyed due to human action. In yet another move that undermines anthropocentrism, the film thus becomes a way for humans (both the characters and the audience of the film) to imagine how threatened animals experience the world.

The film further inverts anthropocentrism by presenting the nearly absolute dependency of humans on the machines, since even their food is industrially produced. Here lies the film's second implication: humans are not only surrounded by machines (due to the city) but also constantly mediated by technology (through their consumption of industrially produced food). The technological mediation of humans has ontological implications through the Net Terminal Gene, meaning that humans and technologies are connected genetically at the level of existence itself. Both instances of the technological mediation of human bodies arguably provoke a radical revision of the relations between humans and technology from one of conflict to an understanding that humans and technology are always already deeply and ontologically intertwined and need to be understood as forces that complement each other to envisage sustainable futures.

In the following sections, I first elaborate on the city in *BLAME!* as an allegory of urban sprawl. In the second section, I cite instances from the film that show how the technologized urban sprawl arguably inverts anthropocentrism to the effect of presenting humans as victims of more powerful technological forces. In the third section, I illustrate how this bleak vision is challenged by the presentation of the entwined relationship between humans and technology, the acknowledgement of which paves the way for a more collaborative relationship between humans and technology.

The City as a Parallel of Urban Sprawl

BLAME! opens with this narration: "Nobody knows when the world became this way. One day the contagion suddenly started, and humans lost the power to connect with the city. After that, the city expanded on its own and humans were seen as illegal residents . . . and exterminated."[22] While the film gives no direct explanation about what it means to "connect" with the city, the term has ontological implications. Since the city is arguably coterminous with the machines, "to connect with the city" could mean a relationship of mutual influence and growth between the humans and the machines. Consequently, the loss of this connection indicates a one-sided influence of the machine-dominated city on the living conditions of the humans while the humans have no influence on the city. The disconnect results in the machines' uncontrolled expansion of the city. The city's expansion corresponds to the general definition of urban sprawl as "the rapid expansion of the geographic extent of cities and towns."[23] However, as mentioned earlier, the situation is markedly different, as the city's continued expansion in *BLAME!* is not due to human activities but rather due to sentient technological forces.

Notably, the reason behind the constant expansion remains elusive to humans. As one character comments with reference to a Builder, "It's making more weird stuff."[24] The "weirdness" can be attributed to the fact that the city's expansion seems to have no evident function. While the film's depiction is exaggerated, actual urban sprawl can also lead to reduced functionality. For instance, in the Japanese context, rapid and haphazard development in the 1960s in the urban fringe made future urbanization difficult, resulting in a landscape that led to greater environmental degradation and increased problems of pollution.[25] Through the continuous expansion of the city, the film shows that in actual urban sprawl, the unplanned and unregulated expansion of cities can spiral out of human control as well. The lack of human control over their situation is visually achieved in terms of framing in *BLAME!*, wherein the technologized environment is depicted as expansive and limitless while humans are diminutive figures (figure 15.2). Traditionally, low-angle shots are meant to present the subject as a powerful force; however, in *BLAME!*, the use of such shots has the opposite effect of depicting the helplessness of humans who are surrounded by technology, thereby visually imparting the almost nonexistent control humans have over their environment.

It is notable that certain machines like the Builders do not directly harm the humans. Indirectly, however, their expansion of the city restricts the human habitat to a limited number of areas. Allegorically, this parallels what urban sprawl, in reality, does to nature, in that "to make way for human dwellings and their associated infrastructure, natural land is plowed under, graded, and paved."[26] As mentioned earlier, there is a conspicuous and total absence of flora and fauna, making the landscape in *BLAME!* essentially a wasteland. This is an extreme consequence of urban sprawl, which can cause or hasten the dying out of various organic lifeforms as it adversely affects natural landscapes. For instance, in the context of Japan's urban sprawl, "beaches and coastal areas disappeared beneath landfills for industrial complexes, hills and forests were razed and paddies filled in for new housing."[27] The "disappearance" of natural landscapes and their associated wildlife is literalized in *BLAME!*, allowing the audience to see their futuristic

Figure 15.2. The expansive, technologized environment in BLAME! Hiroyuki
Seshita, 2017, Tsutomu Nihei, KODANSHA/BLAME! Production Committee.

consequences. Additionally, in the film, while nonhuman organic life has gone
extinct, human life also faces near extinction and worsening living conditions.

The near extinction of humans is indicated when a character explains that the
maximum number of people who have lived in the enclave was four hundred and
that the number has dwindled to 150. The head of the community also expresses
a complete lack of knowledge about the possible existence of other human
communities in the city. In the film, traversing the machine-controlled landscape
to find them is also deemed too dangerous due to the threat of the Safeguard.
However, traveling is required, as the community faces imminent starvation and
despairs that "the hunting grounds near here have all dried up and we have to go
out farther."[28] Furthermore, the population is decimated even more in the climactic
moment of the film, in which an advanced Safeguard machine manages to "pose as
a human" and infiltrate and attack the humans in the enclave.

These scenarios indirectly comment on the impact of urban sprawl on
wildlife. The isolation of the human enclave is mirrored in "the fragmentation of
remaining natural areas" in real life, in which habitats may consequently become
"widely separated from one another."[29] The dangerous but required journey to
source food is very similar to situations that compel species to "cross dangerous
human-dominated landscapes to find food or mates."[30] The direct attack on the
human enclave echoes the way in which urban sprawl causes destruction to
wildlife habitats.

While the situation in *BLAME!* is unlike the sudden and explosive nature
of nuclear disasters, earthquakes, or typhoons that have been allegorized in
Japanese anime like *Gojira* and Toshio Yoshitaka's *Japan Sinks: 2020*, respectively,

the disastrous consequences of phenomena like urban sprawl also need to be represented and critiqued before they cause irreparable damage in the real world. In this context, *BLAME!* imagines a *future* in which the irrevocable effects of urban sprawl have led to a hostile environment for organic life-forms, both human and nonhuman.

Inversion of Anthropocentrism

In the film, the cause of the sprawl can be traced to the machines becoming independent of human control due to a contagion that afflicted all of the humans, which, as mentioned earlier, inverts the anthropocentric nature of sprawl in the real world. Between the Authority, the Safeguard, the Exterminators, and the Builders, the entire terrain in the film is mediated and controlled by machines. The machines have strength in numbers as well as bodies that are less prone to damage. Advanced Safeguard machines have seemingly indestructible bodies, given that they fall from great heights and have limbs blown off but still manage to continue performing their functions. This extreme survivalist ability of the machines is not only a theme of apocalyptic anime but also an important aspect of animation as a form. In animation, bodies have an uncanny "seemingly infinite ability to expand, contract, stretch, bulge, flatten, implode, explode, fragment, and yet return to their original shapes."[31] This ability is arguably tied to the anxiety regarding the increasing "subjection of human, animal, and plant bodies to industrial regimes of categorization and control."[32] This anxiety is reflected in *BLAME!* as well because the relatively stronger bodies of the machines are contrasted with the humans' far more fragile bodies, which make them vulnerable.

Apart from physical vulnerability, the humans are also completely dependent on machines for food. Since there is no organic life, the food is industrially sourced at a "factory." This places the humans in a position that is both dependent on some machines (the factory) and hunted by others (the Safeguard). These factors further the inversion of anthropocentrism, meaning that humans are no longer in a position to exploit either natural or technological forces solely for their own benefit. Instead, in this imaginary scenario, humans are at the mercy of sentient machines that have their own inscrutable agenda.

Inversion of Technological Supremacy

The machines are relatively more powerful than humans in this fictional world; however, the film destabilizes the idea of technological supremacy by showing that the machines are also governed by rules and orders. For instance, the Safeguard that infiltrates the enclave cites "Elimination Ordinance 5" to begin "auxiliary elimination."[33] This shows that the machines are still confined by programming in conducting the extermination. While humans presumably originally invented and programmed the machines, it is unclear whether the source of this human-exterminating program was intentional or the result of a coding error or a corrupting virus. According to the limited information provided by the scientist Cibo in the film, the program can be traced to the "contagion" (which could be biological or technological in nature, or both) that affected the Net Terminal Gene and cost the humans their ability to operate the machines. The implication I want to highlight is that both the humans and the machines are governed by forces beyond them, which negates the idea of absolute superiority of the latter.

The negation of the idea of absolute technological control is reinforced when the scientist Cibo makes contact with the Authority and requests that the humans be saved. The Authority replies, "Without an order from someone with the Net Terminal Gene, we, the Authority, cannot take any such action."[34] The implication of the Net Terminal Gene will be discussed in the following section. At this point in the film, we come to understand that neither humans nor the machines have any form of omnipotent control, although the machines do have an advantage over the humans in terms of strength and numbers. Despite this advantage, Killy's search for humans with the Net Terminal Gene, and Cibo's proposal that a synthetic version of the gene could be made to regain control, suggest that this advantage could shift in favor of humans. Though both Killy and Cibo are unsuccessful in the film's narrative, the end of the film suggests that Killy continues his search for it. The Net Terminal Gene is not only a chief factor that drives the plot of the film ahead, but it also has further implications for the human-technology relationship, as explained in the following section.

The Interconnectedness of Humans and Technology

The conflict between the humans and the machines is attributable to a disconnect between them—as specified in the film's opening narration—rather than a need for supremacy. As mentioned earlier, the disconnect is synonymous with the one-sided influence of the machines on the humans due to the contagion. However, the film offers a potential union of humans and technology as well in the form of the Net Terminal Gene. The term brings together technology ("Net" and "Terminal") and genetics ("Gene"), signifying that access to the city's programming can be achieved through a gene in the human body. Furthermore, Killy's assertion that all humans had it prior to the contagion indicates evidence of an *evolutionary path* connecting humans and technology. Both of these implications suggest that in this fictional and futuristic evolution in the film, human bodies are already mediated by technology at the genetic level.

On the film's official website, the gene is described as "the key to restoring order to the world," which could have two implications.[35] First, in accordance with the human characters' interpretation, the gene could grant control over the Safeguard and the Builders back to the humans. They imagine that such control would allow them to order the Builders to stop the expansion of the city and potentially make the terrain less dangerous for the humans. This could be considered one way of "restoring the order," albeit at the expense of reaffirming anthropocentrism. The second implication, however, challenges anthropocentrism and is revealed by the Safeguard's agenda. At the climactic moment of the film, a Safeguard machine announces, "We, the Safeguard, will eliminate all illegal residents lacking the Net Terminal Gene."[36] The Safeguard's correlation of legal residency with the gene (considering, specifically, its properties that would enable the humans to program technology again) arguably implies that it is programmed to eliminate anyone *who cannot work with the machines.*

While both implications given above are plausible, the film problematizes the first one by having a human character ask a pertinent question regarding the possibility of human control over the machines: "But why did people want to do that in the first place?"[37] The significance of this question lies in the character's knowledge that his lived reality is desolate and unconducive for continued human existence *despite this possible history of human supremacy over technology.* The question also indicates the need for alternative possibilities for our future in which neither humans nor technology are considered to be supreme but instead work with each other, as hinted in the second implication. To understand this, we have to go beyond the spectacle of technologically caused genocide that the film presents and consider the second implication's alternative possibility to anthropocentrism. According to this possibility, the machines are programmed to work *with* the humans (which is only possible with the Net Terminal Gene), thereby making them both complicit in the co-construction of any possible future.

BLAME! also reflects the human-technology connection at a more visible level by blurring the boundaries between human and machine bodies. The first indication of this blurring is evidenced in "Safeguards that look just like humans," just like the Safeguard who enters the enclave to exterminate the humans.[38] The second example of human-machine bodies is Killy, who introduces himself as "human" but is accused by an advanced Safeguard machine of being "a body that was stolen from us, the Safeguard."[39] The film thus foregrounds Killy as neither fully human nor fully machine, thereby blurring the boundaries between the categories. The boundaries are blurred even more when Killy and the Safeguard machine are able to enter the enclave, which is believed to be only accessible to humans and invisible to the machines. Since the perimeter allows both Killy and the Safeguard entry, it can be claimed that the film questions the criteria of being human. A question might even be raised about the "humanness" of the human characters as well, who are constantly mediated by industrially produced food. All these instances point to the idea that humans are always already mediated by technological forces, which arguably makes the idea of a hierarchy between humans and technology redundant.

Conclusion

In order to address our current environmental crises, a shift in the way we perceive the relations between technological and human forces is required. Animated films in particular have a way of treating "natural or man-made environments" as "alive and populated by all manner of nonhuman agents," instead of treating them as passive backdrops.[40] In this regard, *BLAME!* illustrates the liveliness of technology that leads to the creation of an ever-expanding city. In other words, *BLAME!* allegorizes unsustainable urban sprawl by depicting humans at the mercy of a vast city populated by sentient technologies. In the film, the human struggle for survival mimics the extreme conditions of threatened wildlife in the real world. Moreover, depicting humans as the victims of sprawl instead of its cause arguably inverts the anthropocentrism of sprawl in the real world. However, the inversion of anthropocentrism does not lead to the valorization of technological supremacy, even though the machines nearly drive the humans to extinction. This "apocalypse" of technologically caused human extinction has deeper critical implications.

To understand what the apocalypse in *BLAME!* reveals, I compare the film with Napier's apocalyptic continuum of anime as diverse as Hayao Miyazaki's *Nausicaä of the Valley of the Wind* (1984), Katsuhiro Otomo's *Akira* (1988), Hideki Takayama's *Legend of the Overfiend* (1987–1991), and Hideaki Anno's series *Neon Genesis Evangelion* (1997). Napier categorizes the apocalypse in *Nausicaä* as signifying a nostalgia for the past, the visions of *Akira* as achieving cathartic exhilaration, and those of *Legend of the Overfiend* and *Neon Genesis Evangelion* as nihilistic.[41]

The question arises: Where would *BLAME!* fit in this continuum of nostalgia, exhilaration, and nihilism? The answer is complex. In *BLAME!*, while there is an element of wonder for a time when humans controlled machines, it is accompanied by bewilderment regarding *why* humans would want to do so. Second, *BLAME!* offers several action scenes that pit humans against machines. However, the excitement is accompanied by the fear that the destruction would lead to an end of human civilization permanently. Despite the constant threats, however, *BLAME!* stops short of nihilism, as the machines are temporarily defeated, the survivors move to another haven, and an element of hope for survival is revealed in the form of the continued search for humans with the Net Terminal Gene. In sum, the apocalyptic vision that *BLAME!* frames is one of immense change that neither nostalgically valorizes a past where humans could control technology nor expresses exhilaration at temporarily winning the human-machine conflict because it comes at a great cost to the survivors' community. In the process,

BLAME! positions neither humans nor the machines as the supreme force. Instead, *BLAME!* illustrates instances where humans and technologies are enmeshed, from genetic to bodily levels, and finally at the level of the city.

Moreover, the film's imaginative take on a machine-generated sprawl that ironically endangers human life addressed in this chapter may not "solve" the problem of urban sprawl in the real world but may lead to rethinking ways to make urban expansion more sustainable by popularizing environmentalist ideas and working "on the ethical and philosophical underpinnings for sustainability"— specifically, a nonhierarchical perception of the evolving human-technology relationship.[42] Even in present times, technology is already a mediator of social relations as well as human-environment relations. Technology also consistently redefines what it means to be human. Rejecting it at this stage of postindustrial development is not feasible. The alternative is to imagine nonhierarchical and co-constructive relations between humans and technology that might lead to more sustainable futures. In this context, despite their own environmental cost, films not only can be a medium to continue imagining such visions, but they can also help bring forth imaginative critiques of current crises for a more sustainable future. Thus, while films may not be a panacea, they can help maintain a continued effort to imagine and eventually manifest sustainable futures.

Notes

[1] Gabriele Hadl cites ecomedia critic Antonio López from his 2011 article, "A Manifesto for Media Education: Greening Media Education" in Hadl, "Nature, Media and the Future," 349.

[2] López, "Ecomedia Literacy."

[3] Chu, "The Imagination of Eco-Disaster," 255.

[4] John Berger has argued that representations of animals in media can alienate us further from environmental consequences, as they create a deception regarding the health and conditions of the natural world. See Hadl, "Nature, Media, and the Future," 350.

[5] Hadl, "Nature, Media, and the Future," 358.

[6] I have used the Netflix Original film and its English subtitles for the terms and the dialogues from Seshita, *BLAME!*

[7] Cholodenko, "Apocalyptic Imagination."

[8] "Anime" is a contraction of the Japanese term *animēshon*, meaning "animation." See Novielli, "From Pre-Cinema to the Birth of Industry," 4.

[9] Napier, *Anime: From Akira to Princess Mononoke*, 196.

[10] Napier, *Anime: From Akira to Princess Mononoke*, 196.

[11] Napier, *Anime: From Akira to Princess Mononoke*, 194.

[12] Napier, *Anime: From Akira to Princess Mononoke*, 197.

[13] Napier, *Anime: From Akira to Princess Mononoke*, 198.

[14] Heise, "Plasmatic Nature," 316.

[15] *BLAME!*, 0:00:32.

[16] In the film, the Safeguards and the Exterminators are often synonymously used.

[17] Merriam-Webster.com, "ecology."

[18] Ursini, "Social Control and Closed Worlds in Manga and Anime," 50.

[19] Pernice, "Urban Sprawl in Postwar Japan," 239.

[20] Kondo and Lizarralde, "Maladaptation, Fragmentation, and Other Secondary Effects of Centralized Post-Disaster Urban Planning," 12.

[21] Poon, "Mapping the 'Conflict Zones' between Sprawl and Biodiversity."

[22] *BLAME!*, 0:00:41–0:00:48

[23] Rafferty, "Urban Sprawl."

[24] *BLAME!*, 0:05:44

[25] Sorensen, "Environmental Crisis and the New City Planning System of 1968," 207.

[26] Rafferty, "Urban Sprawl."

[27] Sorensen, "Environmental Crisis and the New City Planning System of 1968," 207.

[28] *BLAME!*, 0:25:29–0:25:31.

[29] Rafferty, "Urban Sprawl."

[30] Rafferty, "Urban Sprawl."

[31] Heise, "Plasmatic Nature," 304.

[32] Heise, "Plasmatic Nature," 304.

[33] *BLAME!*, 1:15:51–1:15:54.

[34] *BLAME!*, 1:29:38–1:29:44.

[35] *BLAME!*, "Story."

[36] *BLAME!*, 1:12:41–1:12:46.

[37] *BLAME!*, 1:06:54–1:06:59.

[38] *BLAME!*, 0:17:07–0:17:09.

[39] *BLAME!*, 1:23:44–1:23:47.

[40] Heise, "Plasmatic Nature," 303.

[41] Napier, *Anime: From Akira to Princess Mononoke*, 214–215.

[42] Hadl, "Nature, Media, and the Future," 358.

Bibliography

BLAME! "Story." Accessed on September 1, 2022. http://blame.jp/story/.

Cholodenko, Alan. "Apocalyptic Imagination: In the Wake of Hiroshima, Nagasaki,

Godzilla, and Baudrillard." In *Introducing Japanese Popular Culture*, edited by Alisa
Freedman and Toby Slade. London: Routledge, 2018.
https://doi.org/10.4324/9781315723761.

Chu, Kiu-Wai. "The Imagination of Eco-Disaster: Post-Disaster Rebuilding in Asian
Cinema." *Asian Cinema* 30, no. 2 (2019): 255–72. https://doi.org/10.1386/
ac_00007_1.

Hadl, Gabriele. "Nature, Media and the Future: Unnatural Disaster, Animist Anime and
Eco-Media Activism in Japan." In *Routledge Handbook of Japanese Media*, edited by
Fabienne Darling-Wolf, 336–362. London: Routledge, 2018.

Heise, Ursula K. "Plasmatic Nature: Environmentalism and Animated Film." *Public
Culture* 26, no. 2 (2014): 301–318. https://doi.org/10.1215/08992363-2392075.

Kondo, Tamiyo, and Gonzalo Lizarralde. "Maladaptation, Fragmentation, and Other
Secondary Effects of Centralized Post-Disaster Urban Planning: The Case of the 2011
'Cascading' Disaster in Japan." *International Journal of Disaster Risk Reduction* 58
(2021): 1–15. https://doi.org/10.1016/j.ijdrr.2021.102219.

López, Antonio. "Ecomedia Literacy." Accessed August 31, 2022. https://antonio-lopez.
com/ecomedia-literacy/.

Merriam-Webster.com. "ecology." Accessed September 1, 2022. https://www.merriam-
webster.com/dictionary/ecology.

Napier, Susan J. *Anime: From Akira to Princess Mononoke*. New York: Palgrave Macmillan,
2001.

Novielli, Maria Roberta. "From Pre-Cinema to the Birth of Industry." In *Floating Worlds:
A Short History of Japanese Animation*, 1–18. Boca Raton: CRC Press, 2018.

Pernice, Raffaele. "Urban Sprawl in Postwar Japan and the Vision of the City Based on
the Urban Theories of the Metabolists' Projects." *Journal of Asian Architecture and
Building Engineering* 6, no. 2 (2007): 237–244.

Poon, Linda. "Mapping the 'Conflict Zones' between Sprawl and Biodiversity," *Bloomberg*
Asia edition, last modified February 17, 2018. https://www.bloomberg.com/news/
articles/2018-02-16/mapping-how-urban-sprawl-will-clash-with-biodiversity.

Rafferty, John P. "Urban Sprawl," *Encyclopedia Britannica*, last modified November 17,
2021. https://www.britannica.com/topic/urban-sprawl.

Seshita, Hiroyuki, dir. *BLAME!*. 2017; Tokyo: Polygon Pictures. Netflix.

Sorensen, André. "Environmental Crisis and the New City Planning System of 1968."
In *The Making of Urban Japan: Cities and Planning from Edo to the Twenty-First
Century*, 200–223. London: Routledge, 2005.

Ursini, Francesco-Alessio. "Social Control and Closed Worlds in Manga and Anime." In
Dialogues between Media, edited by Paul Ferstl, 47–58. Berlin: De Gruyter, 2021.

16

Stranded among Eternal Ruins:
Three Films about "Fukushima"

Aidana Bolatbekkyzy

This chapter examines three post-"Fukushima" feature films directed by Sono Sion, known domestically and internationally for his idiosyncratic works.[1] Sono's *Himizu* (2011) and *The Land of Hope* (2012) are among the earliest works in the 3/11 body of fiction films. While the former (*Himizu*) dwells on the unflinchingly grim sociopsychological depiction of society on the brink of collapse in the aftermath of the tsunami, the latter *(The Land of Hope)* exposes the underbelly of "uncanny anxiety" of the nuclear meltdown.[2] The third feature, the meditative sci-fi *The Whispering Star* (2015), takes us into the far future, in which humankind is facing extinction as a result of environmental collapse. Although *The Land of Hope* in particular garnered significant scholarly attention in this chapter, I treat all three films as a disaster trilogy for the first time to unravel their eco-disaster aspects (refugee crisis, state abandonment, and the *longue durée* of the nuclear fallout), which become more apparent when reading these films together. I argue that in tandem, Sono's films form a kind of triptych that offers an expansive and complex panoramic view of how the 3/11 disaster unfolds across time—in the immediate present and in the near and far future.

Drawing on Kiu-wai Chu's 2019 essay on clichéd representations of eco-disasters in Asian cinema, in this chapter, I compare how each film grapples with "post-disaster realism" and issues of national reconstruction, demonstrating the films' resistance toward the pitfalls of the "formulaic spectacles" of mainstream

Asian eco-disaster films that render prescient environmental issues into generic commercial entertainment.[3] Amid the official slogans of recovery that promoted political apathy, early on, Sono's 3/11 films articulated the radical break between pre- and post-3/11 Japan as one of impossible return. Sono's trilogy resists the entropy of forgetting and reminds us of cinema's social function, for "what goes unrecorded never happened."[4] In doing so, Sono's films also contribute to "the preservation of the memory of an inconvenient past," not only in Japan but also within the larger body of East Asian eco-disaster cinema.[5]

Introduction

In his 2019 essay, "The Imagination of Eco-Disaster: Post-Disaster Rebuilding in Asian Cinema," environmental humanities scholar Kiu-wai Chu examines a select few Asian post-catastrophe films dealing with real-world tsunamis and earthquakes. The films range from typically uplifting commercial blockbusters, to aestheticized and culturally ambiguous cosmopolitan films, to more personal yet critical narratives. While the former two categories are more mainstream, it is less common to find movies that zoom in on the unresolved and ongoing effects of a catastrophe, which Chu calls "post-disaster realism." Chu defines post-disaster realism as a critical perspective that "reconfigures our way in perceiving time and temporality of eco-disaster, enables us to see the often-neglected prolonged impacts and consequences."[6]

Following the events of 3/11, countless documentaries (independent and pro-government) were made about the disasters, which cannot be said of fictional responses. Likely as a result of the far-reaching influence of the *genshiryoku mura* (nuclear village), the players in the mainstream conservative film industry remained quiet, so Sono became the first filmmaker to create a fictional account of the tragedy, and as a result, he was stigmatized "as strange for engaging with 'Fukushima.'"[7] This is attested by *Eiga Geijutsu* magazine's bashing of both *Himizu* and *The Land of Hope*, ranking them as two of the worst films of 2012 because "making such films so soon after such a big, shocking disaster is just shallow," a criticism that documentaries were curiously spared.[8] By contrast, Sono's commitment to create a "film which would appear more 'real' than a documentary" was inspired by interviews he conducted with survivors of the 3/11 disasters.[9] Thus, *The Land of Hope* was written as a "proxy spokesman" for the dozens of interviewed victims from Fukushima, functioning similarly to what Fujiki Hideaki dubbed the "therapeutic mode of filmic narration."[10]

Released less than a year apart, *Himizu* and *The Land of Hope* tackle different aspects of the 2011 Tōhoku earthquake, tsunami, and nuclear meltdown. *Himizu* zooms in on the anguished everyday life of the fifteen-year-old Sumida, the son of a violent father and absentee mother. He is surrounded by other underdogs—

refugee characters from Tōhoku who dwell in cardboard shelters around Sumida's boathouse, and his classmate Chazawa Keiko, who also comes from a dysfunctional family. Conversely, *The Land of Hope* presents the almost idyllic traditional Ono family, generational cattle and vegetable farmers, whose lives are irreversibly altered after the nuclear meltdown.

The location of both films is markedly different, with *Himizu* set in Ibaraki Prefecture (between Tokyo and Tōhoku) and *The Land of Hope* in the fictional Ōba town, Nagashima Prefecture (which combines the names of Nagasaki, Hiroshima, and Fukushima). As observed by Kristina Iwata-Weickgenannt, the choice to fictionalize the setting "significantly unlinks nuclear disaster from a specific location such as Fukushima, suggesting that a similar catastrophe could occur anywhere at any time."[11] Moreover, by situating the story in the future, the film not only openly criticizes the government's inadequate handling of the disasters but also serves as a warning sign that it could happen again.[12] The sci-fi aspect culminates in Sono's third Fukushima film, *The Whispering Star*, a black-and-white feature set in the far future where only 20 percent of outer space is populated by humans facing extinction, and the other 80 percent is populated by machines.[13] Doing so, Sono goes even further in picturing the *longue durée* of the nuclear fallout on a planetary scale, visualizing the catastrophic environmental impact of 3/11 far beyond the immediate present, a rare perspective within the post-Fukushima body of fiction films.

Significantly, Sono abstains from presenting a dramatic reenactment of the instance of the reactor explosion or even the tsunami, thereby avoiding the spectacle of disaster films. In *The Land of Hope*, after the earthquake occurs, the film cuts to black for ten full seconds, breaking the temporality to "before" and "after." As time passes, and as the Onos struggle to learn about what happened, the viewers are placed in the shoes of the characters in the film, who, like the public after 3/11, were misinformed by media that continuously downplayed the disasters. In *Himizu*, the low grumbling noise of the tsunami, combined with the sounds of a Geiger counter, repeatedly ring throughout the film in tandem with the imagery of debris. But more so than the protagonist Sumida, it is the tsunami refugee characters, such as Yoruno, who are continuously reliving the disaster flashbacks, unable to move on. Thus, the films focus on the prolonged temporality of the environmental calamities: the televised news coverage is a constant reminder, a background noise, even as the characters go on with their daily lives.

One of the key areas of the long-term effects of the disasters is on social ties, as, for example, in *The Land of Hope*, which centers around the fracturing of households due to environmental catastrophe. The disaster is a turning point of no return for the Ono family's previously tranquil everyday life: the crumbling of the traditional family structure is suggested not only by the eventual demise of the elderly couple, Yasuhiko and Chieko, but also by the repetitive iconography of the empty *kotatsu* table, which they use daily. The camera dwells on the objects that show signs of the characters' recent presence, such as Chieko's drawings, but the absence of people produces an uncanny effect of spectrality. It is reminiscent of the way documentary filmmaker Toshi Fujiwara frames the remaining survivors in Fukushima as ghosts in *No Man's Zone* (2012). As Fujiwara noted, the elderly people he interviews in the film are "out of place, out of time. They don't belong anymore in this modern world."[14]

Post-Disaster Realism

Although the disaster in *Himizu* is recent, the social ailments portrayed in the film are longer-term problems for Japan, including forced prostitution, pickpocketing, murder sprees, urban alienation, yakuza violence, drug dealing, pachinko gambling, and looting. In this way, Sono situates this story within the continuum of wider systemic issues, an important aspect of Kiu wai-Chu's notion of "post-disaster realism." For instance, in *Himizu*, the institution that is satirized the most is a local school, a mouthpiece of the government. Throughout the film, the homeroom teacher is portrayed regurgitating the official version of not only recent events but also the controversial memory of World War II. Moreover, as the teacher repeatedly preaches about the need for post-disaster national reconstruction, Sumida is the only student who objects that "not everyone is able to recover" (*tachinaoranai hito mo ippai iru*). In return, the teacher mocks Sumida's unstable home environment, downplaying the issue of recovery as an individual responsibility (*jikosekinin*) rather than a governmental duty. Yet when Keiko later confronts the teacher about his speeches, he is at a loss for words, exposing the lack of critical thinking behind his words. The sense of abandonment by the government is further mirrored by Sumida's parental absence. His mother, who initially lived with him, flees with her boyfriend without prior notice, leaving fifteen-year-old Sumida only a few thousand yen to survive on and a note saying, "Good luck" (*ganbatte*). This parting message would ring even more hollow in *The Land of Hope*, where a giant banner reading "Ganbarō, Nagashima!" (Let's Do Our Best, Nagashima!) hangs outside the temporary shelter inside the local school. Further juxtaposing the hopelessness of the situation with the official slogans, the camera shows a banner saying "Hope" (*kibō*) plastered on the wall above the makeshift cardboard beds in the same temporary shelter.

Sono's biting commentary reaches its peak in the uncanny television broadcast sequence, which juxtaposes Ono Yoichi's and his wife, Izumi's, diverging views of the disaster. Izumi, an expectant mother, sits parallel to the TV reading a book (signaling her distrust) about the effects of radiation on children, idly criticizing the broadcast, while Yoichi faces the screen (suggesting his susceptibility to the official propaganda) and nods along to the broadcast (figure 16.1).

Figure 16.1. Izumi and Yoichi disagree about the news broadcast.
Sono Sion, 2012, Shochiku Co., Ltd.

The broadcast shows an interview with a group of housewives speaking about their experiences with radiation anxiety. Since such acts of self-protection, like wearing a mask in public, disrupted the social harmony, the housewives gave up on this measure of self-protection in favor of "forgetting the bad feelings and waiting for something positive." As the male host sympathetically nods along, he exclaims, "Da da dum! Let's produce and eat to that," unmistakably referring to the infamous "eat to support" (*tabete ōen shiyō*) campaign, which urged the population to consume produce from Tōhoku to support the economy, without considering radiation risks. In *Himizu*, though such direct antinuclear commentary is absent, a Nazi yakuza character viewing a different television broadcast exclaims, "nuclear energy rules!" (*genpatsu saikō*).

"We Are All Refugees Now": Home(lessness) across Time and Space

Across this trilogy, the fate of humanity in the deteriorating post-catastrophic world is expressed most vividly through the depiction of environmental refugee characters. Untethered, they struggle to find a new permanent home and the sense of safety and security it would grant. But the futility of their attempts is expressed chiefly by the state of residential architecture, which appears as an important leitmotif in all three films. Far from granting a sense of shelter—and buttressing the threshold between public and private in the social order— houses no longer operate as domestic spaces but are instead made strange and uncanny in the aftermath of the calamities. The camera lingers on the temporary school shelters, cardboard box dwellings, lost ancestral homes, and even a freight vessel that looks like a traditional Japanese house. In *The Land of Hope,* Yoichi is expelled from the ancestral home of the Onos and forced into relocation with Izumi, perpetually on the move in futile attempts to escape radiation. However, as indicated in the ending scenes with the murder-suicide of his parents and the Geiger counter at the beach, there is nowhere to run and nowhere to return to.

But while they have the means and ability to relocate, the refugees in *Himizu* see no actual improvement of their living conditions by the end of the film. Sumida himself inhabits a boat rental shop instead of a regular house. In fact, after Yoruno's fallout with Sumida, the refugees are pushed further into poverty, and at the end of the film, they are shown living under a bridge. There are no active social welfare institutions to help them reintegrate into society, and Yoruno's dream of regaining affluence is futile. He is plagued by the memory of walking through the ruins of his home in the aftermath of the tsunami and looking for his loved ones among the debris. Throughout the film, the half-submerged shed in the middle of the lake near Sumida's house serves as a visual memento for the tsunami (figure 16.2).

For example, in one scene, Yoruno looks at the shed, and the camera cuts to a close-up of his eyes. The instant he closes his eyes, the camera then cuts to an image of disaster debris that fills the screen. Later, when the new refugees visit Yoruno, seeing the shed triggers traumatic memories for the photographer, who shouts that it reminds him of "that day." In this way, the film confronts the viewer with a realization that for environmental refugees, the disaster is ever present.

In *The Whispering Star,* which envisions environmental collapse in the aftermath of Fukushima far into the posthuman future, shots of outer space and various planetary landscapes are often framed from within dilapidated buildings or the rental spaceship that resembles a traditional Japanese house, which is used by the android deliverywoman. In fact, the spaceship might be the only house in the film that is inhabited, though it remains unclear. Paradoxically, the house is mobile, an allegory for always being on the move and not quite home anywhere in the world. In their analysis of *The Land of Hope,* Kiu-wai Chu and Winnie L. M. Yee note a sense of "uncanniness, unhomeliness, and inhospitality of post-disaster Japan" that conveys the interconnectedness of the deterioration of the human and natural world.[15] In this film, we see humans appearing in a state of limbo, such as the figures on the beach standing still as if frozen in time amongst the disaster debris. Their "somnambulistic manner"[16] erases not only the visual difference between humans and androids but also emphasizes the lack of purpose and the possibility that by "living their lives as social beings in communities, they are only co-existing in a decaying post-disaster landscape."[17] Needless to say, there is no reconstruction or regeneration in sight on any planet visited in the film; if *Himizu* and *The Land of Hope* depicted the fractured relationship between the state and

Figure 16.2. A half-submerged shed in *Himizu*. Sono Sion, 2011, Gaga.

people, there is no such relationship to begin with in *The Whispering Star*, as the very fabric of a unified human society as we know it is absent.

On a related note, the most major loss we witness is the breakdown of a modern temporal orientation as one of continuous progress. This is evident in the undifferentiated flow of days and even years in *The Whispering Star*. The android deliverywoman not only fails to age, but she also ponders the importance of the concept of time and space for the remaining humans, who are stranded amid the barren landscapes with seemingly nothing to look forward to. In the far future depicted in *The Whispering Star*, although teleportation is possible, many still choose the antediluvian method of delivery that takes years. Only in this way can humans feel the flow of time, convey their feelings to the addressee, and experience the excitement of waiting and the rush of nostalgia produced by the objects inside the parcels.

Gender and Nonreproductive Future

One of the direct links between humanity's future and environmental disaster lies within the purview of the effect of the latter on human reproduction, and the threat of the possible extinction of humanity. In this regard, the issue of gender is a fecund space for the discussion of humanity's fragility amid environmental crises. As has been noted elsewhere, Sono's treatment of women in *The Land of Hope* is rather conventional, especially in the portrayal of Izumi as a hysterical mother.[18] But in *Himizu*, the mothers are either absent, like Sumida's mother who runs away, or outright destructive, like Keiko's mother, who wishes her daughter to hang herself. Notably, Sumida and Keiko evoke Fyodor Dostoevsky's Rodion Raskolnikov and Sonya Marmeladova in *Crime and Punishment*.[19] Keiko, like

Sonya, functions as a symbol of love to help the mentally anguished protagonist who was driven to murder attain a spiritual redemption. At the same time, the film makes it clear that her own disturbed home situation drives her to seek love elsewhere, adding complexity to her character. Neither is their relationship devoid of violence, as attested to by her physical fights with Sumida during the first half of the film. Yet they still cling to the dream of starting a family one day after Sumida is released from prison, as a promise of normalcy in the future. It is a dream which is ultimately undone by the ending of the film, as discussed in the conclusion.

Furthermore, in both *Himizu* and *The Land of Hope*, the older generation expresses their faith in youth, and Yoruno even goes so far as to participate in robbery and manslaughter to save Sumida from the yakuza who are hounding him for his father's debts. When asked by the leader of the gang why he is paying off Sumida's debt, Yoruno replies, "for the future" (*mirai*). In *The Land of Hope*, the patriarch Yasuhiko drives his son, Yoichi, away so that he and Izumi have a chance at having healthy progeny. Although Yoichi and Izumi escape the "zone" and flee as far as possible, the final scene on the seashore (the limits of the Japanese archipelago), in which a Geiger counter alarm goes off, exposes the absurdity of borders for radiation containment. Moreover, given the vulnerability of children to radiation, the effects of such slow violence cannot be known until much later.[20]

Thus, while the burden of reconstruction is placed on the young, "who will bear the yoke of elders who've been wiped out—financially, geographically, emotionally—by recent events," both *Himizu* and *The Land of Hope* end before confirming that the young can succeed in fulfilling their function as the nation's future, given the backdrop of brutal environmental and socioeconomic conditions.[21] Even the two children who appear in the dilapidated landscape of Nagashima in *The Land of Hope*, encountered by the young couple Suzuki Mitsuru and Yōko, are merely ghostly apparitions. Andreas Jacobsson suggests they could be read as representing the ancestors and their connection to the land. He contends that "in the radiation-infused Nagashima the future has expired and the ancestors will disappear forever."[22]

Finally, in *The Whispering Star*, there are almost no children to begin with (except for one boy who receives a parcel), only fragmentary figures, such as the ship's computer voice that sounds like a young boy, images of children on photo negatives and a photograph in some of the parcels, or, finally, among the moving human shadows in the corridor made of paper at the end of the film. The scene takes place on the last planet inhabited entirely by humans, where making a sound above thirty decibels is deadly. Andreas Jacobsson suggests that "this final sequence deconstructs the belief in images with this shadow play depicting human life before the disaster, a past life that is lost forever."[23] This impression is further strengthened by the sequence where Suzuki Yoko hands the package to the

Figure 16.3. Family in shadow corridor in *The Whispering Star*. Sono Sion, 2015, Happinet.

recipient family. As the door opens, we only see the impenetrable darkness of the interior and a female hand reaching out for the package and signing the receipt. As the woman reads the name of the sender, an expression of grief overcomes her as the rest of the family rushes in to witness the scene (figure 16.3).

Although the deliverywoman Suzuki Yoko spends years of interstellar travel attending to domestic chores in a feminine manner, her robot nature is highlighted by her inability to comprehend human emotions and sentimentality; she can only be an observer to those expressions.

Conclusion

In the documentary about the making of *The Land of Hope*, Megumi Kagurazaka, who portrayed Izumi, muses that despite finishing the shooting of the film, she does not feel the usual sense of completion (*owari wa nai kanji*).[24] At the end of the documentary, as the intertitles, "to engrave hope," appear on screen, the sound of a stake being hammered in mixes with the noise of the Geiger counter. It is the same sound that was used in the film to signify the establishment of the twenty-kilometer exclusion zone that drew the arbitrary borderline between safety and danger from nuclear exposure that Sono satirized. On a metaphorical level, the use of stakes signals the rift between the past and present, and between home and homelessness, for the unmoored refugees.

At the end of *Himizu*, Sumida and Keiko run toward the police station so Sumida can turn himself in for the murder of his father. Keiko cheers Sumida with the same phrases previously uttered by their teacher in the classroom (*Sumida, ganbare! Yume o mote!*), phrases that Sumida repeats to himself out loud. But unlike the empty rhetoric coming from a source of authority, it emerges from their own trampled yet persistent will to live. And for a while, it seems as if the ending is offering hope that the youth can make it. However, in the final scene, as the dolly shot frames the young protagonists (notably dressed in white and red, evoking the Japanese flag) running toward Sumida's redemption, the image of the road with thickly growing grass is subtly superimposed upon the disaster landscape. In other words, as they circle back to the beginning, the hope for the young ones is undone the instant it flashes up as a possibility.

Finally, *The Whispering Star* ultimately rejects the progressive modernist notion of linear time and futurity, rendering them meaningless in the face of environmental collapse. The surviving humans are dispersed throughout the dying planets in a state of limbo. There is no hope or optimism left, only nostalgia for objects reminding us of the past in the dilapidated wasteland world. In the words of Andreas Jacobsson, "these films are not a eulogy that directs a nostalgic eye backwards to better times; rather they problematise a future that is both timeless and without a Future as we understand the concept."[25] Perhaps it is in this film that Sono most definitively shows the impossibility of going back to normalcy as we knew it, as social and environmental impacts caused by the calamities are slowly unfolding over time for generations to come.

Notes

[1] In April 2022, numerous reports have surfaced of sexual abuse allegations made against Sono by actresses he has worked with on set. This chapter was written before these allegations were made public, and it does not intend to lionize the director.

[2] Kimura, "Uncanny Anxiety: Literature after Fukushima."

[3] Chu, "The Imagination of Eco-Disaster: Post-Disaster Rebuilding in Asian Cinema," 256.

[4] Long, "Fukushima, Media, Democracy: The Promise of Documentary Film. An Interview with Kamanaka Hitomi with Introduction by Katsuya Hirano."

[5] Geilhorn and Iwata-Weickgenannt, *Fukushima and the Arts*.

[6] Chu, "The Imagination of Eco-Disaster: Post-Disaster Rebuilding in Asian Cinema," 258.

[7] Iwata-Weickgenannt, "Gendering 'Fukushima': Resistance, Self-Responsibility, and Female Hysteria in Sono Sion's Land of Hope," 111.

[8] Schilling, "In the Cinematic Wake of the Fukushima Nuclear Disaster."

[9] *70min-Making-of Documentary*.

[10] Fujiki, "Problematizing Life: Documentary Films on the 3/11 Nuclear Catastrophe," 91.

[11] Iwata-Weickgenannt, "Gendering 'Fukushima': Resistance, Self-Responsibility, and Female Hysteria in Sono Sion's Land of Hope," 113.

[12] For instance, through the voices of the victims retelling their 3/11 experience in a meeting attended by Izumi and Yoichi.

[13] For a more detailed discussion of Sono's science fiction aesthetic, see Jacobsson, "Remembering the Future."

[14] Fujiwara, "A Conversation with Toshi Fujiwara about No Man's Zone."

[15] Yee and Chu, "Local Stories, Global Catastrophe," 683.

[16] Jacobsson, "Remembering the Future," 186.

[17] Jacobsson, "Remembering the Future," 190.

[18] Thouny, "The Land of Hope: Planetary Cartographies of Fukushima, 2012"; Iwata-Weickgenannt, "Gendering 'Fukushima': Resistance, Self-Responsibility, and Female Hysteria in Sono Sion's Land of Hope."

[19] Dostoevsky, *Crime and Punishment*.

[20] See, for instance, Hirano and Kasai, "'Take Science Seriously and Value Ethics Greatly.'"

[21] McCahill, "Himizu—Review."

[22] Jacobsson, "Remembering the Future," 185.

[23] Jacobsson, "Remembering the Future," 189.

[24] *70min-Making-of Documentary*.

[25] Jacobsson, "Remembering the Future," 190.

Bibliography

70min-Making-of Documentary. Third Window Films, 2012.

Chu, Kiu-wai. "The Imagination of Eco-Disaster: Post-Disaster Rebuilding in Asian Cinema." *Asian Cinema* 30, no. 2 (October 2019): 255–272.

Dostoevsky, Fyodor. *Crime and Punishment*. 1st ed. The Russian Messenger, 1866.

Fujiki, Hideaki. "Problematizing Life: Documentary Films on the 3/11 Nuclear Catastrophe." In *Fukushima and the Arts: Negotiating Nuclear Disaster*, edited by Barbara Geilhorn and Kristina Iwata-Weickgenannt, 90–109. London: Routledge, 2017.

Fujiwara, Toshi. "A Conversation with Toshi Fujiwara about No Man's Zone." Interview by Chris Fujiwara, 2015.

Geilhorn, Barbara, and Kristina Iwata-Weickgenannt, eds. *Fukushima and the Arts: Negotiating Nuclear Disaster*. London: Routledge, 2017.

Hirano, Katsuya, and Hirotaka Kasai. "'Take Science Seriously and Value Ethics Greatly': Health Effects of Fukushima Nuclear Disaster." Translated by Akiko Anson. *Asia-Pacific Journal: Japan Focus* 18, issue 19, no. 5 (October 1, 2020): 1–21.

Iwata-Weickgenannt, Kristina. "Gendering 'Fukushima': Resistance, Self-Responsibility, and Female Hysteria in Sono Sion's Land of Hope." In *Fukushima and the Arts: Negotiating Nuclear Disaster*, edited by Barbara Geilhorn and Kristina Iwata-Weickgenannt 110–126. London: Routledge, 2017.

Jacobsson, Andreas. "Remembering the Future: Sion Sono's Science Fiction Films." *Nordic Journal of English Studies* 19, no. 4 (2020): 169–194. https://doi.org/10.35360/njes.607.

Kimura, Saeko. "Uncanny Anxiety: Literature after Fukushima." In *Fukushima and the Arts: Negotiating Nuclear Disaster*, edited by Barbara Geilhorn and Kristina Iwata-Weickgenannt 74–90. London: Routledge, 2017.

Long, Margherita, trans. "Fukushima, Media, Democracy: The Promise of Documentary Film: An Interview with Kamanaka Hitomi with Introduction by Katsuya Hirano." *Asia-Pacific Journal: Japan Focus* 16, issue 16, no. 3 (August 15, 2018).

McCahill, Mike. "Himizu—Review." *The Guardian*, May 31, 2012.

Schilling, Mark. "In the Cinematic Wake of the Fukushima Nuclear Disaster," *Japan Times*, March 4, 2015.

Thouny, Christophe. "The Land of Hope: Planetary Cartographies of Fukushima, 2012." *World Renewal* 10 (January 1, 2015): 17–34. https://doi.org/10.5749/mech.10.2015.0017.

Yee, Winnie L. M., and Kiu-wai Chu. "Local Stories, Global Catastrophe: Reconstructing Nation, Asian Cinema, and Asian Eco-Consciousness in Japan's 3/11 Films." In *The Palgrave Handbook of Asian Cinema*, 667–687. London: Palgrave Macmillan UK, 2018. https://doi.org/10.1057/978-1-349-95822-1_32.

17

Disaster and the Landscape of the Heart in *Asako I & II* (2018)

Dong Hoon Kim

As is widely known, the subject of catastrophe has always been pervasive in the postwar Japanese mediascape. As Susan Napier aptly observes, Japan's location in the Pacific Ring of Fire, which frequently causes earthquakes and tsunami; the country's turbulent modern historical events such as imperialism, the Pacific War, and the atomic bombing of Hiroshima and Nagasaki; and a series of environmental disasters that occurred during the economic growth period have collectively contributed to prevailing images of catastrophe in Japanese film and media.[1] The 9.0-magnitude Tōhoku earthquake that triggered a massive tsunami and the Fukushima nuclear meltdown on March 11, 2011, once again inspired Japanese filmmakers to produce a flurry of disaster-themed films, ranging from explicitly political independent documentaries to commercial movie blockbusters, in their attempts to confront one of the worst disasters in modern history. Among these films are a handful of melodramas that recount a story informed by ecological, natural, or other forms of disaster. While attesting to how prevalent the theme of disaster is across media outlets and genres in Japan in the aftermath of the 2011 triple disaster, this confluence of melodrama and disaster films is distinctive from other disaster-themed films, as it focuses principally on emotional and affective responses to disaster. In these melodramas, disaster provokes a seismic shift in and between characters, driving them to reflect on their lives, reestablish human connectivity and emotional links, and restore their social relations. In such films as *Your Name* (2016), *Asako I & II* (2018), *Weathering with You* (2019), *Bubble* (2022), and *I Am a Hero* (2015), for instance, it takes massive destruction, grand disasters, or even the end of the world for lovers to discover their love and/or to commit themselves to a romantic relationship. In *Happy Hour* (2015), *Survival Family* (2016), *River's Edge* (2018), *The Asadas* (2020), and *Drive My Car* (2021), disasters prompt characters to contemplate themselves and their social lives and reconstruct their relationships with their families, friends, and other loved ones. Though varied in tone, style, and approach, these melodramas examine not only disaster's lasting impacts on individuals but its potentially generative power, which can be positively used to remedy social isolation, the lack of a social life, and diminishing interpersonal interactions that are considered grave social problems that need to be urgently tackled in contemporary Japanese society.

This chapter examines disaster as an emerging genre trope of Japanese melodrama. In probing how experiences of disaster lead to a rediscovery of interiority in recent melodramas, it focuses on *Asako I & II*, in which the titular protagonist's internal transformation, personal evolution, and reestablishing of her social relationships are marked directly by her experiences of the 2011 triple disaster. Adapted from Shibasaki Tomoka's best-selling novel of the same name,[2] *Asako I & II* (*Netemo sametemo/Whether Sleep or Awake*)—which portrays Asako's rather unusual romance with Baku and Ryohei, Asako's two lovers who uncannily have the same appearance but radically different personalities—appears to be an "enigmatic romance"[3] that "flips the gaze to tell the same old story."[4] Indeed, Shibasaki's romance story takes the form of a *bildungsroman* by delicately describing and revealing Asako's innermost thoughts, desires, and emotional fluctuations through the first-person narration, and it strives to reverse the conventional gender roles in the romance genre. In contrast, Hamaguchi Ryūsuke's film version relates Asako's personal story in a substantially different fashion by presenting the 2011 disaster as a central narrative element that triggers Asako's inner transformation and stimulates her to develop new perspectives on her romantic and social life. In the film, the triple disaster, often referred to simply as "3/11," functions as the decisive event that shakes Asako to the core, continues to affect her, and—as the film's English title, *Asako I & II*, implicitly suggests— eventually transforms her, while she struggles between her lingering feelings toward Baku, a free-roaming soul who suddenly vanishes and leaves Asako, and her growing feelings toward Ryohei, a reliable, personable, and capable office worker who devotedly loves her. Without exploiting the visceral pleasure the image of destruction might offer, and without probing the sociopolitical consequences of the catastrophic event, *Asako I & II* centers exclusively on the disaster's tremendous impact on the landscape of the heart. By analyzing the film's representation of how a disaster and its lasting effects seep into individuals' everyday life and affect their inner, emotional, and psychological landscape in a gradual and persistent manner, this chapter ultimately aims to shift the focus in examining the cinematic representation of catastrophe toward the emotional and affective effects of disasters.

Walking through the Ruined Landscapes

Asako I & II opens with Asako strolling through downtown Osaka on a fine day. After the establishing shot, the camera captures Asako, a college student, walking on a pedestrian path alongside the waterfront. A series of following insert shots feature Osaka's landmarks, such as the Tsūtengaku tower, the line of skyscrapers, and the bridges over Osaka's famous waterways that give the city its nickname, "aqua metropolis." The subsequent long shot presents the famous eco-friendly facade of the National Museum of Art, Osaka, located on Nakano Island (Nakanoshima), which is sandwiched between the Dojima River and the Tosabori River. The island is a fifty-hectare sandbank developed into a business district, which is home to Osaka City Hall, Osaka City Central Public Hall, Nakanoshima Park, and many office buildings and cultural facilities. Asako enters from the left side of the frame, and the static camera shows her walking toward the museum. The following slow, horizontal, and tight tracking shots showcase a museum exhibit of photos by the photographer Gochō Shigeo from his self-published *Self and Others* (1977), and the camera movement stops at a photo of identical twin girls in a park. The close-up, a reverse shot, shows the face of Asako, who gazes at the picture of twin girls inside the Gochō exhibit. While Asako continues to appreciate the picture, a man (Baku), who hums and makes noise by dragging his flip-flops, wanders into the shot, has a quick glance at the portrait, and exits from the shot. The subsequent POV shot of Asako tracks the man browsing carelessly through the exhibit. A series of shots then captures Baku and Asako, who walks a few steps behind him, in the same frame as they exit from the museum and walk on the sidewalk alongside the river. Then the sound of fireworks makes Baku turn around, and Asako and Baku begin to stare at each other. After a while, Baku slowly walks up to Asako, and they exchange their names and have their first kiss.

This opening scene, which introduces the serendipitous nature of Asako's romance with Baku, is filled with metaphors and motifs that repeatedly appear throughout the film: the act of walking, the image of water, the photos from the Gochō exhibit, and the fortuities and coincidences that often redefine interpersonal relations in the film. In examining Asako's transformation caused by her disaster experiences, I primarily focus on the narrative functions and symbolic meanings of the photography exhibit and the act of walking. First, the exhibit (and in particular, the photo of twin girls) where Baku and Asako first encounter one another introduces the doppelgänger motif that implies not only Asako's romantic relationships with two men who resemble each other but also her transformation from "Asako I" to "Asako II." Later in the film, Asako visits another Gochō exhibit, where her second romance begins to develop. Asako's "love-at-first-sight" turns out to be a disruptive event with lingering consequences in her life. Baku is a gorgeous, mysterious, and free-spirited college student who likes to follow his heart without any regard for the people around him or their feelings. Six months later, he vanishes without telling Asako or their friends, as everyone had feared he would do. After Baku disappears from Asako's life, the film leaps forward in time two years, and the audience is reintroduced to Asako, who now lives in Tokyo. While delivering coffee from the café where she works as a barista to a meeting at a sake company next door, Asako meets Ryohei, Baku's exact double. She mistakes Ryohei, a marketing manager, for Baku, impulsively confessing her frustrated feelings about Baku's disappearance to the wrong man. The intrigued Ryohei develops an interest in Asako, and one evening, he runs into her and her friend Maya, a stage actress, in front of a gallery where a Gochō exhibit is held, and he visits the exhibit together with them. This exhibit is where Asako's romance evolves into a rather unusual one, and, significantly, it is where the contrast between Baku and Ryohei is quickly established. When Ryohei spots Asako standing at the entrance of the Gochō exhibit, he tries to start a conversation with her. When Asako touches his face with her hand without saying anything, the startled Ryohei tries to leave. As he starts to leave, however, Ryohei eavesdrops on the conversation Asako and Maya have with a gallery staff member who won't let them enter the exhibit because they arrived a few minutes after the last entry time. Ryohei spontaneously joins the group, pretending to be their friend who traveled from a remote city just to visit the exhibit. Using his wits and people skills, he successfully persuades the gallery staff member to let them in. The next shots, consisting of three inserts of Gochō's photos and a close-up of Asako's face, are identical to those from the opening scene that show Asako at the Osaka exhibit; these inserts end with the same shot of the photo of the twin girls, followed by a reverse close-up shot of Asako looking at the picture. The two Gochō exhibits, along with the repetition of shots that present Gochō's works and Asako's reactions to them, therefore, visually represent the doppelgänger motif and establish a connection between Asako's love stories with two men who look identical.

In addition to the doubling motif, another important parallel that can be made between the exhibit and the film is the exploration of truths in human relationships. Gochō was a leading figure of Japanese con-pora (a Japanese abbreviation of *contemporary*), a photography movement that emerged in the late 1960s. His *Self and Others* is regarded as a seminal work that epitomizes con-pora photographers' attempts to challenge modernist photography by finding their subjects from everyday life and portraying them in a simple and candid manner.[5] As the book title demonstrates, *Self and Others* intimately presents the personal life of Gochō—who died a few years after the publication of the book at the age of thirty-six due to a lifelong illness—by showcasing a series of portraits of his

Figure 17.1. Asako exchanges gazes with the twins.
Hamaguchi Ryusuke, 2018, Comme des Cinémas.

friends, families, neighbors, and himself. Yet Gochō's portraits do more than simply present him and the people around him as they seek to explore the meaning of interpersonal experience. His photos blur the boundary between *self* and *others* by having his subjects—who are shot from a close distance, in medium or full shot— look directly at a camera. Gochō's subjects are not simply the camera's subjects, in this sense, because they return the observer's gaze. Both the subject and the observer are the self and the other at the same time, and the self and the other are constantly shifting in the endless return and exchange of gazes that establish mutual dependence in their relations. In a similar manner to Gochō's photos that raise existential questions concerning human relations, Hamaguchi's film contemplates these questions by tracing Asako's evolution as an individual and as a social being. The portrait of twin girls that Asako intently observes at both exhibits deserves a more in-depth discussion here. The photo further complicates Gochō's photographic interrogation of notions of self and others due to the apparent mirror-image motif that comes with twins. Also importantly, the reverse close-ups of Asako gazing at the photo take Gochō's exploration of the self-other boundary and distance to another level, as they insert Asako (and even the audience, who exchanges gazes with both Asako and the twins when they look at Asako staring at the twins, and at the twins returning Asako's gaze) into Gochō's photographic world (figure 17.1). Asako's interactions with the twins and her exchange of gazes with them foreshadow the exploration of Asako's own forthcoming interpersonal relations. The audience members are not distant observers; rather, they are invited to immerse themselves into Asako's story of metamorphosis.

The film's doubling motif and its implications for Asako's romances are additionally augmented by Asako's action after the two exhibits, her act of walking. At the dinner after the visit to the exhibit, Ryohei and Maya enjoy a lively conversation, but Asako remains quiet throughout the meal and eventually leaves. The subsequent tracking shot begins to follow a weeping Asako walking and then running through the night streets of Tokyo. Asako's walking here echoes her and

Baku's walking after they left the Osaka exhibit, and it creates another connection between the two men and between Asako's two love stories. The act of walking that characters frequently undertake throughout the film, however, connotes much more than the doppelgänger motif. It should be noted that walking, strolling, driving, and traveling on public transportation serve significant narrative and aesthetic functions in Hamaguchi's films. These acts of motion typically signify everyday mundaneness, but in Hamaguchi's works, they frequently offer his characters a chance to be liberated momentarily from their daily routine, and they are turned into a meditative time during which characters can reflect on their lives, open up about themselves, and engage in deeply intimate conversations with those who walk or ride with them, including strangers. These contemplative acts often result in an enlightening moment for the characters as they discover something new about themselves, their close ones, and their relationships with others. *Drive My Car*, the winner of the 2022 Oscar for Best International Feature Film, which depicts the bond created between a grieving theater director and his new driver, is the film in which Hamaguchi positions the acts of motion at the very center of the narrative, as key events, conversations, and revelations occur inside moving cars. Similarly, in *Asako I & II*, many events, interactions, and self-discoveries take place while Asako, Ryohei, Baku, and others walk or drive.

As mentioned earlier, the film begins with Asako's urban strolling that leads her to her romance with Baku, a major (and the first) event that changes the course of her life. The urban walking returns later in the film, when Ryohei walks along the streets of earthquake-hit Tokyo on March 11, 2011, like tens of thousands of Tokyoites who walked home for hours due to aftershocks and the failure of much of the city's infrastructure. After their visit to the Gochō exhibit, Ryohei confesses his feelings toward Asako, and they begin to date. Feeling guilty about not telling her new lover that she is attracted to him because of his resemblance to Baku, Asako soon tells Ryohei that they should break up and stops talking to him. In the hope of seeing Asako, Ryohei goes to a stage play Maya is in. Upon learning that Asako is not coming, Ryohei sits down to watch the show alone, but the earthquake ensues and cancels the show. Initially, Ryohei decides to return to his company. Due to roadblocks and unavailable public transportation, however, he takes many detours, and it becomes unclear to the viewer whether he continues on to his company or decides to go back home instead. Ryohei's walking scene that lasts for almost four minutes reveals not just the devastated urban landscape and the city's dismayed residents but also what kind of person he is. In a clear contrast to his aghast fellow Tokyo residents, Ryohei remarkably maintains his composure, consoling people in shock and calmly interacting with others to get more information about the situation. Ryohei walks on into the night with the crowd until he accidently runs into Asako, who, at the sight of Ryohei, paces up to him and hugs him. They hold each other tightly, whispering each other's name, and begin to silently weep. The next scene, which takes place five years later, shows the couple living together, suggesting that the disaster made Asako change her mind and begin to build her life with Ryohei.

Both of Asako's romances, therefore, are achieved through walking, but an obvious distinction is made between the two respective acts of walking. While Asako's leisurely strolling at the outset of the film brings about a deviation from her everyday life, Ryohei's walking, an outcome of an extraordinary event, ends in a return to normalcy and stability for both Ryohei and Asako. Baku is the one who walks up to Asako, asks her name, and kisses her in the opening scene, but at the end of Ryohei's walk, Asako comes to Ryohei, and thus she is the one who initiates (or reinitiates) their relationship. These differences connote the substantially different nature of Asako's two romantic relationships. Unlike her romance with Baku, which involves exciting and reckless activities such as partying, late-night drinking, and riding motorcycles, Asako and Ryohei's life as a couple after the disaster appears to be stable, calm, and even complacent. The couple is often shown at their home, preparing meals together, having everyday conversations, or hanging out with their friends. Importantly, it is not just Ryohei who provides Asako with balance in her life. Maya and Kushihashi, Ryohei's colleague who often hung out with Asako and Ryohei before the disaster, become close friends with Ryohei and Asako. Maya and Kushihashi are now a family, expecting a baby. Haruyo, Asako's friend from Osaka, who returns from Singapore to Tokyo, soon joins them, and the five of them form a tightly knit group. Additionally, Asako's social life greatly expands owing to the disaster, as the couple volunteers to support tsunami survivors of the Tōhoku region. They regularly drive for hours to help the residents of Sendai who still live in temporary housing. Asako's life seems to be secure and well-balanced with a dependable partner and a social support group. Given the severity of the disaster, Asako's seemingly steady relationship with Ryohei, and the expansion of her social circle, it is tempting to see the 2011 disaster as the event that marks the point where "Asako I" transforms into "Asako II." However, when Baku unexpectedly reappears in Asako's life and urges her to restart their relationship with no regard for Asako's situation or her feelings, her life is quickly destabilized. She is still "Asako I." Her true breakthrough comes much later in the film, and it symbolically happens right at ground zero.

Baku's timing could not be worse, since Asako and Ryohei are planning to move to Ryohei's hometown of Osaka after he accepts a position at his company's branch office. Asako learns from Haruyo that Baku traveled overseas after he left Asako, and upon his return, he was recruited by a talent agency and became a model-actor. At first, Asako shows no visible response to the news about her ex-lover and continues with her plan to relocate to Osaka with Ryohei. However, while on a location shooting at a park, Baku spots Asako, pays a surprise visit to her at her and Ryohei's home, and pushes her to return to him. Asako refuses Baku's proposal but is clearly shaken up. She finally gives in to Baku on the eve of her departure for Osaka, when he barges in on the farewell dinner thrown for Asako and Ryohei by their friends. Asako leaves the devastated Ryohei and their shocked friends at the restaurant and drives with Baku to his hometown in Hokkaido to live together at his parents' abandoned house. While driving through the night with Baku to Hokkaido, Asako receives a call from Maya, who tries to persuade her to return. Upon hearing Asako will not go back to Ryohei, Maya informs her that her friends will sever their relations with her in support of Ryohei. Therefore, it is not just Ryohei that Asako leaves to be with Baku but her entire social network, including the circle she and Ryohei formed.

On the way to Hokkaido, Japan's northernmost prefecture, Baku makes a stop near the ocean in Sendai at dawn while Asako sleeps. Upon waking, Asako learns from Baku where they are and looks anxious. The couple soon gets out of the car, and Baku begins walking up the massive sea embankment built after the 2011 tsunami, a giant wall that completely blocks the ocean view. Asako suddenly tells Baku that she cannot go any further, and he cannot replace Ryohei for her. Baku calmly accepts Asako's decision without showing any emotional response and leaves. Asako then climbs the embankment and begins to stare at the ocean (and the audience). The next shot shows Asako on the embankment from afar and then cuts to a close-up of Asako's face. She does not say a word or express any clear emotion, but this close-up shot, which mirrors the close-ups of her face from the two Gochō exhibits when she looks at the photo of the twin girls, visually suggests she is pondering the social distance between herself and others. This is the moment when Asako finally transforms into "Asako II" (figure 17.2). The camera then goes behind her and begins to move horizontally to capture Asako in a medium shot as she begins to slowly walk on the embankment and eventually exits the frame, with huge breaking waves that create thunderous sounds in the background. The spatial setting of this pivotal event becomes even more illuminating when it is revealed in the subsequent shot that Asako is in the village where she and Ryohei have been volunteering; Asako's walk takes her to the temporary houses of the tsunami survivors. Nature in this scene, therefore, is neither otherized nor romanticized. Rather, the motif of the self-other boundary extends beyond social bonds to include the relationship between Asako and her environment, suggesting the possibility of ecological interdependence. Asako's awakening at the site of the disaster foregrounds connections between the protagonist and her natural environment, or the mutually constitutive relationship "between human culture and the physical world."[6] The protagonist is healed and empowered by the very place she comes to rebuild, and thus the transformation is reciprocal. Also importantly, this is the scene that most tellingly demonstrates that her experience of place (ground zero) is more affective and visceral than cognitive. Asako's regular

Figure 17.2. "Asako I" transforms into "Asako II" at ground zero.
Hamaguchi Ryusuke, 2018, Comme des Cinémas.

visits to the Tōhoku region with Ryohei, and her enlightenment there, reveal that Asako's relationship with Ryohei is conditional, as the disaster—or more precisely, the memories of the disaster—are what keep her committed to her partner. Asako needs to be constantly reassured at ground zero that it is the disaster that started their relationship and nurtured their emotional bond, and it is why she needs the stability she can get from the life she is building with Ryohei. In contrast, Baku does not extend her social horizons. Rather, Asako had to cut all her social connections to pursue a passionate but precarious relationship with him. Even worse, Baku himself is a rupture that destabilizes Asako's life. The intense, emotionally charged relationship with Baku, therefore, is replaced by the more steady but less exciting one with Ryohei.

The film's conclusion once again confirms that disaster is certainly a motivation for Asako to actively pursue human connectivity. It also continues to emphasize how profoundly place shapes characters' emotional lives and relations. After leaving ground zero, Asako travels all the way to Osaka to return to Ryohei. The relocation to Osaka is noteworthy because Osaka, Asako's hometown, is where her story commenced, so Osaka is a fitting place to wrap up her romantic journey. Indeed, the film's circular narrative ends with Asako walking on the riverbank of the Amano River where Ryohei's house is located. The Amano is a tributary of the Yodo River, as are the Dojima and Tosabori Rivers featured in the film's opening scene. Equally importantly, Osaka is a city located far from the epicenter of the 2011 disaster. The catastrophic event and the memories of disaster are what keep

Asako committed to her social relations, so her moving to Osaka seems to suggest a new departure for her. However, even in Osaka, disaster lurks, which is ironically a positive sign for the couple's future and also indicates that Asako still needs to hold on to the memories of the disaster to sustain her social relations. When Asako arrives at Ryohei's new residence, the hurt and angry Ryohei refuses to accept her at first. Intriguingly, their eventual reconciliation also involves walking. During their conversation, Asako asks Ryohei about their cat, Chintan, and Ryohei lies to Asako in frustration, bluntly telling her that he let the cat go. Toward the end of the film, Asako roams across the riverbank full of long reeds in the heavy rain in search for Chintan, a scene which clearly parallels the beginning of the film. More importantly, her walking near the Amano River suggests a potential future disaster. While house hunting in Osaka earlier in the film, Asako and Ryohei find their future house, which is located right next to the Amano River in the outskirts of Osaka. The Amano River also bears a disaster implication, as the river is notorious for its frequent flooding, and when the couple first visit the house during their house-hunting trip, they bring this issue up. While Asako and Ryohei look out to the river from the balcony, Ryohei jokingly says, "When it floods, we will be the first ones getting swept away." Despite the grim nature of Ryohei's comment, Asako, looking unusually excited, tells him she loves the place, and she expresses her desire to find a new job when they move in. The couple's new house next to the river signifies that Asako needs constant reminders about a possible disaster in order to motivate her to maintain and enhance her social life. In this regard, Asako's desperate search in the heavy rain for Chintan, a symbol of the stable, comfortable, and dependable relationship Asako has built with Ryohei, once again validates the generative power of disaster that can nurture Asako's romantic and social relations. Not surprisingly, Ryohei soon appears to "rescue" her from a potential disaster. After yelling at Asako to stop the search, Ryohei begins to run, and Asako follows him in the hope of talking to him again. The following static, extreme long shot portrays the couple's odd chase scene in the rainy scenery of the Amano River.

After the long chase, Ryohei gives in to Asako, hands Chintan over, and reluctantly accepts Asako into his (or their) home. Ryohei coldly tells Asako he is not sure if he can trust her after what happened. Asako replies that she understands, and she tells Ryohei that even though she loves him, she will try not to be too dependent on him. The film ends with the couple together on the balcony, looking out to the Amano River after making an incomplete reconciliation. After several intercuts between the couple and their POV shots of the rising river, Ryohei murmurs in an emotionless tone, "The water is rising . . . what an ugly river." Still staring at the river, Asako responds, "But it is beautiful," and with Asako's last word, the camera stays on the couple for a while until the film ends (figure 17.3). For Asako, the Amano River is a symbol of a potentially destructive, unpredictable

Figure 17.3. Asako and Ryohei look out to the rising Amano River
from the balcony after their incomplete reconciliation.
Hamaguchi Ryusuke, 2018, Comme des Cinémas.

event that can damage her inner peace at any moment. The disaster is not a single disruptive event but rather persists in the lives of those who experience it, simply lurking around a corner and ready to spring out. Yet the disaster is also a positive force that prompts Asako to pursue stability and balance in her life through her relationship with the reliable, calm, social, and personable Ryohei and through her support network.

Conclusion: Reconnecting *Self* with *Others*

The restoration of human connectivity through disasters, as represented in *Asako I & II* and other recent Japanese melodramas, certainly evinces a renewed interest in the subject of disaster in the aftermath of the triple disaster. Yet as my discussion of *Asako I & II* has shown, these melodramas are as much about recovery, restoration, and reconciliation as they are about disaster and its dire consequences. When placed in a larger cultural context, this emphasis on recovery and rebuilding resonates with the prevailing cultural trend of post-3/11 Japan. In her book *Gender, Culture, and Disaster in Post-3.11 Japan*, Mire Koikari cogently illuminates the advent of the culture of safety and security in the wake of the 2011 disaster that underscores themes of recovery, reconstruction, and resilience in a nationwide effort to build a new Japan.[7] Rachel DiNitto makes a similar observation in *Fukushima Fiction*, arguing that 3/11. was perceived as the long-awaited opportunity to inspire social and political change in Japan after the initial shock, although the sense of change has turned to resignation and disappointment over time.[8] In these stories, the disaster becomes a facilitator for couples, families, friends, and communities to ruminate on and reestablish interpersonal relations. Yet why do they need such an excessive crisis to restore their faith in social relations, and what kind of "new Japan" are these stories trying to suggest? To put it simply, this new melodrama trope evokes a desperate need to rebuild human relations in contemporary Japanese society. It should be noted that social isolation is recognized as one of the most serious social problems in Japan, so much so that in 2021, the Japanese government appointed its first cabinet member, "the minister of loneliness," to tackle social isolation and the collapsing social safety net after years of studies consistently showed that Japanese citizens were suffering from a significant lack of social life and interactions.[9] Indeed, as the acclaimed sociologist Furuichi Noritoshi and many other social scientists have demonstrated, romance, sex, marriage, and family are becoming a luxury in Japan as more and more young people accept social immobility as a reality in the stagnant, overdeveloped Japanese society.[10] In such a social milieu, a conventional melodramatic tale of a romantic couple or family members overcoming or conforming to social pressures—such as class difference, morality, and gender, sexuality, and other social norms—no longer strongly resonates with viewers. In response, Japanese filmmakers resort to new and more drastic obstacles like earthquakes, radiation, endless rain, meteor strikes, or even zombie outbreaks to make their melodramatic stories more plausible. These stories, however, are typically optimistic, hopeful, and forward-looking. In exploring the desolate landscape of Japanese hearts in the aftermath of yet another catastrophic disaster, *Asako I & II* and other melodramas discover the productive power of disaster and cautiously suggest that this crisis may allow Japanese to cope with a social calamity that has had devastating effects on their society.

Notes

1 Napier, "The Anime Director," 3.

2 Shibasaki Tomoka, *Netemo sametemo.*

3 Maggie Lee, "Film Review: 'Asako I & II.'"

4 Peter Bradshaw, "*Asako I & II* Review."

5 Arai Naomi, "Gochō Shigeo," 3–4.

6 Cheryll Glotfelty, "Introduction," xx.

7 Mire Koikari, *Gender, Culture, and Disaster in Post-3.11 Japan*, 2–3.

8 Rachel DiNitto, *Fukushima Fiction*, 16–17.

9 Kawagochi Shun, "Kodokutantōshōni."

10 Furuichi Noritoshi, *Zetsubō no kuni no kōfukuna wakamonodachi.*

Bibliography

Arai, Naomi. "Gochō Shigeo no futatsu no jikan." *Niigatashi niitsubijutsukan kenkyūgiyō* 3 (March 2015): 3–11.

Bradshaw, Peter. "*Asako I & II* Review—Japanese Romcom Flips the Gaze to Tell the Same Old Story." *The Guardian*, May 15, 2018. https://www.theguardian.com/film/2018/may/15/asako-i-ii-review-japanese-romcom-flips-gaze-ryusuke-hamaguchi.

DiNitto, Rachel. *Fukushima Fiction: The Literary Landscape of Japan's Triple Disaster.* Honolulu: University of Hawai'i Press, 2019.

Furuichi, Noritoshi. *Zetsubō no kuni no kōfukuna wakamonodachi.* Tokyo: Kōdansha, 2015.

Glotfelty, Cheryll. "Introduction: Literary Studies in an Age of Environmental Crisis." In *The Ecocriticism Reader*, edited by Gheryll Glotfelty and Harold Fromm, xv–xxxvii. Athens: The University of Georgia Press, 1996.

Kawagochi, Shun. "Kodokutantōshōni kaigaimediaga aitsugi shuzai." *Mainichi Shimbun*, May 13, 2021. https://mainichi.jp/articles/20210513/k00/00m/010/140000c.

Koikari, Mire. *Gender, Culture, and Disaster in Post-3.11 Japan.* London: Bloomsbury Publishing, 2020.

Lee, Maggie. "Film Review: 'Asako I & II.'" *Variety,* May 15, 2018. https://variety.com/2018/film/asia/asako-i-ii-review-netetemo-sametemo-1202809972/

Napier, Susan J. "The Anime Director, the Fantasy Girl and the Very Real Tsunami." *Asia-Pacific Journal* 10, issue 11, no. 3 (March 05, 2012): 1–11.

Shibasaki, Tomoka. *Netemo sametemo*, Tokyo: Kawade Shobō Shinsha, 2014.

List of Films Discussed
in this Volume

Air Doll / Kūki ningyō (Kore-eda Hirokazu, 2009, TV Man Union, Inc., Bandai Visual, Asmik Ace, Engine Film Inc., Eisei Gekijo)

Asako I & II / Netemo sametemo (Hamaguchi Ryūsuke, 2018, Comme des Cinémas)

Ashes to Honey / Mitsubachi no haoto to chikyū no kaiten (Kamanaka Hitomi, 2010, Group Gendai)

BLAME! (Hiroyuki Seshita, 2017, Tsutomu Nihei, KODANSHA/BLAME! Production Committee)

Charisma / Karisuma (Kurosawa Kiyoshi, 1999, Nikkatsu)

Evangelion: 1.0 You Are (Not) Alone / Evangerion shin gekijōban: jo (Anno Hideaki, 2007, Khara)

Evangelion: 2.0 You Can (Not) Advance / Evangerion shin gekijōban: ha (Anno Hideaki, 2009, Khara)

Evangelion: 3.0 You Can (Not) Redo / Evangerion shin gekijōban: Q (Anno Hideaki, 2012, Khara)

Evangelion: 3.0+1.0 Thrice Upon a Time / Shin evangerion gekijōban :‖ (Anno Hideaki, 2021, Khara)

Future Boy Conan / Mirai shōnen Konan (Miyazaki Hayao, 1978, Studio Ghibli)

Godzilla / Gojira (Honda Ishirō, 1954, Tōhō)

Godzilla (Gareth Edwards, 2014, Warner Bros./Legendary Pictures)

Godzilla versus the Smog Monster / Gojira tai Hedorah (Banno Yoshimitsu, 1971, Tōhō)

Himizu (Sono Sion, 2011, Gaga)

Japan Sinks 2020 Theatrical Edition / Nihon chinbotsu 2020 gekijō henshū-ban shizumanu kibō (Yuasa Masaaki, 2020, Science SARU)

Japan Sinks or Sinking of Japan / Nihon chinbotsu (Higuchi Shinji, 2006, Tōhō)

Japan Sinks or Submersion of Japan / Nihon chinbotsu (Moritani Shirō, 1973, Tōhō)

Jellyfish Eyes / Mememe no kurage (Murakami Takashi, 2013, Takashi Murakami/Kaikai Kiki Co., Ltd)

Land of Hope / Kibō no kuni (Sono Sion, 2012, Shochiku)

Laputa: Castle in the Sky / Tenkū no shiro Rapyuta (Miyazaki Hayao, 1986, Studio Ghibli)

Little Voices from Fukushima / Chiisaki koe no kanon: Sentakusuru hitobito (Kamanaka Hitomi, 2015, Bunbun Films)

Minamata (Andrew Levitas, 2020, Minamata Film LLC)

Minamata Diary: Visiting Resurrected Souls / Minamata nikki: Yomigaeru tamashii o tazunete (Tsuchimoto Noriaki, 2004, Cine Associé)

Nausicaä of the Valley of the Wind / Kaze no tani no Naushika (Miyazaki Hayao, 1984, Studio Ghibli)

Neon Genisis Evangelion / Shin seiki evangerion (Anno Hideaki, 1995-6, Gainax)

Nuclear Gypsies / Ikiteru uchi ga hana na no yo, shindara sore made yo (Morisaki Azuma, 1985, Kinoshita)

Rhapsody in August / Hachigatsu no kyōshikyoku (rapusodī) (Kurosawa Akira, 1991, Shochiku)

Shin Godzilla / Shin Gojira (Anno Hideaki and Higuchi Shinji, 2016, Tōhō)

Space Battleship Yamato / Uchūsenkan Yamato (Matsumoto Leiji, 1974, Tohokushinsha Film Co.)

The End of Evangelion / Shin seiki evangerion gekijōban Air / magokoro o, kimi ni (Anno Hideaki, 1997, Gainax)

The Man Who Stole the Sun / Taiyō wo nusunda otoko (Hasegawa Kazuhiko, 1979, Tōhō)

The Whispering Star / Hiso hiso boshi (Sono Sion, 2015, Happinet)

About the Editor and Contributors

Editor

Rachel DiNitto, Professor of Japanese Literature at the University of Oregon, researches the nuclear environmental humanities through contemporary cultural production including literature, film, and manga. Her book *Fukushima Fiction: The Literary Landscape of Japan's Triple Disaster* (2019) was a winner of the Choice Magazine Outstanding Academic Title award. See her chapters and articles on Japanese film in *The Japanese Cinema Book, Japan Forum, Journal of Japanese Studies,* and *The Asia-Pacific Journal.* Her current project *Environmental Echoes and Nuclear Traces in Japanese Literature* pairs post-Fukushima fiction with novels and short stories from earlier eras of environmental and nuclear harm.

Contributors

Jonathan E. Abel is a Professor in the Asian Studies and Comparative Literature Departments at the Pennsylvania State University. His teaching and research focus on the production, circulation, and reception of cultural products. His books *Redacted* (2012) on literary censorship and *The New Real* (2023) on media, marketing, and mimesis examine the cultural lifecycle of the creative arts in Japan and how they can transform the world. His current book project *Fake News or MicroFiction: How Imagination Transforms the World* focusses on the power of literature circulating on microblogs and social media since 2010 to spin the latest news cycles.

Andrea Gevurtz Arai is acting assistant professor of Japan and East Asian studies and cultural anthropology in the Jackson School of International Studies at the University of Washington. She was the interim chair of the Korea Studies Program 2023–2024. Arai is the author of *The Strange Child: Education and the Psychology of Patriotism in Recessionary Japan* (2016); co-editor (with Clark W. Sorensen) of *Spaces of Possibility: In, Between and Beyond Korea and Japan* (2016), and (with Ann Anagnost) of *Global Futures in East Asia* (2013); and editor of *Spaces of Creative Resistance: Social Change Projects in East Asia* (2025). Arai is completing a second monograph: *The 3.11 Generation: Changing the Subjects of Labor, Gender and Environment in Trans-Local Japan.* She is starting a third book on global activism and solidarity movements, and a new collaborative project on feminist biopolitics of low-fertility; eco-socialism and the peripheral in East Asia.

Davinder L. Bhowmik is an associate professor of Japanese at the University of Washington, Seattle. She teaches and publishes research in the field of modern Japanese literature with a specialization in prose fiction from Okinawa, where she was born and lived until the age of 18. Other scholarly interests include regional fiction, the atomic bombings, and Japanese film. Her publications include "Unruly Subjects in Shun Medoruma's 'Walking a Street Named Peace' and Miri Yū's *Tokyo Ueno Station*" (2020); *Islands of Protest: Japanese Literature from Okinawa* (co-edited with Steve Rabson, 2016); and *Writing Okinawa: Narratives of Identity and Resistance* (2008).

Dr. Adam Bingham is an English lecturer in Film and Television studies at the University of Nottingham in the UK. He has taught Film and TV Studies with a specialism in East Asian Cinemas around England for almost 20 years – in Sheffield, Edge Hill University, SOAS in London and at Nottingham Trent University – and has designed courses and organized community widening participation events and festival programming. He is the author of the book *Japanese Cinema Since Hana-Bi*, as well as numerous journal articles and book chapters covering subjects such as Shohei Imamura, Hiroshi Teshigahara and Japanese authorship, Hong Sang-soo and Yasujiro Ozu among others. He is consultant for Asian cinemas at CineAste in the US and is currently preparing a monograph on variant masculinities in contemporary Japanese and South Korean films and television.

Aidana Bolatbekkyzy is a PhD Candidate in the Department of East Asian Languages and Literatures at the University of Oregon. Her dissertation examines the intersection of law, confinement, and writing in contemporary Japanese dystopian literature. Aidana is the author of "Real Eyes Realize Real Lies: Writing Fukushima through the Child's Gaze" in *Literature After Fukushima: From Marginalized Voices to Nuclear Futurity* (Routledge, 2023), and the co-author of "Writing back to the Capitalocene: Radioactive foodscapes in Japan's Post-3/11 literature" (2023) published in *Contemporary Japan*.

Eugenio De Angelis is Assistant Professor of Japanese and Korean cinema in the Department of Asian and North African Studies at Ca' Foscari University of Venice. His main fields of research include Japanese cinema of the 1960s and 1970s, examining its cultural-political context and its relation to other artistic avant-gardes, as well as film festival studies from an Asian perspective. He is the author of the monograph *Terayamago. The Cinema and Theater of Terayama Shūji in the Intermedial Context of the 1960s and 1970s* (2018, in Italian) and co-editor of *J-Movie. Japanese Cinema from 2005 to 2015* (2016, in Italian).

Jeff DuBois is associate professor of Japanese Studies at the College of St. Benedict and St. John's University in Collegeville, MN. His research, writing, and teaching focuses on Japanese literature, films, culture and media inflected by nuclear issues, and Japan's emperor system. Recent essays include studies of the films of Obayashi Nobuhiko and Ichikawa Kon's adaptations of Yokomizo Seishi's detective novels.

Hideaki Fujiki is professor in screen studies at Nagoya University, Japan. His publications include *Making Audiences: A Social History of Japanese Cinema and Media* (Oxford University Press, 2022), *Making Personas: Transnational Film Stardom in Modern Japan* (Harvard University Asia Center, 2013), and *The Japanese Cinema Book* (co-edited with Alastair Phillips, British Film Institute, 2020). He is also completing the monograph titled *Ecology from Fukushima: Local Communities and Planet by Screen Media*, which discusses cinema and media in relation to a range of ecological issues, such as energy, waste, animals, disabilities, memories, radiation, and the Anthropocene.

Amrita Iyer is a Ph.D. candidate at Nanyang Technological University, Singapore. Her thesis focuses on how philosophies of technology can inform the analysis of science fiction to envision possible sustainable futures, which fits into her broader academic interests of ecocriticism and narratives surrounding intelligent technologies. In addition, she has co-authored an article for Duke University Press's journal *Environmental Humanities* (forthcoming November 2024). She has also contributed a chapter to the forthcoming volume *Shaping Transfuturism: Identity, Representation, and Agency in Science Fiction Literature* (under review) and has a contracted chapter in the forthcoming *The Palgrave Handbook of Monsters and Monstrous Bodies*.

Dong Hoon Kim is an associate professor of the Department of Cinema Studies at the University of Oregon. His research and teaching interests include visual culture, early cinema, film and media spectatorship, and East Asian film, media, and popular culture. Kim is the author of *Eclipsed Cinema: the Film Culture of Colonial Korea* (Edinburgh University Press, 2017) and the co-editor, with Travis Workman and Immanuel Kim, of *The Bloomsbury Handbook of North Korean Cinema* (Bloomsbury Publishing, forthcoming in 2025).

Laura Lee is an associate professor of cinema and visual culture at Florida State University, where she teaches in the College of Motion Picture Arts. Her research centers on film and animation in Japan and her published work on histories and aesthetics of intermedia, screen technologies, popular arts and new media, and special effects has appeared in numerous venues. She is also the author of *Japanese Cinema Between Frames* (2017) and *Worlds Unbound: the Art of teamLab* (2022). Lee's most recent research area focuses on social media and interactive immersive technologies.

Christine Marran specializes in the fields of environmental humanities, critical theory, and gender studies. She is Professor of Japanese Literature and Cultural Studies in the Department of Asian and Middle Eastern Studies and Co-Director of the Environmental Humanities Initiative at the University of Minnesota. Through a new materialist approach, Marran's work addresses how those in area studies can more deliberately contend with the more-than-human world in this age of rising seas. In her analysis of animal and plant life, archipelagoes and climate in narrative and moving images, Marran offers strategies for reading and interpreting more-than-human elements in the work of activist-writers and filmmakers in the Japanese archipelago. Selected works include *Ecology Without Culture: Aesthetics for a Toxic Age*, "Planetarity" in *boundary 2*; "Animal Stranger in a Tokyo Canal" in *Japan at Nature's Edge: The Environmental Context of a Global Power; Fukushima Diary: Diary of Shuhei Tomisawa: 20th Generation Sake Brewer &* other works.

Shan Ren is a Ph.D. candidate in the Department of East Asian Languages and Literatures at the University of Oregon. Shan was a visiting scholar at Aoyama Gakuin University from 2023 to 2024. Her research interests encompass early modern and modern Japanese popular literature, transnational studies, and environmental studies. Her dissertation examines the literary exchange between Japan and China in the 19th century, focusing on the role of popular literature in this transnational dialogue.

Roman Rosenbaum, PhD is an Honorary Associate at the University of Sydney Australia. He specialises in Postwar Japanese Literature, Popular Cultural Studies and translation. He received his Ph.D. in Japanese Literature at the *University of Sydney*. In 2010/11, he spent one year as a Visiting Research Professor at the *International Research Centre for Japanese Studies* (Nichibunken). His latest book publication is: Roman Rosenbaum, Yasuko Claremont (eds) *Art and Activism in the Nuclear Age: Exploring the Legacy of Hiroshima and Nagasaki* (Routledge, 2023). His latest research publications includes: 'The Relationship Between Culture and Political Humor in Japanese Manga,' in Ofer Feldman (ed) *Communicating Political Humor in the Media: How Culture Influences Satire and Irony* (Springer, 2024).

Christopher Smith is an assistant professor of modern Japanese literature and culture at the University of Florida, where he teaches courses on modern Japanese literature, culture, manga, and anime. His research focuses on postwar Japanese literature, particularly contemporary literature (Heisei-Reiwa), as well as Japanese pop culture, including manga and anime. He recently published a translation of Tanaka Yasuo's *Somehow, Crystal* (Kurodahan Press). His first monograph, *Samurai with Telephones: Anachronism in Japanese Literature*, is available from the University Michigan Press.

Kaoru Tamura was born in Niigata Prefecture, Japan and emigrated to the United States as an adult. After a career as a graphic designer, she returned to school and completed an MA in East Asian Studies at Washington University in St. Louis, writing a thesis on Moto Hagio's *Heart of Thomas*. She is currently a PhD candidate at the University of Oregon, where she is writing a dissertation on pre-war Japanese children's literature. She is the co-translator of Tsushima Yuko's short story, "Wisteria Vine," in the forthcoming volume, *Bold Breaks: Japanese Women and Literary Narratives of Divorce.*